INSURANCE: PRINCIPLES, APPLICATIONS AND PRACTICES

INSURANCE: PRINCIPLES, APPLICATIONS AND PRACTICES

Dheeraj Razdan

CYBER TECH PUBLICATIONS
4264/3, Ansari Road, Daryaganj, New Delhi-110002 (India)
Ph.: 011-23244078. Fax: 011-23280028
E-Mail: cyberpublicationsdelhi@yahoo.com

INSURANCE: PRINCIPLES, APPLICATIONS AND PRACTICES

Dheeraj Razdan

First Edition 2027

Published by :

G.S. Rawat for **Cyber Tech Publications**
4264/3, Ansari Road, Daryaganj, New Delhi-110002 (India)
Ph.: 011-23244078. Fax: 011-23280028
E-Mail: cyberpublicationsdelhi@yahoo.com

Printed at : Asian Offset Printers

Preface

Most of the technical and service professions as we know them today developed in the nineteenth century. They initially depended on education through apprenticeship. Later, examinations and other qualifications were established by their professional organizations. These followed the patterns set earlier by the older professions, such as medicine and law. Central in value for these professions were personal service and ethical conduct. In newer professions providing technical and commercial services to industry and business, such as engineering and accountancy, emphasis soon come to be placed on the specialized knowledge and skills that defined the professional. Increasing employment of professionals in organizations raised issues of professional authority and independence.

The essential characteristic of a profession has come to be expertise in the area where professional services are performed. This requires setting of selective standards for admission to the profession, intellectual and practical training to acquire professional competence, and an organization to rest such competence. To ensure that professional services are delivered in a manner expected of professionals, it has become necessary to lay down canons of professional performance and behavior in work situations, as well as procedures for maintaining discipline.

Professional services have been performed in a variety of settings. The older professions, such as medicine and law, were carried on overwhelmingly by independent entrepreneurs, hedged around only with professional restrictions. Increasingly, however, these professions and especially the new professions, such as engineering and accountancy, have come to act largely in professional groups or as employees of business organizations. Professional services provided by business organizations are a means to the financial ends of such organizations. Professionals employed by a business organization share responsibility for their actions with the employer, whereas professionals in private practice bear their responsibility alone. Regardless of their employment status, professionals have a mandate from their profession to act in the public interest.

This book is all about the principles and practices of insurance, I hope that readers will appreciate the work.

—Author

CONTENTS

1

INSURANCE: AN INTRODUCTION

Insurance, in law and economics, is a form of risk management primarily used to hedge against the risk of a contingent loss. Insurance is defined as the equitable transfer of the risk of a loss, from one entity to another, in exchange for a premium. Insurer is the company that sells the insurance. Insurance rate is a factor used to determine the amount, called the premium, to be charged for a certain amount of insurance coverage. Risk management, the practice of appraising and controlling risk, has evolved as a discrete field of study and practice.

PRINCIPLES OF INSURANCE

Commercially insurable risks typically share seven common characteristics.

1. A large number of homogeneous exposure units. The vast majority of insurance policies are provided for individual members of very large classes. Automobile insurance, for example, covered about 175 million automobiles in the United States in 2004. The existence of a large number of homogeneous exposure units allows insurers to benefit from the so-called "law of large numbers," which in effect states that as the number of exposure units increases, the actual results are increasingly likely to become close to expected results. There are exceptions to this criterion. Lloyd's of London is famous for insuring the life or health of actors, actresses and sports figures. Satellite Launch insurance covers events that are infrequent. Large commercial property policies may insure exceptional properties for which there are no 'homogeneous' exposure

units. Despite failing on this criterion, many exposures like these are generally considered to be insurable.

2. Definite Loss. The event that gives rise to the loss that is subject to insurance should, at least in principle, take place at a known time, in a known place, and from a known cause. The classic example is death of an insured on a life insurance policy. Fire, automobile accidents, and worker injuries may all easily meet this criterion. Other types of losses may only be definite in theory. Occupational disease, for instance, may involve prolonged exposure to injurious conditions where no specific time, place or cause is identifiable. Ideally, the time, place and cause of a loss should be clear enough that a reasonable person, with sufficient information, could objectively verify all three elements.
3. Accidental Loss. The event that constitutes the trigger of a claim should be fortuitous, or at least outside the control of the beneficiary of the insurance. The loss should be 'pure,' in the sense that it results from an event for which there is only the opportunity for cost. Events that contain speculative elements, such as ordinary business risks, are generally not considered insurable.
4. Large Loss. The size of the loss must be meaningful from the perspective of the insured. Insurance premiums need to cover both the expected cost of losses, plus the cost of issuing and administering the policy, adjusting losses, and supplying the capital needed to reasonably assure that the insurer will be able to pay claims. For small losses these latter costs may be several times the size of the expected cost of losses. There is little point in paying such costs unless the protection offered has real value to a buyer.
5. Affordable Premium. If the likelihood of an insured event is so high, or the cost of the event so large, that the resulting premium is large relative to the amount of protection offered, it is not likely that anyone will buy insurance, even if on offer. Further, as the accounting profession formally recognizes in financial accounting standards, the premium cannot be so large that there is not a reasonable

chance of a significant loss to the insurer. If there is no such chance of loss, the transaction may have the form of insurance, but not the substance. (See the U.S. Financial Accounting Standards Board standard number 113)

6. Calculable Loss. There are two elements that must be at least estimable, if not formally calculable: the probability of loss, and the attendant cost. Probability of loss is generally an empirical exercise, while cost has more to do with the ability of a reasonable person in possession of a copy of the insurance policy and a proof of loss associated with a claim presented under that policy to make a reasonably definite and objective evaluation of the amount of the loss recoverable as a result of the claim.
7. Limited risk of catastrophically large losses. The essential risk is often aggregation. If the same event can cause losses to numerous policyholders of the same insurer, the ability of that insurer to issue policies becomes constrained, not by factors surrounding the individual characteristics of a given policyholder, but by the factors surrounding the sum of all policyholders so exposed. Typically, insurers prefer to limit their exposure to a loss from a single event to some small portion of their capital base, on the order of 5 percent. Where the loss can be aggregated, or an individual policy could produce exceptionally large claims, the capital constraint will restrict an insurers appetite for additional policyholders. The classic example is earthquake insurance, where the ability of an underwriter to issue a new policy depends on the number and size of the policies that it has already underwritten. Wind insurance in hurricane zones, particularly along coast lines, is another example of this phenomenon. In extreme cases, the aggregation can affect the entire industry, since the combined capital of insurers and reinsurers can be small compared to the needs of potential policyholders in areas exposed to aggregation risk. In commercial fire insurance it is possible to find single properties whose total exposed value is well in excess of any individual insurer's capital constraint. Such properties are generally shared among

several insurers, or are insured by a single insurer who syndicates the risk into the reinsurance market.

INDEMNIFICATION

The technical definition of "indemnity" means to make whole again. There are two types of insurance contracts; 1) an "indemnity" policy and 2) a "pay on behalf" or "on behalf of" policy. The difference is significant on paper, but rarely material in practice.

An "indemnity" policy will never pay claims until the insured has paid out of pocket to some third party; i.e. a visitor to your home slips on a floor that you left wet and sues you for $10,000 and wins. Under an "indemnity" policy the homeowner would have to come up with the $10,000 to pay for the visitors fall and then would be "indemnified" by the insurance carrier for the out of pocket costs (the $10,000).

Under the same situation, a "pay on behalf" policy, the insurance carrier would pay the claim and the insured (the homeowner) would not be out of pocket for anything. Most modern liability insurance is written on the basis of "pay on behalf" language.

An entity seeking to transfer risk (an individual, corporation, or association of any type, etc.) becomes the 'insured' party once risk is assumed by an 'insurer', the insuring party, by means of a contract, called an insurance 'policy'. Generally, an insurance contract includes, at a minimum, the following elements: the parties (the insurer, the insured, the beneficiaries), the premium, the period of coverage, the particular loss event covered, the amount of coverage (i.e., the amount to be paid to the insured or beneficiary in the event of a loss), and exclusions (events not covered). An insured is thus said to be "indemnified" against the loss events covered in the policy.

When insured parties experience a loss for a specified peril, the coverage entitles the policyholder to make a 'claim' against the insurer for the covered amount of loss as specified by the policy. The fee paid by the insured to the insurer for assuming the risk is called the 'premium'. Insurance premiums from many insureds are used to fund accounts reserved for later payment of claims—in theory for a relatively few claimants—and for overhead costs. So long as an insurer maintains adequate funds set aside for anticipated losses (i.e., reserves), the remaining margin is an insurer's profit.

INSURER'S BUSINESS MODEL

Profit = earned premium + investment income-incurred loss-underwriting expenses.

Insurers make money in two ways: (1) through underwriting, the process by which insurers select the risks to insure and decide how much in premiums to charge for accepting those risks and (2) by investing the premiums they collect from insureds.

The most difficult aspect of the insurance business is the underwriting of policies. Using a wide assortment of data, insurers predict the likelihood that a claim will be made against their policies and price products accordingly. To this end, insurers use actuarial science to quantify the risks they are willing to assume and the premium they will charge to assume them. Data is analyzed to fairly accurately project the rate of future claims based on a given risk. Actuarial science uses statistics and probability to analyze the risks associated with the range of perils covered, and these scientific principles are used to determine an insurer's overall exposure. Upon termination of a given policy, the amount of premium collected and the investment gains thereon minus the amount paid out in claims is the insurer's underwriting profit on that policy. Of course, from the insurer's perspective, some policies are winners (i.e., the insurer pays out less in claims and expenses than it receives in premiums and investment income) and some are losers (i.e., the insurer pays out more in claims and expenses than it receives in premiums and investment income).

An insurer's underwriting performance is measured in its combined ratio. The loss ratio (incurred losses and loss-adjustment expenses divided by net earned premium) is added to the expense ratio (underwriting expenses divided by net premium written) to determine the company's combined ratio. The combined ratio is a reflection of the company's overall underwriting profitability. A combined ratio of less than 100 percent indicates underwriting profitability, while anything over 100 indicates an underwriting loss.

Insurance companies also earn investment profits on "float". "Float" or available reserve is the amount of money, at hand at any given moment, that an insurer has collected in insurance premiums but has not been paid out in claims. Insurers start investing insurance premiums as soon as they are collected and continue to earn interest on them until claims are paid out.

In the United States, the underwriting loss of property and casualty insurance companies was $142.3 billion in the five years ending 2003. But overall profit for the same period was $68.4 billion, as the result of float. Some insurance industry insiders, most notably Hank Greenberg, do not believe that it is forever possible to sustain a profit from float without an underwriting profit as well, but this opinion is not universally held. Naturally, the "float" method is difficult to carry out in an economically depressed period. Bear markets do cause insurers to shift away from investments and to toughen up their underwriting standards. So a poor economy generally means high insurance premiums. This tendency to swing between profitable and unprofitable periods over time is commonly known as the "underwriting" or insurance cycle.

Property and casualty insurers currently make the most money from their auto insurance line of business. Generally better statistics are available on auto losses and underwriting on this line of business has benefited greatly from advances in computing. Additionally, property losses in the US, due to natural catastrophes, have exacerbated this trend.

Finally, claims and loss handling is the materialized utility of insurance. In managing the claims-handling function, insurers seek to balance the elements of customer satisfaction, administrative handling expenses, and claims overpayment leakages. As part of this balancing act, fraudulent insurance practices are a major business risk that must be managed and overcome.

COMPARISON WITH GAMBLING

Both gambling and insurance transfer risk and reward.

Gambling transactions offer the possibility of either a loss or a gain. Gambling creates losers and winners. Insurance transactions do not present the possibility of gain. Insurance offers financial support sufficient to replace loss, not to create pure gain.

Gamblers can continue spending, buying more risk than they can afford to pay for. Insurance buyers can only spend up to the limit of what carriers would accept to insure; their loss is limited to the amount of the premium. Gamblers, by creating new risk transfer, are risk seekers. Insurance buyers are risk avoiders, transferring risks away from themselves.

Gambling or (euphemistically) "gaming" is designed at the outset so that the odds are not affected by the players' conduct or behavior, and the players not required to conduct risk mitigation practices. But players can prepare and increase their odds of winning in certain games such as poker or blackjack. In contrast to gambling, to obtain certain types of insurance, such as fire insurance, policyholders can be required to conduct risk mitigation practices, such as installing sprinklers and using fireproof building materials to reduce the odds of loss to fire. In addition, after a proven loss, insurers specialize in providing rehabilitation to minimize the total loss.

Insurance, the avoiding, mitigating and transferring of risk, creates greater predictability for individuals and organizations.

HISTORY OF INSURANCE

In some sense we can say that insurance appears simultaneously with the appearance of human society. We know of two types of economies in human societies: money economies (with markets, money, financial instruments and so on) and non-money or natural economies (without money, markets, financial instruments and so on). The second type is a more ancient form than the first. In such an economy and community, we can see insurance in the form of people helping each other. For example, if a house burns down, the members of the community help build a new one. Should the same thing happen to one's neighbour, the other neighbours must help. Otherwise, neighbours will not receive help in the future. This type of insurance has survived to the present day in some countries where modern money economy with its financial instruments is not widespread (for example countries in the territory of the former Soviet Union).

Turning to insurance in the modern sense (i.e., insurance in a modern money economy, in which insurance is part of the financial sphere), early methods of transferring or distributing risk were practiced by Chinese and Babylonian traders as long ago as the 3rd and 2nd millennia BC, respectively. Chinese merchants travelling treacherous river rapids would redistribute their wares across many vessels to limit the loss due to any single vessel's capsizing. The Babylonians developed a system which was recorded in the famous Code of Hammurabi, c. 1750 BC, and practiced by early Mediterranean sailing merchants. If a merchant received a loan to fund his shipment, he would pay the lender an additional sum in exchange for the lender's guarantee to cancel the loan should the shipment be stolen.

Achaemenian monarchs were the first to insure their people and made it official by registering the insuring process in governmental notary offices. The insurance tradition was performed each year in Norouz (beginning of the Iranian New Year); the heads of different ethnic groups as well as others willing to take part, presented gifts to the monarch. The most important gift was presented during a special ceremony. When a gift was worth more than 10,000 Derrik (Achaemenian gold coin) the issue was registered in a special office. This was advantageous to those who presented such special gifts. For others, the presents were fairly assessed by the confidants of the court. Then the assessment was registered in special offices.

The purpose of registering was that whenever the person who presented the gift registered by the court was in trouble, the monarch and the court would help him. Jahez, a historian and writer, writes in one of his books on ancient Iran: "[W]henever the owner of the present is in trouble or wants to construct a building, set up a feast, have his children married, etc. the one in charge of this in the court would check the registration. If the registered amount exceeded 10,000 Derrik, he or she would receive an amount of twice as much."

A thousand years later, the inhabitants of Rhodes invented the concept of the 'general average'. Merchants whose goods were being shipped together would pay a proportionally divided premium which would be used to reimburse any merchant whose goods were jettisoned during storm or sinkage. The Greeks and Romans introduced the origins of health and life insurance c. 600 AD when they organized guilds called "benevolent societies" which cared for the families and paid funeral expenses of members upon death.

Guilds in the Middle Ages served a similar purpose. The Talmud deals with several aspects of insuring goods. Before insurance was established in the late 17th century, "friendly societies" existed in England, in which people donated amounts of money to a general sum that could be used for emergencies.

Separate insurance contracts (i.e., insurance policies not bundled with loans or other kinds of contracts) were invented in Genoa in the 14th century, as were insurance pools backed by pledges of landed estates. These new insurance contracts allowed insurance to be separated from investment, a separation of roles that first proved useful in marine insurance. Insurance became far more sophisticated in post-Renaissance Europe, and specialized varieties developed.

Toward the end of the seventeenth century, London's growing importance as a centre for trade increased demand for marine insurance. In the late 1680s, Mr. Edward Lloyd opened a coffee house that became a popular haunt of ship owners, merchants, and ships' captains, and thereby a reliable source of the latest shipping news. It became the meeting place for parties wishing to insure cargoes and ships, and those willing to underwrite such ventures. Today, Lloyd's of London remains the leading market (note that it is not an insurance company) for marine and other specialist types of insurance, but it works rather differently than the more familiar kinds of insurance.

Insurance as we know it today can be traced to the Great Fire of London, which in 1666 devoured 13,200 houses. In the aftermath of this disaster, Nicholas Barbon opened an office to insure buildings. In 1680, he established England's first fire insurance company, "The Fire Office," to insure brick and frame homes.

The first insurance company in the United States underwrote fire insurance and was formed in Charles Town (modern-day Charleston), South Carolina, in 1732.

Benjamin Franklin helped to popularize and make standard the practice of insurance, particularly against fire in the form of perpetual insurance. In 1752, he founded the Philadelphia Contributionship for the Insurance of Houses from Loss by Fire. Franklin's company was the first to make contributions toward fire prevention. Not only did his company warn against certain fire hazards, it refused to insure certain buildings where the risk of fire was too great, such as all wooden houses.

In the United States, regulation of the insurance industry is highly Balkanized, with primary responsibility assumed by individual state insurance departments.

Whereas insurance markets have become centralized nationally and internationally, state insurance commissioners operate individually, though at times in concert through a national insurance commissioners' organization. In recent years, some have called for a dual state and federal regulatory system for insurance similar to that which oversees state banks and national banks.

In the state of New York, which has unique laws in keeping with its stature as a global business centre, former New York Attorney General Eliot Spitzer was in a unique position to grapple with major national insurance brokerages.

Spitzer alleged that Marsh & McLennan steered business to insurance carriers based on the amount of contingent commissions that could be extracted from carriers, rather than basing decisions on whether carriers had the best deals for clients. Several of the largest commercial insurance brokerages have since stopped accepting contingent commissions and have adopted new business models.

TYPES OF INSURANCE

Any risk that can be quantified can potentially be insured. Specific kinds of risk that may give rise to claims are known as "perils". An insurance policy will set out in detail which perils are covered by the policy and which are not.

Below are (non-exhaustive) lists of the many different types of insurance that exist. A single policy may cover risks in one or more of the categories set forth below. For example, auto insurance would typically cover both property risk (covering the risk of theft or damage to the car) and liability risk (covering legal claims from causing an accident). A homeowner's insurance policy in the U.S. typically includes property insurance covering damage to the home and the owner's belongings, liability insurance covering certain legal claims against the owner, and even a small amount of health insurance for medical expenses of guests who are injured on the owner's property.

Business insurance can be any kind of insurance that protects businesses against risks. Some principal subtypes of business insurance are (a) the various kinds of *professional liability insurance,* also called *professional indemnity insurance,* which are discussed below under that name; and (b) the business owners policy (BOP), which bundles into one policy many of the kinds of coverage that a business owner needs, in a way analogous to how homeowners insurance bundles the coverages that a homeowner needs.

Life & Annuity Coverages

- Life insurance provides a monetary benefit to a decedent's family or other designated beneficiary, and may specifically provide for income to an insured person's family, burial, funeral and other final expenses. Life insurance policies often allow the option of having the proceeds paid to the beneficiary either in a lump sum cash payment or an annuity.
- Annuities provide a stream of payments and are generally classified as insurance because they are issued by insurance companies and regulated as insurance and require the same kinds of actuarial and investment management expertise that life insurance requires. Annuities and pensions that pay a benefit for life are sometimes regarded as insurance against the possibility that a retiree will outlive his or her financial resources. In that sense, they are the complement of life insurance and, from an underwriting perspective, are the mirror image of life insurance.

Health Coverages

- Health insurance policies will often cover the cost of private medical treatments if the National Health Service in the

UK (NHS) or other publicly-funded health programs do not pay for them. It will often result in quicker health care where better facilities are available.

- Dental insurance, like medical insurance, is coverage for individuals to protect them against dental costs. In the U.S., dental insurance is often part of an employer's benefits package, along with health insurance.

Disability Coverages

- Disability insurance policies provide financial support in the event the policyholder is unable to work because of disabling illness or injury. It provides monthly support to help pay such obligations as mortgages and credit cards.
- Total permanent disability insurance insurance provides benefits when a person is permanently disabled and can no longer work in their profession, often taken as an adjunct to life insurance.
- Disability overhead insurance allows business owners to cover the overhead expenses of their business while they are unable to work.
- Workers' compensation insurance replaces all or part of a worker's wages lost and accompanying medical expense incurred because of a job-related injury.

Property & Casualty Coverages

Property insurance provides protection against risks to property, such as fire, theft or weather damage. This includes specialized forms of insurance such as fire insurance, flood insurance, earthquake insurance, home insurance, inland marine insurance or boiler insurance.

Casualty insurance insures against accidents, not necessarily tied to any specific property.

- Automobile insurance, known in the UK as *motor insurance,* is probably the most common form of insurance and may cover both legal liability claims against the driver and loss of or damage to the insured's vehicle itself. Throughout the United States auto insurance policy is required to legally operate a motor vehicle on public roads. In some jurisdictions, bodily injury compensation for automobile accident victims has been changed to a no-fault system, which reduces or eliminates the ability to sue for compensation but provides automatic eligibility for benefits. Credit card companies insure against damage on rented cars.

- o Driving School Insurance insurance provides cover for any authorized driver whilst under going tuition, cover also unlike other motor policies provides cover for instructor liability where both the pupil and driving instructor are both equally liable in the event of a claim.

- Aviation insurance insures against hull, spares, deductible, hull wear and liability risks.
- Boiler insurance (also known as boiler and machinery insurance or equipment breakdown insurance) insures against accidental physical damage to equipment or machinery.
- Builder's risk insurance insures against the risk of physical loss or damage to property during construction. Builder's risk insurance is typically written on an "all risk" basis covering damage due to any cause (including the negligence of the insured) not otherwise expressly excluded.
- Crime insurance is a form of casualty insurance that covers the policyholder against losses arising from the criminal acts of third parties. For example, a company can obtain crime insurance to cover losses arising from theft or embezzlement.
- Crop insurance "Farmers use crop insurance to reduce or manage various risks associated with growing crops. Such risks include crop loss or damage caused by weather, hail, drought, frost damage, insects, or disease, for instance."
- Earthquake insurance is a form of property insurance that pays the policyholder in the event of an earthquake that causes damage to the property. Most ordinary homeowners insurance policies do not cover earthquake damage. Most earthquake insurance policies feature a high deductible.

Rates depend on location and the probability of an earthquake, as well as the construction of the home.

- A fidelity bond is a form of casualty insurance that covers policyholders for losses that they incur as a result of fraudulent acts by specified individuals. It usually insures a business for losses caused by the dishonest acts of its employees.
- Fire insurance: See "Property insurance".
- Flood insurance protects against property loss due to flooding. Many insurers in the US do not provide flood insurance in some portions of the country. In response to this, the federal government created the National Flood Insurance Program which serves as the insurer of last resort.
- Hazard insurance: See "Property insurance".
- Home insurance or homeowners insurance: See "Property insurance".
- Marine insurance and marine cargo insurance cover the loss or damage of ships at sea or on inland waterways, and of the cargo that may be on them. When the owner of the cargo and the carrier are separate corporations, marine cargo insurance typically compensates the owner of cargo for losses sustained from fire, shipwreck, etc., but excludes losses that can be recovered from the carrier or the carrier's insurance. Many marine insurance underwriters will include "time element" coverage in such policies, which extends the indemnity to cover loss of profit and other business expenses attributable to the delay caused by a covered loss.
- Political risk insurance is a form of casualty insurance that can be taken out by businesses with operations in countries in which there is a risk that revolution or other political conditions will result in a loss.
- Surety bond insurance is a three party insurance guaranteeing the performance of the principal.
- Terrorism insurance provides protection against any loss or damage caused by terrorist activities.

- Volcano insurance is an insurance that covers volcano damage in Hawaii.
- Windstorm insurance is an insurance covering the damage that can be caused by hurricanes and tropical cyclones.

LIABILITY COVERAGES

Liability insurance is a very broad superset that covers legal claims against the insured. Many types of insurance include an aspect of liability coverage. For example, a homeowner's insurance policy will normally include liability coverage which protects the insured in the event of a claim brought by someone who slips and falls on the property; automobile insurance also includes an aspect of liability insurance that indemnifies against the harm that a crashing car can cause to others' lives, health, or property. The protection offered by a liability insurance policy is twofold: a legal defense in the event of a lawsuit commenced against the policyholder and indemnification (payment on behalf of the insured) with respect to a settlement or court verdict. Liability policies typically cover only the negligence of the insured, and will not apply to results of willful or intentional acts by the insured.

- Environmental liability insurance protects the insured from bodily injury, property damage and cleanup costs as a result of the dispersal, release or escape of pollutants.
- Errors and omissions insurance: See "Professional liability insurance" under "Liability insurance".
- Professional liability insurance, also called *professional indemnity insurance,* protects professional practitioners such as architects, lawyers, doctors, and accountants against potential negligence claims made by their patients/clients. Professional liability insurance may take on different names depending on the profession. For example, professional liability insurance in reference to the medical profession may be called *malpractice insurance.* Notaries public may take out *errors and omissions insurance (E&O).* Other potential E&O policyholders include, for example, real estate brokers, home inspectors, appraisers, and website developers.
- Directors and officers liability insurance protects an organization (usually a corporation) from costs associated

with litigation resulting from mistakes incurred by directors and officers for which they are liable. In the industry, it is usually called "D&O" for short.

- Prize indemnity insurance protects the insured from giving away a large prize at a specific event. Examples would include offering prizes to contestants who can make a half-court shot at a basketball game, or a hole-in-one at a golf tournament.

Credit Coverages

- Credit insurance repays some or all of a loan back when certain things happen to the borrower such as unemployment, disability, or death. Mortgage insurance is a form of credit insurance, although the name *credit insurance* more often is used to refer to policies that cover other kinds of debt.
- Mortgage insurance insures the lender against default by the borrower.

Other Types of Coverage

- Defense Base Act Workers' compensation or DBA Insurance insurance provides coverage for civilian workers hired by the government to perform contracts outside the US and Canada. DBA is required for all US citizens, US residents, US Green Card holders, and all employees or subcontractors hired on overseas government contracts. Depending on the country, Foreign Nationals must also be covered under DBA. This coverage typically includes expenses related to medical treatment and loss of wages, as well as disability and death benefits.
- Expatriate insurance provides individuals and organizations operating outside of their home country with protection for automobiles, property, health, liability and business pursuits.
- Financial loss insurance protects individuals and companies against various financial risks. For example, a business might purchase cover to protect it from loss of sales if a fire in a factory prevented it from carrying out its business for a time. Insurance might also cover the

failure of a creditor to pay money it owes to the insured. This type of insurance is frequently referred to as "business interruption insurance." Fidelity bonds and surety bonds are included in this category, although these products provide a benefit to a third party (the "obligee") in the event the insured party (usually referred to as the "obligor") fails to perform its obligations under a contract with the obligee.

- Kidnap and ransom insurance
- Locked funds insurance is a little-known hybrid insurance policy jointly issued by governments and banks. It is used to protect public funds from tamper by unauthorized parties. In special cases, a government may authorize its use in protecting semi-private funds which are liable to tamper. The terms of this type of insurance are usually very strict. Therefore it is used only in extreme cases where maximum security of funds is required.
- Nuclear incident insurance covers damages resulting from an incident involving radioactive materials and is generally arranged at the national level. (For the United States, see the Price-Anderson Nuclear Industries Indemnity Act.)
- Pet insurance insures pets against accidents and illnesses-some companies cover routine/wellness care and burial, as well.
- Pollution Insurance. A first-party coverage for contamination of insured property either by external or on-site sources. Coverage for liability to third parties arising from contamination of air, water, or land due to the sudden and accidental release of hazardous materials from the insured site. The policy usually covers the costs of cleanup and may include coverage for releases from underground storage tanks. Intentional acts are specifically excluded.
- Purchase insurance is aimed at providing protection on the products people purchase. Purchase insurance can cover individual purchase protection, warranties, guarantees, care plans and even mobile phone insurance. Such insurance is normally very limited in the scope of problems that are covered by the policy.

- Title insurance provides a guarantee that title to real property is vested in the purchaser and/or mortgagee, free and clear of liens or encumbrances. It is usually issued in conjunction with a search of the public records performed at the time of a real estate transaction.
- Travel insurance is an insurance cover taken by those who travel abroad, which covers certain losses such as medical expenses, lost of personal belongings, travel delay, personal liabilities, etc.

Types of Insurance Financing Vehicles

- Protected Self-Insurance is an alternative risk financing mechanism in which an organization retains the mathematically calculated cost of risk within the organization and transfers the catastrophic risk with specific and aggregate limits to an Insurer so the maximum total cost of the program is known. A properly designed and underwritten Protected Self-Insurance Program reduces and stabilizes the cost of insurance and provides valuable risk management information.
- Retrospectively Rated Insurance is a method of establishing a premium on large commercial accounts. The final premium is based on the insured's actual loss experience during the policy term, sometimes subject to a minimum and maximum premium, with the final premium determined by a formula. Under this plan, the current year's premium is based partially (or wholly) on the current year's losses, although the premium adjustments may take months or years beyond the current year's expiration date. The rating formula is guaranteed in the insurance contract. Formula: retrospective premium = converted loss + basic premium × tax multiplier. Numerous variations of this formula have been developed and are in use.
- Fraternal insurance is provided on a cooperative basis by fraternal benefit societies or other social organizations.
- Formal self insurance is the deliberate decision to pay for otherwise insurable losses out of one's own money. This can be done on a formal basis by establishing a separate fund into which funds are deposited on a periodic basis,

or by simply forgoing the purchase of available insurance and paying out-of-pocket. Self insurance is usually used to pay for high-frequency, low-severity losses. Such losses, if covered by conventional insurance, mean having to pay a premium that includes loadings for the company's general expenses, cost of putting the policy on the books, acquisition expenses, premium taxes, and contingencies. While this is true for all insurance, for small, frequent losses the transaction costs may exceed the benefit of volatility reduction that insurance otherwise affords.

- No-fault insurance is a type of insurance policy (typically automobile insurance) where insureds are indemnified by their own insurer regardless of fault in the incident.
- Reinsurance is a type of insurance purchased by insurance companies or self-insured employers to protect against unexpected losses. Financial reinsurance is a form of reinsurance that is primary used for capital management rather than to transfer insurance risk.
- Stop-loss insurance provides protection against catastrophic or unpredictable losses. It is purchased by organizations who do not want to assume 100% of the liability for losses arising from the plans. Under a stop-loss policy, the insurance company becomes liable for losses that exceed certain limits called deductibles.
- Social insurance can be many things to many people in many countries. But a summary of its essence is that it is a collection of insurance coverages (including components of life insurance, disability income insurance, unemployment insurance, health insurance, and others), plus retirement savings, that mandates participation by all citizens. By forcing everyone in society to be a policyholder and pay premiums, it ensures that everyone can become a claimant when or if he/she needs to. Along the way this inevitably becomes related to other concepts such as the justice system and the welfare state. This is a large, complicated topic that engenders tremendous debate, which can be further studied in the following articles (and others):

- o Social welfare provision
- o Social security
- o Social safety net
- o National Insurance
- o Social Security (United States)
- o Social Security debate (United States)

Types of Insurance Companies

Insurance companies may be classified as

- *Life* insurance companies, which sell life insurance, annuities and pensions products.
- *Non-life* or *general* insurance companies, which sell other types of insurance.

General insurance companies can be further divided into these sub categories.

- Standard Lines
- Excess Lines.

In most countries, life and non-life insurers are subject to different regulatory regimes and different tax and accounting rules. The main reason for the distinction between the two types of company is that life, annuity, and pension business is very long-term in nature — coverage for life assurance or a pension can cover risks over many decades. By contrast, non-life insurance cover usually covers a shorter period, such as one year.

In the United States, standard line insurance companies are your "main stream" insurers. These are the companies that typically insure your auto, home or business. They use pattern or "cookie-cutter" policies without variation from one person to the next. They usually have lower premiums than excess lines and can sell directly to individuals. They are regulated by state laws that can restrict the amount they can charge for insurance policies.

Excess line insurance companies (aka Excess and Surplus) typically insure risks not covered by the standard lines market. They are broadly referred as being all insurance placed with non-admitted insurers. Non-admitted insurers are not licensed in the states where the risks are located. These companies have more flexibility and can react faster than standard insurance companies because they are not required to file rates and forms as do the "admitted" carriers do. However, they still have substantial regulatory requirements placed upon them. State laws generally require insurance placed with surplus line agents and brokers to not be available through standard licensed insurers.

Insurance companies are generally classified as either *mutual* or *stock* companies. This is more of a traditional distinction as true mutual companies are becoming rare. Mutual companies are owned by the policyholders, while stockholders (who may or may not own policies) own stock insurance companies. Other possible forms for an insurance company include reciprocals, in which policyholders 'reciprocate' in sharing risks, and Lloyds organizations.

Insurance companies are rated by various agencies such as A. M. Best. The ratings include the company's financial strength, which measures its ability to pay claims. It also rates financial instruments issued by the insurance company, such as bonds, notes, and securitization products.

Reinsurance companies are insurance companies that sell policies to other insurance companies, allowing them to reduce their risks and protect themselves from very large losses. The reinsurance market is dominated by a few very large companies, with huge reserves. A reinsurer may also be a direct writer of insurance risks as well.

Captive insurance companies may be defined as limited-purpose insurance companies established with the specific objective of financing risks emanating from their parent group or groups. This definition can sometimes be extended to include some of the risks of the parent company's customers. In short, it is an in-house self-insurance vehicle. Captives may take the form of a "pure" entity (which is a 100 percent subsidiary of the self-insured parent company); of a "mutual" captive (which insures the collective risks of members of an industry); and of an "association" captive (which self-insures individual risks of the members of a professional, commercial or industrial association). Captives represent commercial, economic and tax advantages to their sponsors because of the reductions in costs they help create and for the ease of insurance risk management and the flexibility for cash flows they generate. Additionally, they may provide coverage of risks which is neither available nor offered in the traditional insurance market at reasonable prices.

The types of risk that a captive can underwrite for their parents include property damage, public and products liability, professional indemnity, employee benefits, employers liability, motor and medical aid expenses. The captive's exposure to such risks may be limited by the use of reinsurance.

Captives are becoming an increasingly important component of the risk management and risk financing strategy of their parent. This can be understood against the following background:

- heavy and increasing premium costs in almost every line of coverage;
- difficulties in insuring certain types of fortuitous risk;
- differential coverage standards in various parts of the world;
- rating structures which reflect market trends rather than individual loss experience;
- insufficient credit for deductibles and/or loss control efforts.

There are also companies known as 'insurance consultants'. Like a mortgage broker, these companies are paid a fee by the customer to shop around for the best insurance policy amongst many companies.

Similar to an insurance consultant, an 'insurance broker' also shops around for the best insurance policy amongst many companies. However, with insurance brokers, the fee is usually paid in the form of commission from the insurer that is selected rather than directly from the client. Neither insurance consultants nor insurance brokers are insurance companies and no risks are transferred to them in insurance transactions.

Third party administrators are companies that perform underwriting and sometimes claims handling services for insurance companies. These companies often have special expertise that the insurance companies do not have.

LIFE INSURANCE AND SAVING

Certain life insurance contracts accumulate cash values, which may be taken by the insured if the policy is surrendered or which may be borrowed against. Some policies, such as annuities and endowment policies, are financial instruments to accumulate or liquidate wealth when it is needed.

Further Information: Life Insurance

In many countries, such as the U.S. and the UK, the tax law provides that the interest on this cash value is not taxable under certain circumstances. This leads to widespread use of life insurance as a tax-efficient method of saving as well as protection in the event of early death.

In U.S., the tax on interest income on life insurance policies and annuities is generally deferred. However, in some cases the benefit derived from tax deferral may be offset by a low return. This depends upon the insuring company, the type of policy and other variables (mortality, market return, etc.). Moreover, other income tax saving vehicles (e.g., IRAs, 401(k) plans, Roth IRAs) may be better alternatives for value accumulation. A combination of low-cost term life insurance and a higher-return tax-efficient retirement account may achieve better investment return.

SIZE OF GLOBAL INSURANCE INDUSTRY

Global insurance premiums grew by 9.7 percent in 2004 to reach $3.3 trillion. This follows 11.7 percent growth in the previous year. Life insurance premiums grew by 9.8 percent during the year, thanks to rising demand for annuity and pension products. Non-life insurance premiums grew by 9.4 percent, as premium rates increased. Over the past decade, global insurance premiums rose by more than a half as annual growth fluctuated between 2 percent and 10 percent.

Advanced economies account for the bulk of global insurance. With premium income of $1,217 billion in 2004, North America was the most important region, followed by the EU (at $1,198 billion) and Japan (at $492 billion). The top four countries accounted for nearly two-thirds of premiums in 2004. The United States and Japan alone accounted for a half of world insurance premiums, much higher than their 7 percent share of the global population. Emerging markets accounted for over 85 percent of the world's population but generated only 10 percent of premiums. The volume of UK insurance business totaled $295 billion in 2004 or 9.1 percent of global premiums.

Financial Viability of Insurance Companies

Financial stability and strength of an insurance company should be a major consideration when purchasing an insurance contract. An insurance premium paid currently provides coverage for losses that might arise many years in the future.

For that reason, the viability of the insurance carrier is very important. In recent years, a number of insurance companies have become insolvent, leaving their policyholders with no coverage (or coverage only from a government-backed insurance pool or other arrangement with less attractive payouts for losses).

A number of independent rating agencies, such as Best's, Fitch, Standard & Poor's, and Moody's Investors Service, provide information and rate the financial viability of insurance companies.

Accounting Definition (United States)

An operational definition of insurance is that it is

- the benefit provided by a particular kind of indemnity contract, called an insurance policy;
- that is issued by one of several kinds of legal entities (stock insurance company, mutual insurance company, reciprocal, or Lloyd's syndicate, for example), any of which may be called an insurer;
- in which the insurer promises to pay on behalf of or to indemnify another party, called a policyholder or insured;
- that protects the insured against loss caused by those perils subject to the indemnity in exchange for consideration known as an insurance premium.

In recent years this kind of operational definition proved inadequate as a result of contracts that had the form but not the substance of insurance. The essence of insurance is the transfer of risk from the insured to one or more insurers. How much risk a contract actually transfers proved to be at the heart of the controversy.

This issue arose most clearly in reinsurance, where the use of Financial Reinsurance to reengineer insurer balance sheets under US GAAP became fashionable during the 1980s. The accounting profession raised serious concerns about the use of reinsurance in which little if any actual risk was transferred, and went on to address the issue in FAS 113, cited above. While on its face, FAS 113 is limited to accounting for reinsurance transactions, the guidance it contains is generally conceded to be equally applicable to US GAAP accounting for insurance transactions executed by commercial enterprises.

Risk Transfer Requirement

FAS 113 contains two tests, called the '9a and 9b tests,' that collectively require that a contract create a reasonable chance of a significant loss to the underwriter for it to be considered insurance.

Indemnification of the ceding enterprise against loss or liability relating to insurance risk in reinsurance of short-duration contracts requires both of the following, unless the condition in paragraph 11 is met:

a. The reinsurer assumes significant insurance risk under the reinsured portions of the underlying insurance contracts.
b. It is reasonably possible that the reinsurer may realize a significant loss from the transaction.

Paragraph 10 of FAS 113 makes clear that the 9a and 9b tests are based on comparing the present value of all costs to the PV of all income streams. FAS gives no guidance on the choice of a discount rate on which to base such a calculation, other than to say that all outcomes tested should use the same rate.

Statement of Statutory Accounting Principles ("SSAP") 62, issued by the National Association of Insurance Commissioners, applies to so-called 'statutory accounting'-the accounting for insurance enterprises to conform with regulation. Paragraph 12 of SSAP 62 is nearly identical to the FAS 113 test, while paragraph 14, which is otherwise very similar to paragraph 10 of FAS 113, additionally contains a justification for the use of a single fixed rate for discounting purposes. The choice of an "reasonable and appropriate" discount rate is left as a matter of judgment.

No Brightline Test

Neither FAS 113 nor SAP 62 defines the terms *reasonable* or *significant*. Ideally, one would like to be able to substitute values for both terms. It would be much simpler if one could apply a test of an X percent chance of a loss of Y percent or greater. Such tests have been proposed, including one famously attributed to an SEC official who is said to have opined in an after lunch talk that a 10 percent chance of a 10 percent loss was sufficient to establish both reasonableness and significance. Indeed, many insurers and reinsurers still apply this 10/10" test as a benchmark for risk transfer testing.

It should be obvious that an attempt to use any numerical rule such as the 10/10 test will quickly run into problems. Implicit in the test is keeping the 10/10 that either are upper bonds for the comment made by the SEC official therefore, the rest of this paragraph doesn't apply. Suppose a contract has a 1 percent chance of a 10,000 percent loss? It should be reasonably self-evident that such a contract is insurance, but it fails one half of the 10/10 test.

It does not appear that any brightline test of reasonableness nor significance can be constructed.

Excess of loss contracts, like those commonly used for umbrella and general liability insurance, or to insure against property losses, will typically have a low ratio of premium paid to maximum loss recoverable.

This ratio (expressed as a percentage), commonly called the *rate on line* for historical reasons related to underwriting practices at Lloyd's of London, will typically be low for contracts that contain reasonably self-evident risk transfer. As the ratio increases to approximate the present value of the limit of coverage, self-evidence decreases and disappears.

Contracts with low rates on line may survive modest features that limit the amount of risk transferred. As rates on line increase, such risk limiting features become increasingly important.

"Safe Harbor" Exemptions

The analysis of reasonableness and significance is an estimate of the probability of different gain or loss outcomes under different loss scenarios. It takes time and resources to perform the analysis, which constitutes a burden without value where risk transfer is reasonably self-evident.

Guidance exists for insurers and reinsurers, whose CEO's and CFO's attest annually as to the reinsurance agreements their firms undertake. The American Academy of Actuaries, for instance, identifies three categories of contract as outside the requirement of attestation:

- Inactive contracts. If there are no premiums due nor losses payable, and the insurer is not taking any credit for the reinsurance, determining risk transfer is irrelevant.
- Pre-1994 contracts. The attestation requirement only applies to contracts that were entered into, renewed or amended on or after 1 January 1994. Prior contracts need not be analyzed.
- Where risk transfer is "reasonably self-evident."

"Risk transfer is reasonably self-evident in most traditional per-risk or per-occurrence excess of loss reinsurance contracts. For these contracts, a predetermined amount of premium is paid and the reinsurer assumes nearly all or all of the potential variability in the underlying losses, and it is evident from reading the basic terms of the contract that the reinsurer can incur a significant loss. In many cases, there is no aggregate limit on the reinsurer's loss. The existence of certain experience-based contract terms, such as experience accounts, profit commissions, and additional premiums, generally reduce the amount of risk transfer and make it less likely that risk transfer is reasonably self-evident."— "Reinsurance Attestation Supplement 20-1: Risk Transfer Testing Practice Note,"

American Academy of Actuaries, *November 2005.*

Risk Limiting Features

An insurance policy should not contain provisions that allow one side or the other to unilaterally void the contract in exchange for benefit. Provisions that void the contract for failure to perform or for fraud or material misrepresentation are ordinary and acceptable.

The policy should have a term of not more than about three years. This is not a hard and fast rule. Contracts of over five years duration are classified as 'long-term,' which can impact the accounting treatment, and can obviously introduce the possibility that over the entire term of the contract, no actual risk will transfer. The coverage provided by the contract need not cease at the end of the term (e.g., the contract can cover occurrences as opposed to claims made or claims paid).

The contract should be considered to include any other agreements, written or oral, that confer rights, create obligations, or create benefits on the part of either or both parties. Ideally, the contract should contain an 'Entire Agreement' clause that assures there are no undisclosed written or oral side agreements that confer rights, create obligations, or create benefits on the part of either or both parties. If such rights, obligations or benefits exist, they must be factored into the tests of reasonableness and significance.

The contract should not contain arbitrary limitations on timing of payments. Provisions that assure both parties of time to properly present and consider claims are acceptable provided they are commercially reasonable and customary.

Provisions that expressly create actual or notional accounts that accrue actual or notional interest suggest that the contract contains, in fact, a deposit.

Provisions for additional or return premium do not, in and of themselves, render a contract something other than insurance. However, it should be unlikely that either a return or additional premium provision be triggered, and neither party should have discretion regarding the timing of such triggering.

All of the events that would give rise to claims under the contract cannot have materialized prior to the inception of the contract. If this "all events" test is not met, then the contract is considered to be a retroactive contract, for which the accounting treatment becomes complex.

CONTROVERSIES

Insurance Insulates too Much

By creating a "security blanket" for its insureds, an insurance company may inadvertently find that its insureds may not be as risk-averse as they might otherwise be (since, by definition, the insured has transferred the risk to the insurer).

This problem is known to the insurance industry as moral hazard. To reduce their own financial exposure, insurance companies have contractual clauses that mitigate their obligation to provide coverage if the insured engages in behavior that grossly magnifies their risk of loss or liability.

For example, life insurance companies may require higher premiums or deny coverage altogether to people who work in hazardous occupations or engage in dangerous sports. Liability insurance providers do not provide coverage for liability arising from intentional torts committed by the insured.

Even if a provider were so irrational as to desire to provide such coverage, it is against the public policy of most countries to allow such insurance to exist, and thus it is usually illegal.

Closed Community Self-insurance

Some communities prefer to create virtual insurance amongst themselves by other means than contractual risk transfer, which assigns explicit numerical values to risk.

A number of religious groups, including the Amish and some Muslim groups, depend on support provided by their communities when disasters strike.

The risk presented by any given person is assumed collectively by the community who all bear the cost of rebuilding lost property and supporting people whose needs are suddenly greater after a loss of some kind. In supportive communities where others can be trusted to follow community leaders, this tacit form of insurance can work.

In this manner the community can even out the extreme differences in insurability that exist among its members. Some further justification is also provided by invoking the moral hazard of explicit insurance contracts.

In the United Kingdom The Crown (which, for practical purposes, meant the Civil service) did not insure property such as government buildings.

If a government building was damaged, the cost of repair would be met from public funds because, in the long run, this was cheaper than paying insurance premiums. Since many UK government buildings have been sold to property companies, and rented back, this arrangement is now less common and may have disappeared altogether.

Complexity of Insurance Policy Contracts

Insurance policies can be complex and some policyholders may not understand all the fees and coverages included in a policy.

As a result, people may buy policies on unfavorable terms. In response to these issues, many countries have enacted detailed statutory and regulatory regimes governing every aspect of the insurance business, including minimum standards for policies and the ways in which they may be advertised and sold.

Many institutional insurance purchasers buy insurance through an insurance broker. Brokers represent the buyer (not the insurance company), and typically counsel the buyer on appropriate coverages, policy limitations. A broker generally holds contracts with many insurers, thereby allowing the broker to "shop" the market for the best rates and coverage possible.

Insurance may also be purchased through an agent. Unlike a broker, who represents the policyholder, an agent represents the insurance company from whom the policyholder buys. An agent can represent more than one company.

Redlining

Redlining is the practice of denying insurance coverage in specific geographic areas, purportedly because of a high likelihood of loss, while the alleged motivation is unlawful discrimination. Racial profiling or redlining has a long history in the property insurance industry in the United States. From a review of industry underwriting and marketing materials, court documents, and research by government agencies, industry and community groups, and academics, it is clear that race has long affected and continues to affect the policies and practices of the insurance industry.

In determining premiums and premium rate structures, insurers consider quantifiable factors, including location, credit scores, gender, occupation, marital status, and education level. However, the use of such factors is often considered to be unfair or unlawfully discriminatory, and the reaction against this practice has in some instances led to political disputes about the ways in which insurers determine premiums and regulatory intervention to limit the factors used.

An insurance underwriter's job is to evaluate a given risk as to the likelihood that a loss will occur. Any factor that causes a greater likelihood of loss should theoretically be charged a higher rate. This basic principle of insurance must be followed if insurance companies are to remain solvent.

Thus, "discrimination" against (i.e., differential treatment of) potential insureds in the risk evaluation and premium-setting process is a necessary by-product of the fundamentals of insurance underwriting.

For instance, insurers charge older people significantly higher premiums than they charge younger people for term life insurance. Older people are thus treated differently than younger people (i.e., a distinction is made, discrimination occurs).

The rationale for the differential treatment goes to the heart of the risk a life insurer takes: Old people are likely to die sooner than young people, so the risk of loss (the insured's death) is greater in any given period of time and therefore the risk premium must be higher to cover the greater risk. However, treating insureds differently when there is no actuarially sound reason for doing so is unlawful discrimination.

What is often missing from the debate is that prohibiting the use of legitimate, actuarially sound factors means that an insufficient amount is being charged for a given risk, and there is thus a deficit in the system.

The failure to address the deficit may mean insolvency and hardship for all of a company's insureds. The options for addressing the deficit seem to be the following: Charge the deficit to the other policyholders or charge it to the government (i.e., externalize outside of the company to society at large).

Health Insurance

Health insurance, which is coverage for individuals to protect them against medical costs, is a highly charged and political issue in the United States, which does not have socialized health coverage. In theory, the market for health insurance should function in a manner similar to other insurance coverages, but the skyrocketing cost of health coverage has disrupted markets around the globe, but perhaps most glaringly in the U.S. See health insurance & Health insurance in the United States.

Insurance Patents

New insurance products can now be protected from copying with a business method patent in the United States.

A recent example of a new insurance product that is patented is telematic auto insurance. It was independently invented and patented by a major U.S. auto insurance company, Progressive Auto Insurance (U.S. Patent 5,797,134) and a Spanish independent inventor, Salvador Minguijon Perez (EP patent 0700009).

The basic idea of telematic auto insurance is that a driver's behavior is monitored directly while he or she drives and the information is transmitted to the insurance company.

The insurance company uses the information to assess the likelihood that a driver will have an accident and adjusts premiums accordingly.

A driver who drives great distances at high speeds, for example, might be charged a different rate than a driver who drives short distances at low speeds. The precise effect on charges is not known as it is not clear that a high speed long distance driver incurs greater risk to an insurance pool than the slow around-town driver.

A British auto insurance company, Norwich Union, has obtained a license to both the Progressive patent and Perez patent. They have made investments in infrastructure and developed a commercial offering called "Pay As You Drive" or PAYD.

Recent theoretical economic research on the social welfare effects of Progressive's telematics technology business process patents have questioned whether the business process patents are pareto efficient for society. Preliminary results suggest that they are not, but more work is needed.

Many independent inventors are in favor of patenting new insurance products since it gives them protection from big companies when they bring their new insurance products to market. Independent inventors account for 70 percent of the new U.S. patent applications in this area. Many insurance executives are opposed to patenting insurance products because it creates a new risk for them.

The Hartford insurance company, for example, recently had to pay $80 million to an independent inventor, Bancorp Services, in order to settle a patent infringement and theft of trade secret lawsuit for a type of corporate owned life insurance product invented and patented by Bancorp.

There are currently about 150 new patent applications on insurance inventions filed per year in the United States. The rate at which patents have issued has steadily risen from 15 in 2002 to 44 in 2006.

The Insurance Industry and Rent Seeking

Certain insurance products and practices have been described as rent seeking by critics.

That is, some insurance products or practices are useful primarily because of legal benefits, such as reducing taxes, as opposed to providing protection against risks of adverse events. Under United States tax law, for example, most owners of variable annuities and variable life insurance can invest their premium payments in the stock market and defer or eliminate paying any taxes on their investments until withdrawals are made.

Sometimes this tax deferral is the only reason people use these products. Another example is the legal infrastructure which allows life insurance to be held in an irrevocable trust which is used to pay an estate tax while the proceeds themselves are immune from the estate tax.

Criticism of Insurance Companies

Some people believe that modern insurance companies are money-making businesses which have little interest in insurance. They argue that the purpose of insurance is to spread risk so the reluctance of insurance companies to take on high-risk cases (e.g. houses in areas subject to flooding, or young drivers) runs counter to the principle of insurance.

Other criticisms include:

- Insurance policies contain too many exclusion clauses. For example, some house insurance policies do not cover damage to garden walls.
- Most insurance companies now use call centres and staff attempt to answer questions by reading from a script. It is difficult to speak to anybody with expert knowledge.

2

Life Insurance in India

Life Insurance in India was nationalised by incorporating Life Insurance Corporation (LIC) in 1956. All private life insurance companies at that time were taken over by LIC.

In 1993 the Government of Republic of India appointed RN Malhotra Committee to lay down a road map for privatisation of the life insurance sector.

While the committee submitted its report in 1994, it took another six years before the enabling legislation was passed in the year 2000, legislation amending the *Insurance Act* of 1938 and legislating the *Insurance Regulatory and Development Authority Act* of 2000. The same year that the newly appointed insurance regulator-Insurance Regulatory and Development Authority IRDA — started issuing licenses to private life insurers.

List of Life Insurers (as of Sept, 2006)

Apart from Life Insurance Corporation, the public sector life insurer, there are 14 other private sector life insurers, most of them joint ventures between Indian groups and global insurance giants.

Life Insurer in Public Sector

1. Life Insurance Corporation of India

Life Insurers in Private Sector

1. Bajaj Allianz Life

Pranav,Surat 1

1. Tata AIG Life
2. ICICI Prudential Life Insurance
3. HDFC Standard Life

4. Birla Sunlife
5. SBI Life Insurance
6. Kotak Mahindra Old Mutual Life Insurance
7. Aviva Life Insurance
8. Reliance Life Insurance Company Limited-Formerly known as AMP Sanmar LIC
9. Metlife India Life Insurance
10. ING Vysya Life Insurance
11. Max Newyork Life Insurance
12. Sahara Life Insurance-Now they are not into business
13. Shriram Life Insurance
14. Bharti AXA Life Insurance Co Ltd

Foreign Direct Investment (FDI) Policy in Insurance Sector

As per the current (Mar 06) FDI norms, foreign participation in an Indian insurance company is restricted to 26.0% of its equity / ordinary share capital. The Union Budget for fiscal 2005 had recommended that the ceiling on foreign holding be increased to 49.0%. However, the matter is still under discussions.

Indian Life Insurance Industry Overview

All life insurance companies in India have to comply with the strict regulations laid out by Insurance Regulatory and Development Authority of India (IRDA). Therefore there is no risk in going in for private insurance players. In terms of being rated for financial strength like international players, only ICICI Prudential is rated by Fitch India at National Insurer Financial Strength Rating of AAA(Ind) with stable outlook indicating the highest claims paying ability rating.

Life Insurance Corporation of India (LIC), the state owned behemoth, remains by far the largest player in the market. Among the private sector players, ICICI Prudential Life Insurance(JV between ICICI Bank and Prudential PLC)is the largest followed by Bajaj Allianz Life Insurance Company Limited (JV between Bajaj Group and Allianz).

The private companies are coming out with better products which are more beneficial to the customer. Among such products are the ULIPs or the Unit Linked Investment Plans which offer both life cover as well as scope for savings or investment options as the customer desires.Further, these type of plans are subject to a minimum lock-in period of three years to prevent misuse of the significant tax benefits offered to such plans under the Income Tax Act. Hence, comparison of such products with mutual funds would be erroneous.

Commission / Intermediation fees

- The maximum commission limits as per statutory provisions are:

Agency commission for retail life insurance business:

- 35-40% for 1st year premium if the premium paying term is more than 20 years
- 25-30% for 1st year premium if the premium paying term is more than 15 years
- 10-15% for 1st year premium if the premium paying term is less than 10 years
- 7.5%-yr 2 and 3rd year and 5%-thereafter for all premium paying terms.

In case of Mutual fund related-Unit linked policies it varies between 1.5% to 60% on the premium paid.

o Agency commission for retail pension policies:

  * 7.5% for 1st year premium and 2.5% thereafter

    - Maximum broker commission-30%
    - Referral fees to banks – Max 55% for regular premium and 10% for single premium. However in any case this fee cannot be more than the agency commission as filed under the product.
    - However, the above commission may be further subject to the product wise limits specified by IRDA while approving the product.

LIFE INSURANCE CORPORATION OF INDIA

The Life Insurance Corporation of India (LICI) is the largest life insurance company in India; it is fully owned by the Government of India. It was founded in 1956.

Headquartered in Mumbai, which is considered the financial capital of India, the Life Insurance Corporation of India currently has 8 zonal Offices and 101 divisional offices located in different parts of India, at least 2048 branches located in different cities and towns of India along with satellite Offices attached to about some 50 Branches, and has a network of around one million and 200 thousand agents [1] for soliciting life insurance business from the public.

History

The Oriental Life Insurance Company, the first corporate entity in India offering life insurance cover was established in Calcutta in 1818 by Bipin Behari Dasgupta and others. Europeans in India were its primary target market, and it charged Indians heftier premiums. The Bombay Mutual Life Assurance Society, formed in 1870, was the first native insurance provider. Other insurance companies established in the pre-independence era included

- Bharat Insurance Company (1896)
- United India (1906)
- National Indian (1906)
- National Insurance (1906)
- Co-operative Assurance (1906)
- Hindustan Co-operative (1907)
- Indian Mercantile
- General Assurance
- Swadeshi Life (later Bombay Life)

The first 150 years were marked mostly by turbulent economic conditions. It witnessed, India's First War of Independence, adverse affects of the World War I and World War II on the economy of India, and in between them the period of world wide economic crises triggered by the Great depression. The first half of the 20th century also saw a heightened struggle for India's independence.

The aggregate effect of these events led to a high rate of bankruptcies and liquidation of life insurance companies in India. This had adversely affected the faith of the general public in the utility of obtaining life cover.

The LIFE INSURANCE Act and the Provident Fund Act were passed in 1912, providing the first regulatory mechanisms in the Life Insurance industry. The Indian Insurance Companies Act of 1928 authorized the government to obtain statistical information from companies operating in both life and non-life insurance areas. The subsequent Insurance Act of 1938 brought stricter state control over an industry that had seen several financially unsound ventures fail. A bill was also introduced in the Legislative Assembly in 1944 to nationalize the insurance industry.

NATIONALIZATION

In 1955, parliamentarian Feroze Gandhi raised the matter of insurance fraud by owner's of private insurance companies. In the ensuing investigations, one of India's wealthiest businessmen, Ram Kishan Dalmia, owner of the Times of India newspaper, was sent to prison for two months. Eventually, the Parliament of India passed the Life Insurance of India Act on 1956-06-19, and the Life Insurance Corporation of India was created on 1956-09-01, by consolidating the life insurance business of 245 private life insurers and other entities offering life insurance services. Nationalization of the life insurance business in India was a result of the Industrial Policy Resolution of 1956, which had created a policy framework for extending state control over at least seventeen sectors of the economy, including the life insurance. The company began operations with 5 zonal offices, 33 divisional offices and 212 branch offices.

Current Status

Over its existence of around 50 years, Life Insurance Corporation of India, which commanded a monopoly of soliciting and selling life insurance in India, created huge surpluses, and contributed around 7 % of India's GDP in 2006.

The Corporation, which started its business with around 300 offices, 5.6 million policies and a corpus of INR 459 million, has grown to 2,048 offices servicing around 180 million policies and a corpus of over INR 3.4 trillion.

The organization now comprises 2048 branches, 100 divisional offices and 8 zonal offices, and employs over 1 million agents. It also operates in 12 other countries, primarily to cater to the needs of Non Resident Indians.

With the change in the India's economic philosophy from the early 1990s, and the subsequent relaxation of state control over several sectors of the economy, the monopolistic position of the Life Insurance Corporation of India was diluted, and it has had to compete with a number of other corporate entities, Indian as well as transnational Life Insurance brands.

In the fiscal year 2006-07 Life Insurance Corporation of India's number of policy holders are said to have crossed a whopping 200 million (fourth in terms of population of the countries of the world)

Subsidiaries

LIC owns the following subsidiaries:

- Life Insurance Corporation of India International: This is a joint venture offshore company promoted by LIC which commenced operations in July, 1989 with the objectives of offering US$ denomimated policies to cater to the insurance needs of NRIs and providing insurance services to holders of LIC policies currently residing in the Gulf. LIC International operates in all GCC countries.
- LIC Nepal: A joint venture company formed in 2001 with the Vishal Group of Industries, Nepal.
- LIC Lanka: A joint venture company formed in 2003 with the Bartleet Group of Companies, Sri Lanka.
- LIC Housing Finance: Incorporated in 19th June 1989, its main objective is to provide long term finance forconstruction or purchase of houses or apartments. It has a Dubai office.
    - o LICHFL Care Homes: A wholly owned subsidiary of LIC Housing Finance, it builds and operates "Assisted Community Living Centres" for senior citizens.

Technology Usage

The insurance giant opted for internet services for all its subscribers and developed massive networking for own usage and internal governance. While the pros and cons of internal networking remains concealed within the officials and hidden for the common customers, the customer portal somehow fails to satisfy the 21st century customers. Apparently, low bandwidth, unwise web page hyper linking, illogical page set ups, all just contribute to the irritation of common net age customers.

The portal gives opportunity to register any policy to be tagged up with any one. As a matter of fact, if Mr. 'A' knows the policy number and premium value of certain policy 'X' of Mr. 'B,' 'A' can tag up 'X' with his own Profile in LICI portal and get all the details of the policy. Moreover, though the organization is officially known as Life Insurance Corporation of India, abbreviated, LICI, the portal welcomes a customer to LIC. As a result of all these, online payment of premium through the site could not be a popular option for the customers. The site fails to show the details of all its recognized agents in its Agent locator section.

3

INSURANCE STRUCTURE

INTRODUCTION

Today, only one business, which affects all walks of life, is insurance business. That's why insurance industry occupies a very important place among financial services operative in the world. Owing to growing complexity of life, trade and commerce, individuals as well as business firms are turning to insurance to manage various risks. Therefore a proper knowledge of what insurance is and what purpose does it serve to individual or an organisation is therefore necessary. Insurance is a mechanism that ensures an individual to thrive on adverse consequences by compensating the individual his/her loss financially. Every individual in this world is subject to unforeseen and uncalled for hazards or dangers, which may make him and his family vulnerable. At this place, only insurance helps him not only to survive but also recover his loss and continue his life in a normal manner, which would otherwise be unthinkable.

OBJECTIVES

After going through this lesson you should be able to:

- Explain the meaning of insurance
- Understand the nature and characteristics of insurance
- Discuss the need of getting insured and its benefits to individual and business firms
- Describe the types of insurance and their meaning
- List out the meanings of different terms used in the lesson
- Find out the new insurance products available in the market

- Discuss the historical background and the present state of insurance industry after liberalisation of insurance sector.

Meaning and Nature

The term insurance can be defined in financial as well as in legal terms. The financial definition deals with the funding or financial arrangement of the losses whereas the legal definition deals with provisions relating to legally enforceable contract.

Definition in Financial Sense

Insurance is a financial arrangement, which redistributes the costs of unexpected losses among the members of the pool. The pool is a collection of people facing common risks. All members contribute a fixed amount towards a pool called premium. In exchange for the premium payment, the person gets an assurance that a certain sum of money is to be paid to him on the happening of the event insured against. The assurance is that his loss will be made good. Thus, insurance involves the transfer of loss exposures to an insurance pool and the redistribution of losses among the members of the pool.

Definition in Legal Sense

Insurance can be defined as a contract between two parties by which one party undertakes to make good or indemnify any financial loss suffered by other party, in consideration of a sum of money, on the happening of a specified event e.g. fire, accident or death. We call the party agreeing to pay for the losses the insurer. We call the party whose loss makes the 'insurer' pay the claim the insured. We call the payment insured pays to the insurer the premium. We call the insurance contract a policy. In the end we can sum up that insurance is a transfer of risk from the individual to the group and there is a sharing (pooling) of losses on some equitable basis such that fortuitous losses can be indemnified (paid).

Nature of Insurance

The insurance has the following characteristics, which are observed in case of life, marine, fire and general insurance.

Sharing of risk-Insurance is a device to share the financial losses which might befall on an individual or his family on the happening of a specified event. The event may be death in case of life insurance, fire in fire insurance etc. If insured the loss arising from these events will be shared by all insured in the form of premium.

(1) Co-operative device-The most important feature of every insurance plan is the cooperation of large number of persons who, in effect, agree to share the financial loss arising due to a particular risk which is insured. An insurer would be unable to compensate all losses from his capital. So, by insuring a large number of persons, he is able to pay the amount of loss.

(2) Value of risk-The risk is evaluated before insuring to charge the amount of share of an insured, premium. There are several methods of evaluation of risks. If there is expectation of more risk, higher premium may be charged. So, the probability of loss is calculated at the time of insurance.

(4) Payment at contingency-The payment is made at a certain contingency insured. If the contingency occurs, payment is made. Since the life insurance contract is a contract of certainty, because the contingency, the death or the expiry of term, will certainly occur, the payment is certain. In other insurance contracts, the contingency is the fire or the marine perils etc., may or may not occur. So, if the contingency occurs, payment is made, otherwise no amount is given to the policy-holder.

(5) Amount of payment-The amount of payment depends upon the value of loss occurred due to the particular insured risk provided insurance is there up to that amount. In life insurance, the purpose is not to make good the financial loss suffered. The insurer promises to pay a fixed sum on the happening of an event. If the event or the contingency takes place, the payment falls due if the policy is valid and in force at the time of the event.

(6) Large number of insured persons-To spread the loss immediately, smoothly and cheaply, large number of persons should be insured. Large number of persons or property is insured to lower the cost of insurance and the amount of premium.

(7) Insurance is not a gambling-The insurance serves indirectly to increase the productivity of the community by eliminating worry and increasing initiative. The uncertainty is changed into certainty by insuring property and life because the insurer promises to pay a definite sum at damage or death. From the company's point of view, the life insurance is essentially non-speculative; in fact, no other business operates with greater certainties. From the insured point cf view, too, insurance is also the antithesis of gambling. Nothing is more uncertain than life and life insurance offers the only sure method of changing that uncertainty into certainty.

(8) Insurance is not charity-Charity is given without consideration but insurance is not possible without premium. It provides security and safety to an individual and to the security although it is a kind of business because in consideration of premium it guarantees the payment of loss. It is a profession because it provides adequate sources at the time of disasters only by charging a nominal premium for the service.

Purpose and Need

Beside things mentioned by you, let's discuss in detail the purpose and need of insurance. As we all know life is full of uncertainties and insurance is based on uncertainties and if there are no uncertainties about the occurrence of a disaster, the concept of insurance will cease to exist. If we all are able to predict the future dangers correctly then we can take a safeguard action to move out of the danger but problem is that we cannot predict death, disaster and danger. All individuals as well as their tangible and intangible assets are exposed to all types of unforeseen risks. Thus insurance is done against such possible contingencies to save the owner and his family from all sorts of sufferings by making good the losses of the unfortunate few, through the help of the fortunate many, who were exposed to the same risk, but saved from the misfortune.

As insurance is a system of sharing risk that seems to be too great to be borne by one individual we can list out the benefits derived by individual and society from the insurance.

(1) Indemnifies loss-Insurance restores people to their former financial position as if no loss had occurred. It helps them to remain financially secure without running into debt after a loss. It also helps business firms to carry on their normal business operations without interruption even after the loss occurs.

(2) Reduces worry and fear-Insurance helps in reducing anxiety and fear before and after the loss occurs, as it is known that the insurance company will compensate the loss.

(3) Makes available funds for investment-Investments are the base of an economic development and mostly these investments are the result of savings. An insurance company is a major instrument for the mobilisation of the savings of people, which are thereafter canalised into investment for economic growth. Insurance provides the continuity in trade and commerce, by covering the risks that could retard the economy and thereby indirectly helps the economy to grow.

(4) Provides employment to a large number of people-Insurance industry offers regular full time employment to a large number of people in the country. Besides them a number of agents, professionals etc. are also engaged by the industry to render professional services.

(5) Educates people about loss prevention-Insurance companies also engage themselves in educating people about loss prevention. In our country the GIC has created the loss prevention association of India to promote and propagate loss prevention.

(6) Insurance enhances credit worthiness-Insurance policies are often offered as collateral security for credit as well.

(7) Social benefits-Above all we derive social benefits when people with peaceful minds carry on their operations properly and in a better way. Thus insurance's contribution to the economy as a whole is valuable as it avoids economic hardships to people.

Principles of Insurance

Indemnity

A contract of insurance is a contract of indemnity. Indemnity means that the insured in case of loss against which the policy has been insured, shall be paid the actual amount of loss not exceeding the amount of the policy i.e. he shall be fully indemnified. The purpose of contract of insurance is to place the insured in the same financial position, as he was before the loss. Suppose, a person insured his factory for Rs.20 lakhs against fire, the factory is partially burnt and it is estimated that a sum of Rs.10 lakhs will be required to restore it to the original condition. The insurer is liable to pay Rs.10 lakhs only. The exceptions to the rule are found in Personal Accident policies, Agreed Value policies in marine insurance and Valuables and reinstatement policies in Engineering insurance. These are also contracts of indemnity but by a special application of the principle, the amount of indemnity is decided at the time of entering into the contract itself.

In certain forms of insurance, the principle of indemnity is modified to apply. For example, in marine or fire insurance, sometimes, certain profit margin that would have earned in the absence of the event, is also included in the loss. Under life insurance, the insurer is required to pay the fixed amount in the event of death or on the expiry of the period of the policy. Thus the contract of life insurance is not insurance as such but it is an assurance. This is due to the reason that life cannot be indemnified i.e. the life of a person cannot be valued in terms of money and therefore the question of compensation of actual loss does not arise. Thus a contract of life insurance is a contract of guarantee.

Utmost Good Faith

The doctrine of utmost good faith applies to all forms of insurance. Both parties of the insurance contract must be of the same mind at the time of contract. There should not be any fraud, non-disclosure or misrepresentation concerning the material facts. An insurance contract is a contract of absolute good faith where both parties of the contract must disclose all the material facts truly and fully as insurance shifts risk from one party to another. As in insurance insured knows more about the risks than the insurer, so there must be utmost good faith and mutual confidence between insured and insurer. For instance, if a person suffers from a serious invisible disease but does not disclose this fact while getting his life insured, the insurance company can avoid the contract.

Similarly the insurer must exercise the same good faith in disclosing the scope of the insurance, which he is prepared to grant. Breach of good faith renders the contract voidable ab initio at the discretion of the aggrieved party. A material fact is a fact which would influence the mind of an insurer in deciding whether he should accept the risk, on what terms and what premium he should charge. The utmost good faith says that all material facts should be disclosed in true and full form. It means that the facts should be disclosed in that form in which they really exist. There should no false statement and no half-truth nor any silence on the material facts. What is a material fact depends upon the circumstances of the particular case.

Insurable Interest

For an insurance contract to be valid, the insured must have an insurable interest in the subject matter of insurance. It means that the insured must have an actual pecuniary interest. The insured must be so situated with regard to the thing insured that he would have benefit by its existence and loss from its destruction. For instance, a person has insurable interest in his life or in the life of the spouse but he has no insurable interest in the life of a stranger.

The owner of a building has absolute insurance interest. If this building is financed by banks then financiers too have their interest in the property but is limited to the extent of their financial commitment only. The insurable interest must exist both at the time of the proposal and at the time of claims but in case of life insurance, insurable interest must exist only when the policy is taken.

The essentials of a valid insurable interest are the following:

(a) There must be a subject matter to be insured.

(b) The insured should have monetary relationship with the subject matter.

(c) The relationship between the insured and the subject matter should be recognised by law i.e. there should not be any illegal relationship between the insured and the subject matter.

(d) The financial relationship between the insured and the subject matter should be such that the insured is financially benefited by its existence or survival and will suffer economic loss at the destruction or death of the subject matter.

The subject matter is life in life insurance, property and goods in property insurance, liability and adventure in general insurance. Insurable interest is essentially a pecuniary interest, no emotional or sentimental loss, like an expectation or an anxiety, could be the ground of the insurable interest.

Proximate Cause

The rule of proximate cause says that the cause of the loss must be proximate or immediate and not remote. If the proximate cause of the loss is a risk insured against, the insured can recover. If the risk insured is the outcome of a remote cause, which is not insured against, then the insurer is not bound to pay compensation. Proximate cause means the active efficient cause that sets in motion a chain of events, which brings about a result, without intervention of any force started and working actively from a new and independent source. That means proximate cause is the cause which in a natural and unbroken series of events is responsible for a loss or damage.

If there is a single cause of the loss, the cause will be proximate cause and if the cause of loss was insured, insurer will have to indemnify the loss. When a loss has been brought about by two or more causes, the question arises as to which is the proximate cause. If the causes occurred in form of chain, they have to be observed seriously. For the policy to cover the loss must have an insured peril must occur in the chain of causation that links the proximate cause with the loss. The proximate cause is not necessarily, the cause that was nearest to the damage either in time or in place, but is rather the cause that was actually responsible for loss.

Subrogation

The doctrine of subrogation is a corollary to the principle of indemnity and applies only to fire and marine insurance. According to it, when an insured has received full indemnity in respect of his loss, all rights and remedies which he has against third person will pass on to the insurer.

The insurer's right of subrogation arises only when he has paid for the loss and this right extend only to the rights and remedies available to the insured in respect of the thing to which the contract of insurance relates.

If the insured is in a position to recover the loss in full or in part from a third party due to whose negligence the loss may have been occurred, his right of recovery is subrogated (substituted) to the insurer on settlement of the claim.

The insurers, thereafter, can recover the claim from the third party or in case the lost property is recovered or the damaged property fetches any value, the insurer will be its owner. Suppose, a house is insured for Rs.2 lakhs against fire, the house is damaged by fire and the insurer pays the full value of Rs.2 lakhs to the insured. Later on the damaged house is sold for Rs.20, 000. The insurer is entitled to receive the sum of Rs.20, 000.

Contribution

When an insured obtains more than one policy on one risk, the principle of contribution comes into play. The aim of contribution is to distribute the actual amount of loss among the different insurers who are liable for the same risk under different policies in respect of the same subject matter.

That means the insured may effect more than policy to cover the same risk, he/she cannot recover in total more than a full indemnity (sum insured). In other words, the right of contribution arises when (a) there are different policies which relate to the same subject matter (b) the policies cover the same peril which caused the loss (c) all the policies are in force at the time of the loss and (d) one of the insurers has paid to the insured more than his share of the loss. However, the principle of contribution does not apply to life insurance.

Mitigation of Loss

In the event of a mishap, the insured must take all possible steps to mitigate or minimise the loss to the subject matter of insurance. He should act in the same manner in which he would have acted in the absence of the insurance cover. This means that it is the duty of the insured to make a reasonable effort and take all available precautions to save the insured property.

Warranties

There are certain conditions and promises in the insurance contract which are called warranties. Warranties which are mentioned in the policy are called express warranties. There are certain warranties which are not mentioned in the policy. These warranties are called implied warranties. Warranties, which are answers to the question, are called affirmative warranties. The warranties fulfilling certain conditions or promises are called promissory warranties.

Warranty is the very important condition in the insurance contract which is to be fulfilled by the insured. On breach of warranty the insurer becomes free from his liability. Therefore insured must have to fulfil the condition and promises during the insurance contract whether it is important or not in connection with the risk. If warranties are not followed, the other party may cancel the contract whether risk has occurred or not. However, when the warranty is declared illegal and there is no reverse effect on the contract, the warranty can be waived.

Types of Insurance

The insurance can be divided from two angles: from business point of view and from the risk point of view.

Business Point of View

The insurance from business point of view can be categorised into: (1) Life Insurance, (2) General Insurance, and (3) Social Insurance.

Life Insurance

Life Insurance is different from other insurance in the sense that the subject matter of insurance is life of human being. The insurer will pay the fixed amount of insurance at the death or at the expiry of certain period. At present, life insurance enjoys maximum scope because each and every person requires the insurance. This insurance provides protection to the family at the premature death or gives adequate amount at the old age when earning capacities are reduced. Types of insurance plans offered in our country:

- Term assurance plans
- Whole life plans
- Endowment assurance plans
- Assurances for children
- Family income policy
- Life annuity Joint life assurance
- Pension plans
- Unit linked plan
- Policy for maintenance of handicapped dependent
- Endowment policies with health insurance benefits

General Insurance

The general insurance includes property insurance, liability insurance and other forms of insurance. Fire and marine insurance comes under property insurance. Liability insurance includes motor, theft, fidelity and machine insurances to a certain extent. The strictest form of liability insurance is fidelity insurance whereby the insurer compensates the loss to the insured when he is under the liability of payment to the third party. Types of insurance policies available are:

-Health insurance

-Medi-claim policy

-Personal accident policy

-Group insurance policy

-Automobile insurance

-Worker's compensation

-Liability insurance

-Aviation insurance

-Business insurance

-Fire insurance policy

-Travel insurance policy

Social Insurance

The social insurance is to provide protection to the weaker sections of the society who are unable to pay the premium for adequate insurance. Pension plan, disability benefits, unemployment benefits, sickness insurance and industrial insurance are the various forms of social insurance.

Risk Point of View

Insurance can be divided into property, liability and other forms of insurance.

Property Insurance

Under the property insurance property of a person is insured against a certain specified risks. The risk may be fire or marine perils, theft of property or goods, damage to property at accident. Examples of this are:

-Home insurance

-Business insurance

-Commercial insurance

Marine Insurance

Marine insurance provides protection against loss of marine perils. The marine perils are collision with rock, or ship attacks by enemies, fire and capture by pirates etc. These perils cause damage, destruction or disappearance of the ship and cargo and non-payment of freight. So, marine insurance insures ship (Hull), cargo and freight. Types of policies are:

-Voyage policies

-Time policies

-Valued policies

-Hull insurance

-Cargo insurance

-Freight insurance

Fire Insurance

Fire insurance covers risks of fire. In the absence of fire insurance, the fire waste will increase not only to the individual but to the society as well. With the help of fire insurance, the losses, arising due to fire are compensated and the society is not losing much. The individual is protected from such losses and his property or business or industry will remain in the same position in which it was before the loss. The fire insurance does not protect only losses but it provides certain consequential losses also. Policies available in this insurance are:

-Consequential loss policy

-Comprehensive policy

-Valued policy

-Valuable policy

-Floating policy

-Average policy

Miscellaneous Insurance

The property, goods, machine, furniture, automobile, valuable goods etc., can be insured against the damage or destruction due to accident or disappearance due to theft. There are different forms of insurances for each type of the said property whereby not only property insurance exists but liability insurance and personal injuries are also insured. Miscellaneous insurance covers:

-Motor

-Disability

-Engineering and aviation risks

-Credit insurance

-Construction risks

-Money insurance

-Burglary and theft insurance

-All risks insurance

Liability Insurance

The general insurance also includes liability insurance whereby the insurer is liable to pay the damage of property or to compensate the loss of personal injury or death. The examples of this type of insurance are fidelity insurance, automobile insurance and machine insurance. Examples are:

-Third party insurance

-Employees insurance

-Reinsurance

Other Forms

Besides the property and liability insurances, there are certain other insurances, which are included under general insurance. The examples of such insures are export credit insurances, state employees insurance, etc. whereby the insurer guarantees to pay certain amount at the happening of certain events. Examples are:

-Fiduciary insurance

-Credit insurance

-Privilege insurance

INSURANCE PRODUCTS AND STATE OF INSURANCE INDUSTRY IN INDIA

Terminology

* Loss – Loss means being without something which is previously possessed.
* Total Loss – A total loss implies that the subject matter insured is fully destroyed and is totally lost to its owner.
* Actual Loss – In actual loss subject matter is completely destroyed or so damaged that it ceases to be a thing of the kind insured like complete destruction of cargo by fire.
* Constructive total loss – In case of constructive total loss the ship or cargo insured is not completely destroyed but is so badly damaged that the cost of repair or recovery would be greater than the value of the property saved.
* Partial loss – A partial loss occurs when the subject matter is partially destroyed or damaged.
* General Average – General average refers to the sacrifice made during extreme circumstances for the safety of the ship and the cargo. This loss has to be borne by all the parties who have an interest in the marine adventure.

* Particular Average – Particular average may be defined as a loss arising from damage accidentally caused by the perils insured against. Such a loss is borne by the underwriter who insured the object damaged.
* Peril – A peril is defined as the cause of the loss. Examples of perils include fires, tornadoes, heart attacks and criminal acts. Insurance policies provide financial protection against losses caused by perils.
* Hazards – hazards are conditions that increase either the frequency or the severity of losses.
* Warranties – A warranty is that by which the assured undertakes that some particular thing shall or shall not be done, or that some conditions shall be fulfilled, or whereby he affirms or negatives the existence of a particular state of facts.
* Reinsurance-It is an arrangement whereby an original insurer who has insured a risk insures a part of that risk again with another insurer, that means reinsures a part of the risk in order to diminish his liability.
* Jettison – Jettison means voluntary throwing away of the cargo or part of a vessel's equipment for the lightening or relieving the ship for common safety. The aim of the intentional throwing away of the goods or property is to relieve the vessel from some imminent peril.
* Enemies – The ships belonging to the enemy may cause loss to the insured and is re-underwritten by the marine policy. This policy extends to all the persons of the enemy country and to their hostile acts provided such acts from part of the enemy actions.
* Agent-A licensed person or organization authorized to sell insurance by or on behalf of an insurance company.
* Broker-A licensed person or organization paid by you to look for insurance on your behalf
* Burglary-Coverage against loss as a result of forced entry into premises.
* Claim-Notice to an insurer that under the terms of a policy, a loss maybe covered Disability Insurance-Health insurance

that provides income payments to the insured wage earner when income is interrupted or terminated because of illness, sickness, or accident.

* Grace Period-A period (usually 31 days) after the premium due date, during which an overdue premium may be paid without penalty. The policy remains in force throughout this period.
* Material Misrepresentation-The policyholder / applicant makes a false statement of any material (important) fact on his/her application. For instance, the policyholder provides false information regarding the location where the vehicle is garaged.
* Policy-The written contract of insurance.
* Premium-The amount of money an insurance company charges for insurance coverage.
* Underwriting-The process of selecting applicants for insurance and classifying them according to their degrees of insurability so that the appropriate premium rates may be charged. The process includes rejection of unacceptable risks. Workers Compensation Insurance-Coverage providing four types of benefits (medical care, death, disability, and rehabilitation) for employee job-related injuries or diseases as a matter of right (without regard to fault).

New Insurance Products

Some of the new policies are:

(1) Policies under LIC Mutual Fund – LIC launched its Mutual Fund with promise to the investors to provide high returns along with safety and security of investments. LIC Mutual Fund came up with 5 schemes which provide distinct benefits to various cross sections of investors. The names of scheme are:

- Dhanashree 1989
- Dhan 80 cc(1)
- Dhanavarsha
- Dhanaraksha 1989
- Dhanavridhi 1989

(2) Jeevan Akshay – In return for purchase price paid by the purchaser a monthly pension will be paid during the lifetime of the purchaser of the pension. On the death of the pensioner, the original amount invested by the employee along with an additional bonus will be returned to the nominee or his legal heirs.

(3) Jeevan Dhara – The payment of annuities in respect of policies under Jeevan Dhara has to start one month after the completion of the deferment period.

(4) Jeevan Kishor – Children between the ages of 1(last birthday) and 12(last birthday) are eligible to be proposed for insurance under this plan.

(5) Jeevan Chhaya – Couples having a child of age less than one year can avail of this plan, in order to ensure that an adequate financial provision is made for the higher education of the child. The child should not have completed one year of age on the date of the registration. Either father or mother or each one of them individually can take policies under this plan.

(6) Jeevan Suraksha – This policy enables individuals to provide for retirement income from a chosen date. The policy is with life cover but can be taken without life cover under certain conditions.

(7) Rural insurance – The policies offered under this scheme are:

Personal Insurance

(a) Janta Personal Accident (Individual)
(b) Janta Personal Accident (Group)
(c) Gramin Personal Accident

Property Insurance

(a) Agricultural Pumpset
(b) Animal Driven Carts Insurance
(c) Hut Insurance
(d) Gober Gas Insurance
(e) New Well Insurance

Cattle and Livestock Insurance

(a) Cattle Insurance

(b) Sheep and Goat Insurance

(c) Camel Insurance

(d) Horse Insurance

Poultry Insurance

(a) Duck Insurance

(b) Poultry Insurance Master Policy

(8) Insurance of Species

(9) Package Insurance

(10) Crop Insurance

(11) Medi-claim Hospitalisation and

Domiciliary Hospitalisation Insurance

(12) Overseas Medi-claim Policy

(13) Student's Safety Insurance

(14) Unborn Child Welfare Insurance

(15) Cancer Medical Expenses Policy

(16) Boiler and Pressure Plant Insurance

(17) Machinery Insurance

(18) Cold Storage Insurance

(19) Baggage Insurance

(20) Shopkeeper's Insurance

(21) All Risks Cover Insurance

(22) Social Security Scheme

(23) Wedding Insurance

(24) Kidnap and ransom Insurance

(25) Travel Insurance

4

Present State of Insurance Industry in India

The insurance industry in India can be discussed in two ways – its historical background and its present state. Insurance in India is nothing new. It had its origins in the early 19th century with the arrival of British enterprise in India.

Insurance, particularly non-life remained an urban oriented activity of the Insurance companies operating through their agencies.

HISTORICAL BACKGROUND

Life Insurance Corporation of India

The insurance sector in India dates back to 1818 when first insurance company, The Oriental Life Insurance Company, was established, at Calcutta. Thereafter, Bombay Life Assurance Company in 1823 and Madras Equitable Life Assurance Society in 1829 were established. In 1912, the Indian Life Assurance Companies Act was enacted as the first statute to regulate the life insurance business. In 1928, the Indian Insurance Companies Act was enacted to enable the Government to collect statistical information about both life and non-life insurance businesses. The Insurance Act was subsequently reviewed and a comprehensive legislation was enacted called the Insurance Act, 1938. The nationalisation of life insurance business took place in 1956 when 245 Indian and foreign insurance and provident societies were first amalgamated and then nationalised.

The Life Insurance Corporation of India (LIC) came into existence by an Act of Parliament, viz. LIC act, 1956, with a capital contribution of Rs.5 Crores from the Government of India General Insurance Corporation Of India-The General insurance business in India started with the establishment of Triton Insurance Company Limited in 1850 at Calcutta.In 1907, the first company, The Mercantile Insurance Ltd. Was set up to transact all classes of general insurance business. General Insurance Council, a wing of the Insurance Association of India in 1957, framed a code of conduct for ensuring fair conduct and sound business practices. In 1968 the Insurance Act was amended to regulate investments and to set minimum solvency margins. In the same year the Tariff Advisory Committee was also set up. In 1972, The General Insurance Business (Nationalisation) Act was passed to nationalise the general insurance business in India with effect from 1st January 1973. For these 107 insurers was amalgamated and grouped into four company's viz., the National Insurance Company Ltd., the New India Assurance Company Ltd., the Oriental Insurance Company Ltd. And the United India Insurance Company Ltd. General Insurance Corporation of India was incorporated as a company.

Current Scenario

In new economic policies formulated since 1991, globalisation, privatisation and liberalisation have become new buzzwords. Under new economic policies, many economic and financial reforms took place. Like liberalising licensing policy, attracting FDI, allowing foreign equity in public sector undertakings. The financial reforms restructured banking sector by allowing entry of new private and foreign banks. They also allowed private sector and commercial banks in mutual funds investment business, rationalising the EXIM policy and so on.

Insurance Sector Reforms

After the nationalisation of the life insurance industry in 1956 and the general insurance industry in 1972, the insurance industry confined only to the operations of LIC, GIC and its four subsidiaries viz. The National Insurance Company Limited, New India Assurance Company Limited, Oriental Fire and General Insurance Company Limited and United India Fire and General Insurance Company Limited. Over the years this state monopoly resulted in complacency, use of outdated technologies, inefficient and insufficient customer services and non-coverage of the potential market. Recognising this, the Government set-up a high-powered committee headed by Mr. R. N. Malhotra.

Malhotra Committee

Purpose

In 1993, Malhotra Committee, headed by former Finance Secretary and RBI Governor, was formed to evaluate the Indian Insurance Industry and recommend its future direction. The committee was set up with an objective of complementing the reforms in the Indian Financial sector. The reforms were aimed at "creating a more efficient and competitive financial system suitable for the requirements of the economy keeping in mind the structural changes currently underway and recognising that insurance is an important part of the overall financial system where it was necessary to address the need for similar reforms." Besides this, the Malhotra committee was asked to make recommendations for changing the structure of insurance industry, to make specific suggestions about how to improve the functioning of LIC and GIC and to recommend on regulation and supervision of the insurance sector in India. Besides this, the committee was asked to assess the strengths and weaknesses of the existing insurance industry and to make recommendations for changes in its functioning and the general policy framework keeping in mind the reforms under way in other parts of the financial sector.

Recommendations

In 1994, the committee submitted the report and gave the following recommendations:

Structure

- Government stake in the insurance companies to be brought down to 50%
- Government should take over the holdings of GIC and its subsidiaries so that these subsidiaries can act as independent corporations
- All the insurance companies should be given greater freedom to operate.

Competition

- Entry of private sector companies within well defined parameters of nature of business.
- Private Companies with a minimum paid up capital of Rs.1 billion should be allowed to enter the industry
- No Company should deal in both Life and General Insurance through a single entity
- Selective entry of foreign insurance companies preferably through joint ventures.
- Postal Life Insurance should be allowed to operate in the rural market
- Only one State Level Life Insurance Company should be allowed to operate in each state
- The insurance Act should be changed
- Controller of Insurance should be made independent
- Establishment of a strong and effective Insurance Regulatory Authority (IRA) as a statutory autonomous board.

Investments

- Mandatory Investments of LIC Life Fund in government securities to be reduced from 75% to 50%
- GIC and its subsidiaries are not to hold more than 5% in any company

Customer Service

- LIC should pay interest on delays in payments beyond 30 days
- Insurance companies must be encouraged to set up unit linked pension plans
- Computerisation of operations and updating of technology to be carried out in the insurance industry Overall, the committee strongly felt that in order to improve the customer services and increase the coverage of the insurance industry should be opened up to competition. But at the same time, the committee felt the need to exercise caution as any failure on the part of new players could ruin the public confidence in the industry. The

recommendations of the committee were discussed at different forums. The recommendations to set up an autonomous IRA found wide support. Since enacting legislation for creating the statutory IRA was to take time, the then government constituted an interim IRA, pending the enactment of comprehensive legislation.

It was on the basis of this report that the then Finance Minister P. Chidambaram proposed the opening up of insurance to the private sector, including multinational companies.

IRDA Bill

The IRDA Bill was drafted keeping the Malhotra Committee recommendations in view and hence the government has ruled out privatisation of public sector insurance companies, LIC and GIC. The bill did not provide for any dilution of 100 percent government equity in the two premier companies.

The IRDA bill sought to give a statutory status to the interim Insurance Regulatory Authority and amend the 1938 Insurance Act, the 1956 Life Insurance Corporation Act and the 1972 General Insurance Business (Nationalisation) Act to open up the sector. It provides for a nine-member regulatory body with statutory powers. The bill also fixed minimum capital requirement for life and general insurance at Rs.100 Crores and for reinsurance firms at Rs.200 Crores. The Malhotra Committee Report justified the entry of foreign insurance companies by arguing that if it is permitted, it should be done on selective basis preferably through joint venture with Indian partner. In 1999, the bill was finally passed and IRDA was formed to regulate and promote insurance business in India. The IRDA Act bestows the authority with powers to frame varies regulations, issue licenses, set capital requirements and solvency margins, prepare investment norms and inspect the books of private insurers independent of the government.

Liberalisation of Insurance Markets

Liberalisation of Insurance involves transformation of the industry from a Government monopoly to a competitive environment. Free markets allow for better resource allocation and creation of wealth and prosperity of people and the country. It enables development of health care, education and infrastructure of the country. In a liberalised insurance market, consumers are able to choose from different insurance providers having a wide range of products. A liberal insurance market is one in which the market determines who should be allowed to sell insurance, what, how and the prices at which these insurance products should be sold. The issues like market access and equality of competitive opportunity and national treatment will decide who will be allowed to sell insurance. Second and fourth items commonly deal with issues such as product, price and market conduct regulation.

There are certain pre-conditions to make liberalisation of insurance effective:

- Sound competition law
- Efficient and reliable regulation
- Phased liberalisation
- Consistency and impartiality between competitors
- Optimum quantum of regulation
- Efficient disclose and dissemination of information to the society.

Insurance markets in India possess certain imperfections justifying the need for competition as well as regulation.

Insurance Players in India

Bajaj Allianz General Insurance Company Limited

It is a joint venture between Bajaj Auto Limited and Allianz AG of Germany. The company registered on May 2, 2001 to conduct General Insurance business (incl[illegible]g Health Insurance business) in India. The company has an [illegible]rised and paid up capital of Rs.110 Crores and has a networ[illegible]1 offices across the country.

ICICI Lombard General Insurance Company Limited

It is a joint venture between ICICI Bank Limited India's second largest bank and Lombard Canada Limited, one of the oldest property and casualty insurance companies in Canada. ICICI Lombard offers a wide range of retail and corporate general insurance customised products. The company has over 100 branches across the country.

IFFCO-TOKIO General Insurance Company Limited

It is a joint venture between IFFCO and The Tokio Marine and Fire Insurance Company Limited, Japan Krishak Bharati Cooperative Limited (KRIBHCO), and Indian Potash contributing 49 percent, 26 percent and 5 percent respectively to its Rs.100 Crores capital. After getting the licence the company started operations and is a leading private General Insurance Company in India in launching innovative insurance cover for farmers called the "Sankat Haran Policy" It is operating from 20 cities in India.

National Insurance Company Limited

It was incorporated in 1906 to carry out general insurance business and nationalised in 1972.In the same year, 22 foreign and 11 Indian Insurance Companies were amalgamated with National Insurance Company Limited, as a subsidiary company of General Insurance Corporation of India. In 2002, with the passage of Insurance amendment Bill (2002), National Insurance Company has been delinked from GIC and has been functioning as an independent company. Apart from domestic insurance business the company also undertakes reinsurance and foreign operations.

New India Assurance Company Limited

The New India Assurance Company was incorporated on July 23, 1919 and commenced business from October 14, 1919. In 1972 the Government of India took over the management of the company along with all other non-life insurers in the country. New India Assurance was subsequently reconstituted taking over 23 companies. In2002, with the passage of Insurance amendment Bill, New India Assurance Company Limited has been delinked from GIC and has been functioning as an independent company.

Oriental Insurance Company Limited

The Oriental Insurance Company Limited is a public sector company and is one of the four subsidiary companies of the General Insurance Corporation of India. In 1956, Oriental became a subsidiary of the Life Insurance Corporation of India. On May 13, 1971 Government of India took over the management of all general insurance companies in India and nationalised the Oriental Fire and General Insurance Company under the General Insurance

Corporation of India as one of the four subsidiaries. In 2002, with the passage of Insurance amendment Bill, the Oriental Insurance Company Limited has been delinked from GIC and has been functioning as an independent company.

United India Insurance Company Limited

United India Insurance is one of the four subsidiaries of the General Insurance Company carrying on general insurance business in India. In 2002, with the passage of Insurance amendment Bill (2002), United India Insurance has been delinked from GIC and has been functioning as an independent company.

Tata AIG General Insurance Company Limited

Tata AIG General Insurance Company Ltd. And Tata AIG Life Insurance Company Ltd. (collectively "Tata AIG") are joint venture companies between the Tata group and American International Group Inc. (AIG), the leading U.S. based international insurance and financial services organisation. It has a capital of Rs.125 Crores out of which 74 percent has been brought in by Tata Sons and the remaining 26 percent by American partner. Tata AIG General Insurance Company Limited claims to be the first Indian insurance company to offer a comprehensive policy to cover various risks in the IT sector.

Royal Sundaram General Insurance Company Limited

The joint venture between Royal and Sun Alliance Insurance and Sundaram Finance Limited started its operation from March 2001. Royal and Sun Alliance is one of the world's leading international insurance companies. The Sun was established in 1710 and is the oldest insurance company in existence still trading under its original name. The Alliance was founded in 1824 and the Royal in 1845.

Cholamandalam General Insurance Company Limited

It is promoted by Chennai based Murugappa Group. The company is founded with Rs.105 Crores out of which 75 percent is being held by Tube Investment, a Murugappa group company. While Cholamandalam Investment and Finance Company Limited holds 15 percent stake and the rest is by other privately held Murugappa companies with 5 percent stake each.

Reliance General Insurance Company Limited

Reliance group has announced its plans to enter the Indian insurance sector – both in the life and general insurance businesses. Reliance Industries plans to bring in around Rs.300 Crores into its insurance venture through its financial arm Reliance Capital Limited. The two companies will have an initial authorised capital of Rs.200 Crores each. This is the first Indian company without a foreign tie-up.

Export Credit Guarantee Corporation of India Limited

It was established in the year 1957 by the Government of India to strengthen the export promotion drive by covering the risk of exporting on credit. Being an export promotion organisation, it functions under the administrative control of the Ministry of Commerce, Government of India. It is the fifth largest credit insurer of the world in terms of coverage of national exports. The paid –up capital of the company is Rs.390 Crores.

HDFC Chubb General Insurance Limited

HDFC, India's premier financial services company and Chubb Corporation, leading global non-life insurer, entered into a joint venture agreement for non-life insurance in 2002. HDFC holds 74 percent and Chubb 26 percent in the joint venture company, HDFC Chubb General Insurance Limited with initial capital of Rs.100 Crores.

Life Insurers

Alliance Bajaj Life Insurance Company Limited

Alliance Bajaj Life Insurance Company Limited is a joint venture between Alliance AG and Bajaj Auto Limited. The company was incorporated on March 12, 2001. The company received the IRDA certificate of registration on August 3, 2001 to conduct Life Insurance business in India.

Birla Sun Life Insurance Company Limited

It is a joint venture between Birla Group and Sun Life Corporation of U.S. The products of Birla Sun Life Insurance Company (BSLI) are distributed through a fully owned subsidiary– BSDL Insurance Advisory Services Limited (BSDL IAS) BSDL.

The company claims to have unique products, presenting a powerful combination of returns, liquidity, safety, tax benefits, transparency and convenience.

HDFC Standard Life Insurance Company Limited

HDFC and Standard Life was the first joint venture to enter the life insurance market, in January 1995. In October 1998, the joint venture agreement was renewed and Standard Life purchased 2 percent of Infrastructure Development Finance Company Limited (IDFC). The company as such, was incorporated on August 14, 2000 under the name of HDFC Standard Life Insurance Company Limited. HDFC are the main shareholders in HDFC Standard Life, with 81.4 percent, while Standard Life owns 18.6 percent. HDFC and Standard Life have a long and close relationship built upon shared values and trust.

ICICI Prudential Life Insurance Company Limited

The company was incorporated on July 20, 2000, with an authorised capital of Rs.230 Crores (paid up Rs.190 Crores). It is a joint venture of ICICI (74%) and Prudential plc U.K (26%). The company is on the top of the list of competitors to LIC. The company was granted certificate of incorporation on 26-11-2000 and it started its operations on 19-12-2000.

Life Insurance Corporation of India Limited

LIC was established in 1956 and is the dominant leader in life insurance in India. It has 7 zonal offices, over 100 divisional offices and 204 branches in India with over 6.50 lakhs agents.

Tata AIG Life Insurance Company Limited

It is capitalised at Rs.185 Crores of which 74 percent has been brought in by Tata Sons and the American partner brings in the remaining 26 percent. American Insurance Group (AIG) is the leading U.S. based international insurance and financial services organisation and the largest underwriter of commercial and industrial insurance in the United States. AIG's global businesses also include financial services and asset management. Including aircraft leasing, financial products, trading and market making, consumer finance, institutional, retail and direct investment fund asset management etc.

SBI Life Insurance Company Limited

India's largest bank SBI and Cardiff S.A. a leading insurer in France have firmed SBI Life. It is a 74: 24 venture; with Cardiff the foreign partner contributing 24 percent paid capital of Rs.250 Crores. SBI plans to market the insurance products through select branches of SBI and its seven associate banks.

OM Kotak Mahindra Insurance Company Limited

The joint venture OM Kotak Mahindra Life Insurance started off with an initial net worth of Rs.150 Crores, with 74: 26 stake between KMFL and OM. Kotak Mahindra is one of India's premier financial services groups, with a range of over two dozen highly specialised products and services. Starting as a one-product company in the mid 80's, they have evolved into a full service financial conglomerate.

Old Mutual pic. Is a leading financial services provider in the world, providing a broad range of financial services in the area of insurance, asset management and banking. It is a leading life insurer in South Africa, with more than 30 percent market share. The partnership with Old Mutual plc. provides the Kotak Mahindra group with an international perspective and expertise in the life insurance business.

Max New York Life Insurance Company Limited

It is a partnership between Max India Limited, one of India's leading multi business corporations and New York Life, a Fortune 100 company. The paid up capital of the joint venture is Rs.250 Crores. Max India Ltd. is building businesses in the emerging knowledge based areas of Healthcare, Financial Services and Information Technology.

ING Vyasya Life Insurance Company Ltd.

It is a joint venture between ING, Vyasya Bank, one of India's leading private sector banks and GMR group. As per the joint venture agreement, Vyasya Bank holds 49 percent stake, ING 26 percent, and the GMR Group would hold 25 percent.

The paid up capital of the joint venture is Rs.110 Crores. Vyasya Bank has a very high degree of retail focus with good customer service. ING Group, with an asset base of over Rs.28,

42,000 Crores is a global financial institution of Dutch origin, which is active in the field of banking, insurance and asset management in more than 60 countries.

Aviva Life Insurance Company Ltd.

It is a joint venture between Dabur India and CGU, a wholly owned subsidiary of Aviva Pic, is capitalised at Rs.110 Crores. Aviva Pic is the largest life and general insurance group of UK and the world's largest insurer with worldwide premium income and retail investment sales of £28 billion. Aviva Life has tied up with ABN Amro, Canara Bank, Laxmi Vilas Bank and American Express for distribution of its products.

AMP Sanmar Assurance Company Ltd.

It is a joint venture between AMP having a stake of 26 percent and the Sanmar Group holding 74 percent. The Sanmar group is one of the largest industrial groups in South India. AMP Limited is one of the world's leading financial services businesses.

UNDERSTANDING ANNUAL REPORTS OF LIC AND GIC

The Annual Report of LIC

The contents of annual report of LIC are:

(1) Preamble Under Section 27 of the LIC Act 1956, LIC has to present its Annual report to the members. This also contains the names of the members of the Corporation and its various committees during the year.

(2) Scenario Economic In this, information is provided about GDP (Gross Domestic Product), GDS (Gross Domestic Saving), fiscal position, monetary conditions, inflation, equity market and external sector. What changes have taken place during the year in global life insurance business as well as domestic insurance market? After the opening up of the domestic insurance market in 1999 and with a level playing field provided by the new supervisory framework, what is the position of the state owned and private platers in the insurance business? How the changes in GDS, GDP and disposable income has affected the business performance of the insurance industry.

(3) Impact of Macro Economic Environment on Life Insurance Business Under this, the information is provided about impact of RBI policies and Government of India's Monetary and credit policies on insurance business. Like there is a RBI policy to reduce the exposure of Non-Banking Financial Institutions including LIC, in the call money market. As a result the Corporation has reduced its investment in call money market to meet RBI guidelines. Now, LIC has been actively deploying its funds in other money market instruments like Repo and CBLO (Collateralized Borrowing and Lending Obligation). In addition, what is the impact of changes in the interest rate, inflation on life insurance business? Thus changes taking place on a global and national level affects the life insurance business.

(4) Working results the total working results of the Corporation are divided into two parts:

   (1) New Business and

   (2) Business in Force.

   In new business the report discusses about the Number of Policies, Sum Assured, Annual Premium Receivable in Individual Assurance, General Annuity, Pensions Portfolio, Unit Linked business (Bema Plus and Future Plus) in India as well as out of India. It also gives information about Group insurance business including Social Security. In Social Security Schemes, the LIC provides insurance cover through Janashree Bima Yojana to 43 occupations like Beedi workers, Lady Tailors, Textile, Wood and Paper products, Printing, Physically Handicapped, Self-Employed persons.

   The report also discusses about First Insurance, Rural Thrust, Alternate Distribution Channels, and Product Development. In First Insurance, in pursuance of the corporate objectives LIC provides insurance cover to more and more people who have no previous insurance on their lives. In Rural Thrust, LIC gives information about Life insurance cover provided to people of backward and remote areas. In Alternate Distribution Channels, the LIC provides information about how in competitive market environment LIC targets new market segments and high net worth individuals to increase its customer base. Banks have emerged as strong business partners amongst alternate channels in terms of first premium mobilisation. In order to meet the changing needs of customers, LIC offers a wide variety of products. Thus, in product development, the LIC gives information about new insurance products introduced and some existing withdrawn from the market after periodical review of its product portfolio.

In Business In Force in various segments, the LIC report says about Number of Policies, Sum Assured, and Annual Premium Receivable under Individual Assurance, General Annuity Pension Portfolio, Unit Linked (Bima Plus and Future Plus) in India as well as out of India. In Group Insurance Business the information is given about Number of Schemes, Number of Members, Sum Assured, Premium Income under Group Insurance including Social Security and Group Superannuation.

(5) Capital Redemption and Annuity Certain Business it provides information about Annuity Certain and Capital Redemption Policies in force.

(6) Statutory Statements regarding Policies Under this heading information in statements in the form "DD" prescribed under Insurance Act, 1938 is given about Number of Policies, Sum Insured and Annuities Per Annum, Single Premiums and Yearly Renewal Premium for Ordinary policies (Individual Assurance), Annuity Contracts, Unit Linked Plans (Bima Plus and Future Plus), Jeevan Suraksha, Group Insurance Policies and Group Annuity Contracts etc. in India and out of India in respect of premium paid during the tear for New Life Insurance business. Statutory Statements regarding Policies also provides information about Total Life Insurance business in force at the end of the year in the form of Number of Policies, Sum insured with Bonuses and Annuities per Annum, premium income for which credit has been taken in the Revenue Account in India and out of India.

(7) Life Fund, Surplus and Taxes Paid This provides information about life fund, valuation surplus, surplus retained, share of surplus and taxes paid to the Central Government for the last three years.

(8) Investments and Social Responsibilities This heading gives information about total investments of the Corporation in India and out of India. Besides investing in Stock Exchange Securities, Loans constitute one of the major avenues of investment for the Corporation's funds. Loans have been given to finance projects/ schemes for generation and transmission of electricity for agricultural and industrial use, housing schemes, development of road transport, piped water supply and sewerage projects in rural and urban areas and townships and industrial development.

LIC also fulfils its social responsibilities towards society at large.

To achieve this goal LIC provides security to as many people as possible. To meet this end, the Corporation has been promoting Social Welfare through socially oriented schemes. LIC invested and given loans to Central, State and other Government Guaranteed Marketable Securities and Infrastructure sector.

(9) Marketing Activities, Agents and Diversified Activities under marketing activities, LIC provides information about its operations in India and in Foreign countries. Also its operations through Foreign Subsidiaries/ Joint Venture Companies. In Agents heading, LIC gives information about total number of agents on roll, number of schemes launched by the Corporation to promote the cause of professionalising the agency force. In order to recognize agents who perform consistently year after year, clubs at five levels have been designated viz. Chairman, Zonal Manager, Divisional Manager, Branch Manager and Distinguished Agents by the Corporation. In order to motivate and recognize high performers a premium club called the "Corporate Club" has been formed. Besides providing insurance covers to lakhs of people, how LIC

has diversified its activities through LIC Housing Finance Limited, LIC Mutual Fund Trustee Company Private Limited/ Jeevan Bima Sahayog Asset Management Company (JBS AMC) Limited.

(10) Policy Holders' servicing this heading provides information about how Corporation settles the claims of policyholders on maturity as well as on death. In case Claimants have any grievances, they can present their cases before Zonal/ Central Claims Review Committee. To impart transparency to the decision making process former High Court / District Court Judge is appointed as a sitting member of Review Committee. Also Corporation has Grievance Redressal Officers at Branch / Divisional /Zonal / Central office to redress grievances of customers and for transparency.

(11) Public Relations and Corporate Communications Activities In order to improve public image and to boost the public confidence, Corporation has undergone a transformation, renaming its "PR and Publicity" department as "PR and CC" to revamp corporate image. AD campaigns through various media like Radio, TV, Internet, Press etc. were used to augment its sales and to enhance brand image. For this LIC has received many accolades from diverse entities.

(12) Personnel and Employee Relations In this information is provided about staff strength, new recruitments, relationship with employees and unions, ratio of women workers in the total strength of staff, reservation of SC,ST and OBC, Physically Handicapped and Ex – Servicemen Employees and Sports activities.

(13) HRD / OD initiatives / Training Statistics This heading provides information about training profiles of the Personnel of the Corporation. To sharpen the skills and capabilities of the personnel how training is imparted through in – house training centres, Management Development Centre, National Insurance Academy and Zonal and Divisional Training Centres. Besides this, to strengthen the entrepreneurial ability of the Managers to

have better managerial perception and practices, Management Development Centre (MDC), the apex-training institute of LIC imparts training to Managers.

(14) Engineering Activities and Estates It gives information about new additions to the existing buildings and offices of the LIC. How Estate Portfolio of the Corporation progressed during the year, how much housing loans were given to employees for various staff housing schemes and agents housing schemes.

(15) Information Technology Initiatives This provides information about information technology initiatives undertaken by the Corporation to modernise their offices and to give better alternate options to the customers to do business with LIC like premium collection through ECS, E – Mail and Internet services, on line Data Store Project, a standardised package for Pension Policy Servicing etc.

(16) Internal Audit To help management to take corrective action and to ensure continuous improvement in the overall working of the offices of the Corporation, internal audit department is established by the Corporation. It periodically audits the workings of Branch, Divisional and Zonal offices and all offices of the Corporation.

(17) Inspection and Vigilance Inspection of all the branches, Divisional and Zonal offices in India are carried out by the Corporation. Besides this, Vigilance activities are also undertaken by the Corporation. Here the greater emphasis is on preventive vigilance through the dissemination of information on areas susceptible to vigilance besides expediting disposal of vigilance cases.

(18) Nominee Directors It provides information of directors nominated by the Corporation on the Boards of the Companies where it has substantial stake by way of Debt or Equity. Nominee directors are reviewed and guided by the Corporation from time to time. These Directors are Non – Executive Directors, not connected with day to day operational matters of the Company, who report on important matters discussed at the board meetings/other

related committee meetings or any other issue which deserves attention of the Corporation.

(19) Corporate Governance The practice of good Corporate Governance enables the strengthening of the confidence of the stake holders, maintaining a healthy industrial climate within the organisation improving customer focus and withstanding the pressures of change in the external environment and in making LIC is great and dynamic organisation. This is achieved through various proactive measures, initiatives and guidance by the Government, namely, Board of Directors, Executive committee, Audit Committee, Investment Committee, Consumer Affairs Committee, Zonal Advisory Boards, Divisional level Policy holders Councils and LIC's employees and Agency force.

(20) Board Meetings and Central Management Committee As per regulations, Board meetings should be held at least once in a quarter. Board Meetings are generally held at corporate office of LIC to discuss policy matters to provide guidance and direction to management for Growth, Excellence and Corporate Governance. Board members have access to any information that they may like to have and the recommendations that may be prescribed or desired are implemented within the time frame. The Central Management Committee consists of all Executive Directors, Chief of Central Office and all the Zonal Managers. In the meetings Policy and Strategic issues are discussed and appropriate steps are taken to reformulate the strategies if thought necessary in view of the changes in the market environment.

(21) Zonal Advisory Board(ZAB) Zaps are constituted for each Zone, which are competent to discuss and review all matters and policy affecting the proper development of the LIC within due territorial limits of the Zone and make recommendations thereon.

(22) Policy Holder's Council Policyholder's councils are constituted in each division. Policyholder councils discuss all the matters, which relate to the servicing of the Policyholders. Items discussed are Service to the Policy

Holder, Outstanding claims, Progress of New Business in the Division, Publicity activities etc.

(23) Auditors Appointment of Statutory Auditors with the previous approval of the Central Government. In this the names and addresses of the firms are given.

(24) Plans In this, information about Annual Budget of New Business is given. This heading provides for what LIC wishes to do in the coming financial year under:

(1) Linked Business
- Life Assurance
- Pension Plan
- Total linked Business

(2) Non-linked Business
- Life Assurance
- Pension plan
- Total Linked Business

(3) Composite Business

(25) Acknowledgement In this LIC expresses its sincere thanks to the various Parliamentary Committees, the Union Finance Minister, and Union Minister of state for Finance, the Insurance division of the ministry of Finance and the IRDA for their active support, advice and cooperation on various committees and Board of Directors for their guidance and valuable suggestions.

The Annual Report of GIC

The Annual Report of a GIC has the following contents:

(1) Information about Corporation, board of Directors and Management It provides information about the members of the board of directors, Auditors bankers and registered office of the GIC. It also gives information about composition of the Management, like the names of Chairman-cum-Managing Director, Chief Vigilance officer and Assistant General Manager

(2) Notices It incorporates information about notice given to all the members about Annual General meeting to transact the business. This notice provides information about when

and where the meeting will be held and what will be discussed in the meeting. The notice gives opportunity to the members who are unable to attend the meeting on the designated place that they can appoint another person as his/her proxy to attend the meeting and thereat instead of him/her.

(3) Director's report In this, the director represents the annual report on the working and affairs of the Corporation and the audited statement of account for the year ended to the members. This is the important document as it provides information about financial results of the corporation for the year under review. It informs about the total authorised and paid-up of the corporation, whether any new issues or bonus shares have been issued during the year, what rate of dividend has been proposed by directors. What is the position of capital and funds, assets, investments of the corporation in the current year? Whether there is any increase or decrease as compared to the previous year. As GIC is a Reassurance Company, its working and functions, are governed by the IRDA. So it has to confirm to the requirements of the IRDA about paid-up equity specifications, preparations and presentation of financial statements and auditor's report.

The director's report also provides information about total strength of the corporation, total amount of remuneration paid to the employees, welfare schemes undertaken, if any, for the welfare of the employees like SC/ST?OBC etc., to upgrade the skills of the officers and staff,any training programmes undertaken by the corporation.

The report discloses the names of the board of directors, different board committees like audit committee and investment committee and their composition. To ensure financial and office discipline and also to imbibe a culture of value and ethics in daily office work, vigilance department is constituted which is headed by a chief vigilance officer. There is also an internal audit department in the corporation. The directors present information about how internal audit department conducts audit of business transactions and also renews prevalent systems and makes suggestions and recommendations for the consideration of the Audit committee of the board. And lastly they give information about the domestic as well as the overseas operation of the corporation, their responsibilities to confirm to the requirements of sec217 (2AA) of the companies Act 1956, about observation of applicable accounting standards in the preparation of annual accounts, consistent application of accounting policies and about precautions and care taken to safeguard the assets of the corporation and for prevention and detection of frauds and other irregularities.

(4) Management's discussion and Analysis Report In this management discusses about global economic scenario, in particular Indian economic conditions and the factors which effect the economic conditions. All these factors contribute towards the growth of insurance industry on a global scale and affect Indian insurance industry also.

It also discusses business performance in terms of total premium earned from different classes of business, income from investments, apportionment of overall revenue profit among the policyholders' fund and payment of claims to policyholders'.

It also provides information about global risks affecting the insurance business like Terrorism, Natural Perils, Liability, Environmental issues etc. In order to mitigate these risks, management exchanges information about all these risks with various global players in the insurance market. Besides Global risks, Strategic risks also affect the functioning of the Corporation. Strategic risks arise from an imbalance between the defined corporate strategy and the constantly fluctuating business environment. To reduce such risks, monitoring of mission – critical parameters and regular review of underlying assumptions are done by the management.

As GIC is reinsurance company, Operational risks (technical) is of special importance to it. The risk factors that can affect business are appropriate pricing, accurate estimates of claims liability and establishing adequate reserves for catastrophic losses. To reduce such risks GIC adopts a very conservative loss reserving methodology.

An operational risk (investment) is another type of operational risks. Investment risks mainly consist of market fluctuations, quality of the investments (security ratings) and liquidity. GIC's debt portfolio being of high quality enjoys liquidity benefits and least of credit risk. Corporation follows an active investment policy to earn better returns.

Future outlook of GIC provides information about its future plans. What actions will be taken by the Corporation to achieve these objectives? How it will sense the opportunities to strengthen its position in the domestic as well as international markets to face new threats and challenges.

(5) Management Report In this, in accordance with Part IV of schedule B of the IRDA (Preparation of Financial Statements and Auditor's Report of Insurance Companies) Regulations 2002, the management of the Corporation confirms that all dues payable to the statutory authorities have been duly paid, shareholding pattern as well as transfer of shares is in accordance with the regulatory or statutory requirements, required solvency margins have been maintained and that the Corporation's risk exposure consists of Obligatory Cessions, Facultative Support given to Indian Insurance Companies Corporation's share in Indian Insurance Companies through First / Second Surplus Treaties and Excess of Loss programme and also Foreign Inward Business accepted.Besides this Corporation also declares and certifies that funds of the holders of policies in India are not directly or indirectly invested outside India; the values of all the assets of the Corporation have been reviewed on the date of the Balance Sheet, that the Corporation does not operate directly in any other country except through its representative offices. The

Corporation also confirms that applicable accounting standards, principles and policies have been followed consistently in the preparation of financial statements and sufficient care has been taken for safeguarding the assets of the company as well for prevention and detection of fraud and other irregularities and in the last financial statements are prepared on a going concern basis and internal audit system commensurate with the size and nature of the business exists and is operating effectively. The management also certifies that no payment has been made to individuals, firms, companies and organisations in which the Directors of the corporation are interested.

(6) Comments and Review by Comptroller and Auditor General of India under sec. 619(4) of the Companies Act, 1956 on the accounts of GIC.

(7) Auditors' report In this auditors appointed by the Corporation, audit the attached Balance Sheet of GIC and also the Revenue Accounts of Fire, Marine, Miscellaneous and Life reinsurance and the Profit and Loss Account and the Cash Flow Statement for the year ended on that date annexed thereto. In this report the auditors express their opinion on these financial statements and report to the members of the Corporation that proper books of account have been maintained and the Balance Sheet, Revenue Accounts and Profit and Loss Account and Cash Flow Statement comply with the Accounting Standards as well as IRDA regulations. Auditors also have to certify that after reviewing the management report no apparent mistake or material inconsistencies have been found.

(8) Schedules forming part of Financial Statements In the schedules information about premium earned (net), claims incurred (net) on different forms of insurance, commission paid, about Share Capital, Share Capital pattern of Shareholding, Reserves and Surplus, Investments – Shareholders' fund and Policyholders' Fund, Loans, Fixed Assets, Cash and Bank Balances, Advances and Other Assets, Current Liabilities, Provisions and Miscellaneous Expenditure is given.

SUMMARY

In the end we can sum up that Insurance is a financial arrangement for redistributing the costs of unexpected losses requiring a legal contract whereby an insurer agrees to compensate an insured for loss. A loss is an undesired, unplanned reduction of economic value. The benefits of insurance are too large that it is beneficial for individual as well as business organisations to insure their properties and themselves against uncalled for contingencies.

The principles of Insurance provide us information about those features on which the whole insurance business is based. Types of insurance as well as new insurance products provide us information about availability of different types of insurance covers in the market and different policies under all these categories. It also gives information about new products offered by new players in the market after the opening up of the insurance industry to foreign and multinational companies. What changes that have made in the Indian Insurance Industry. In the next lesson you will study the different Acts and Laws, which has changed the face of the insurance industry in India especially the IRDA Act.

5

LEGAL FRAMEWORK

INTRODUCTION

Insurance is a tool used to help manage financial risk. Financial risk can take many forms. There are risks to our investments, liabilities for our actions, and risks to our ability to earn income. There is insurance to manage all these risks. Insurance is a financial agreement entered by two people to protect one against a certain risk. The contract that binds the two parties to certain obligations is known as Policy. The one who buys the insurance is known as policyholder or insured while the party that sells insurance is known as the insurer. From the time the insured signs the policy he/she has an obligation to pay a certain amount of money known as premium.. In this lesson, we will discuss the various laws governing insurance in India. The Insurance sector in India is governed by Insurance Act, 1938, the Life Insurance Corporation Act, 1956 and General Insurance Business (Nationalization) Act, 1972, Insurance Regulatory and Development Authority (IRDA) Act, 1999 and other related acts.

Objectives

After going through this lesson you should be able to:

- Define the term contract.
- Describe essential features of valid contract.
- Understand meaning of lawful Consideration.
- Define the term 'Consumer'.
- Know the difference between agent and servant.
- Define Complaint Procedure.

- Know redressal of consumer's grievances
- Understand Features of IRDA Act.
- Understand main functions of LIC Act.
- Understand main functions of GIC Act

LESSON 1-GENERAL CONTRACT ACT 1872, LIC ACT 1956 & GIC ACT 1972

Essentials of General Contract (Section 10) of Indian Contract Act 1872

A contract is an agreement made between two or more parties, which the law will enforce.

To be enforceable by law, an agreement must possess the essential elements of a valid contract as contained in Sections 10.

Essential of a valid contract: The contract of insurance, like any other contract must fulfill the following essential requirements of a valid contract as laid down in the Indian contracts act.

A contract is an agreement made between two or more parties, which the law will enforce.

The essential requirements of a valid contract as laid down in the Indian contract act are:

1. Agreement: This involves, one party making the offer and the other party accepting it. The acceptance of the offer must be in the writing or given verbally and must be absolute and unconditional and must be communicated to the proposer.
2. Legal Relationship: when the two parties enter into an agreement their intention must be create legal relationship between them. With many informal and social agreements, such as, an agreement to give a friend a lift in one's car, there is never any intention of legal consequences so the agreement for same reason should not be carried out
3. Lawful Consideration: The, agreement is legally enforceable, only when the contract is supported by consideration, i.e., 'when both the parties give something in return. In insurance both parties provide consideration. Consideration from the insured to the insurer is the

premium while from the insurer to the insured is a promise to compensate the insured or to make certain payment in the event of certain happening s taking place.

4. Capacity of Parties: The parties to the agreement must be competent or capable of entering into a valid contract. A person is competent to contract if he is of the age of majority, is sound mind, and is not disqualified from contracting by any law to which he is subject
5. Free and Genuine Consent: There must also be a free and genuine consent of the parties to the agreement. If the agreement is induced by 44 coercion, undue influence, fraud misrepresentation etc., there is absence of free consent.
6. Lawful Object: The object of the contract must be lawful. Thus, the object of the agreement must not be illegal, immoral, or opposed to public policy. If an agreement suffers from any legal flaw, it would not be enforceable by law. For example a landlord knowingly lets a house to terrorist to carry out his activities, and he cannot recover the rent through the court of law.
7. Agreement Not Declared Void: The agreement, though it might possess all the essential elements, must not have been expressly declared void by any law in force in country. Any contract which is contrary to the law of this country is void, such as insurance on goods being traded with an enemy national in times of war.
8. Certainty and Possibility or Performance: It is essential the creation of every contract that the terms of agreement must be certain and not vague, indefinite, or ambiguous. An agreement to do an act impossible in itself cannot be enforced. For example Q agrees with P, to increase his height by magic. This agreement is not enforceable by law.
9. Legal Formalities: The agreement maybe either oral or in writing. But if it is in writing, it must comply with the necessary legal formalities as to writing, registration, attestation, and stamp and must be issued under seal.

CONTRACTS WHICH ARE DEFECTIVE

Void agreement: An agreement not enforceable by law is said to be void [sec2 (g)]. A void agreement does not create any legal rights or obligations. It is void ab initio, i.e. from very beginning, for example an agreement with minor. Void contracts: A contracts which legally does not exist is known as void contract. In other words, a contract, which ceases to be enforceable, is void when it ceases to be enforceable. It is valid when it is entered into, but something, which happens subsequently to the formation of the contract makes it void. Example: a contract to import goods from foreign country. It may subsequently become void.

Voidable contract: An agreement which is enforceable by law at the option of one or more of the parties thereto, but not at the option of the other or others, is voidable contract. In other words when either party is in breach of the essential terms of the contract, the other party has a right to consider the contract void. If the aggrieved party may decide to overlook the breach or to waive the breach, the contract on this case is unaffected and remains in full force. Example: Anu promises to sell his watch for Rs. 500. Her consent is obtained by use of force. The contract is voidable at the option of Anu. She may accept it or reject it. Unenforceable contracts: Unenforceable contracts are those which are neither void nor voidable but which cannot be enforced through the courts. For example, an insurance policy without proper stamp duty cannot be produced as evidence of a contract in court. Unenforceable contracts are fully valid contracts but the parties cannot enforce them through the courts.

Illegal Agreements: Illegal agreements are those agreements, which involve the breaking of some rule of basic public policy and.are criminal in nature. An illegal agreement is not only void as between immediate parties but also taints the collateral transactions with illegality.

Essential Feature of Insurance Contracts

The purchasers of Insurance have to enter into a contract, where by one party (insured) agrees to pay to other party (insurer) a certain sum of money, determined on the happening of a certain event in consideration of a certain sum of money caned Premium.

Such a contract is known as "Insurance Contract". Like any other contract, Insurance contract are also governed by the provisions of the law of contract as laid down in The Indian Contract Act, 1872. Therefore they have to fulfill the essential features of a valid contract. The essentials of a valid contract have been discussed earlier.

Life Insurance Corporation Act, 1956

An Act to provide for the nationalization of life insurance business in India by transferring all such business to a Corporation established for the purpose and to provide for the regulation and control of the business of the Corporation and for matters connected there with or incidental thereto.

Some of the important provisions are as follows: —

1. Short title and commencement. —

(1) This Act maybe called the Life Insurance Corporation Act, 1956

(2) It shall come into force on such date as the Central Government may, by Notifications in the Official Gazette, appoint. Definitions: In this Act, unless the context otherwise requires,

- (1) "Appointed day," means the date on which the Corporation is established under Section 3;
- (2) "Composite insurer "means an insurer carrying on in addition to controlled business any other kind of insurance business;
- (3) "Controlled business" means—
- (i) In the case of any insurer specified in sub-clause (a) or sub-clause (b) of clause (9) of section 2 of the Insurance Act and carrying on life insurance business—
  - (a) all his business, if he carries on no other class of insurance business;
  - (b) all the business appertaining to his life insurance business, if he carries on any other class of insurance business also;
  - (c) all his business if his certificate of registration under the Insurance Act in respect of general

insurance business stands wholly cancelled for a period of more than six months on the 19th day of January, 1956.

(ii) in the case of any other insurer specified in clause (9) ofsection2 of the Insurance Act and carrying on life insurance business—

(a) all his business in India, if he carries on no other class of insurance business in India;

(b) all the business appertaining to his life insurance business in India, if he carries on any other class of insurance business also in India;

(c) all his business in India if he certificate of registration under the Insurance Act in respect of general insurance business in India stands wholly cancelled for a period of more than six months on the 19th day of January, 1956.

Explanation.

An insurer is said to carry on no class of insurance business other than life insurance business,if in addition to life insurance business, he carries on only capital redemption business or annuity certain business or both;and the expression" business appertaining to his life insurance business" in sub-clause (i) and (ii) shall be construed accordingly; (iii) in the case of a provident society, as defined in section 65 of the Insurance; Act, all its business; (iv) in the case of the Central Government or a State Government, all life insurance business carried on by it, subject to the exceptions specified in section44;

(4) "Corporation" means the Life Insurance Corporation of India established under section 3;

(5) "Insurance Act" means the Insurance Act, 1938(4of1938);

(6) "Insurer" means an insurer as defined in the Insurance Act who carries on life insurance business in India and includes the Government and a provident society as defined in section65 of the Insurance Act;

(7) "Member" means a member of the Corporation;

(8) "Prescribed" means prescribed by rules made under this Act;

(9) "Tribunal" means a Tribunal constituted under section17 and having jurisdiction in respect of any matter under the rules made under this Act;

(10) All other words and expressions used herein but not defined and defined in the Insurance Act shall have the meanings respectively assigned to them in that Act.

Establishment and incorporation of Life Insurance Corporation of India.—

(1) With effect from such date as the Central Government may, by notification in the Official Gazette, appoint, there shall be established a Corporation called the Life Insurance Corporation of India.

(2) The Corporation shall be a body corporate having perpetual succession and a common seal with power subject to the provisions of this Act, to acquire, hold and dispose of property, and may by its name sue and be sued.

Constitution of the Corporation.—

(1) The Corporation shall consist of such number of persons not exceeding 2 as the Central Government may think fit to appoint thereto and one of them shall be appointed by the Central Government to be the Chairman there of.

(2) Before appointing a person to be a member, the Central Government shall satisfy itself that person will have no such financial or other interest as is likely to affect prejudicially the exercise or performance by him of his functions as a member, and the Central Government shall also satisfy itself from time to time with respect to every member that he has no such interest; and any person who is, or whom the Central Government proposes to appoint and who has consented to be, a member shall, whenever required by the Central Government so to do, furnish to it such information as the Central Government considers necessary for the performance of its duties under this sub-section.

(3) A member who is in anyway directly or indirectly interested in a contract made or proposed to be made by the Corporation shall as soon as possible after the relevant

circumstances have come to his knowledge, disclose the nature of his interest to the Corporation and the member shall not take part in any deliberation or discussion of the Corporation with respect to that contact.

Capital of the Corporation.—

(1) The original capital of the Corporation shall be five crores of rupees provided by the Central Government after due appropriation made by Parliament bylaw for the purpose, and the terms and conditions relating to the provision of such capital shall be such as maybe determined by the Central Government.

(2) The Central Government may, on the recommendation of the Corporation, reduce the capital of the Corporation to such extent and in such manner as the Central Government may determine.

Functions of the Corporation.—

1) Subject, to the rules, if any, made by the Central Government in this behalf, it shall be the general duty of the Corporation to carry on life insurance business, whether in or outside India, and the Corporation shall so exercise its powers under this Act as to secure that life insurance business is developed to the best advantage of the community.

2) Without prejudice to the generality of the provisions contained in sub-section (1) but subject to the other provisions contained in this Act, the Corporation shall have power —

   (a) To carryon capital redemption business, annuity certain business or reinsurance business in so far as such re insurance business appertains to life insurance business;

   (b) Subject to the rules, if any, made by the Central Government in this behalf, to invest the funds of the Corporation in such manner as the Corporation may think fit and to take all such steps as may be necessary or expedient for the protection or realization of any investment; including the taking over of and administering any property offered as security for the investment until a suitable opportunity arises for its disposal;

(c) To acquire, hold and dispose of any property for the purpose of its business;

(d) To transfer the whole or any part of the life insurance business carried on outside India to any other person or persons, if in the interest of the Corporation it is expedient so to do;

(e) To advance or lend money upon the security of any movable property or otherwise;

(f) To borrow or raise any money in such manner and upon such security as the Corporation may think fit;

(g) To carry on either by itself or through any subsidiary any other business in any case where such other business was being carried on by a subsidiary of an insurer whose controlled business has been transferred to and invested in the Corporation under this Act;

(h) to carry on any other business which may seen to the Corporation to be capable of being conveniently carried on in connection with its business and calculated directly or indirectly to render profitable the business of the corporation;

(i) to do all such things as maybe incidental or conducive to the proper exercise of any of the powers of the Corporation. In the discharge of any of its functions the Corporation shall act so far as maybe on business principles.

Power to impose conditions, etc.—

(1) In entering into any arrangement, under section 6, with any concern, the Corporation may impose such conditions as it may think necessary or expedient for protecting the interest of the Corporation and for securing that the accommodation granted by it is put to the best use by the concern.

(2) Where any arrangement entered into by the Corporation under section 6 with any concern provides for the

appointment by the Corporation of one or more directors of such concern, such provision and any appointment of directors made in pursuance there of shall be valid and effective notwithstanding anything to the contrary contained in the Companies Act, 1956 (1 of1956),or in any other law for the time being in force or in the memorandum, articles of association or any other instrument relating to the concern, and any provision regarding share, qualification, age limit, number of directorships, removal from office of Directors and such like conditions contained in any such law or instrument aforesaid, shall not apply to any director appointed by the Corporation in pursuance of the arrangement as aforesaid.

(3) Any director appointed as aforesaid shall-

(a) Hold office during the pleasure o f the Corporation any maybe removed or substituted by any person by order in writing by the Corporation;

(b) Not incur any obligation or liability by reason only of his being a director or for anything done or omitted to be done in good faith in the discharge of his duties as a director or anything in relation thereto;

(c) Not be liable to retirement by rotation and shall not be taken into account for computing the number of directors liable to such retirement.

Offices, branches and agencies.—

(1) The central office of the Corporation shall be at such place as the Central Government may, by notification in he Official Gazette, specify.

(2) The Corporation shall establish a zonal office at each of the following places, namely, Bombay, Calcutta, Delhi, Kanpur and Madras, and, subject to the previous approval of the Central Government, may establish such other zonal offices as it thinks fit.

(3) The territorial limits of each zone shall be such as may be specified by the Corporation.

(4) There may be established as many divisional offices and branches in each zone as the Zonal Manager thinks fit.

Committees of the Corporation.—

(1) The Corporation may entrust the general superintendence and direction of its affairs and business to an Executive Committee consisting of not more than five of its members and the Executive Committee may exercise all powers and do all such acts and things as may be delegated to it by the Corporation.

(2) The Corporation may also constitute an Investment Committee for the purpose of advising it in matters relating to the investment of its funds, and the Investment Committee shall consist of not more than eight members of whom not less than four shall be members of the Corporation and the remaining members shall be persons (whether members of the Corporation or not) who have special knowledge and experience in financial matters, particularly, matters relating to investment of funds.

(3) The Corporation may constitute such other Committees as it may thin fit for the purpose of discharging such of its functions as maybe delegated to them.

Funds of the Corporation.—

The Corporation shall have its own fund and all receipts of the Corporation shall be credited thereto and all payments of the Corporation shall be made there from. Audit.—

(1) The accounts of the Corporation shall be audited by auditors duly qualified to act as auditors of companies under the law for the time being in force relating to companies, and the auditors shall be appointed by the Corporation with the previous approval of the Central Government and shall receive such remuneration from the Corporation as the Central Government may fix.

(2) Every auditor in the performance of his duties shall have at all reasonable times access to the books, accounts and other documents of the Corporation.

(3) The auditors shall submit their report to the Corporation and shall also forward a copy of their report to the Central Government.

Annual report of activities of Corporation.—

The Corporation shall, as soon as may be, after the end of each financial year, prepare and submit to the Central Government in such form as maybe prescribed a report giving an account of its activities during the previous financial year, and the report shall also give an account of the activities, if any, which are likely to be undertaken by the Corporation in the next financial year.

General Insurance Contract, 1972

Although Life Insurance was nationalized as early as 1956, general insurance business continued to be in the private sector right up to 1969. In that year the Government imposed strict social control on General Insurance Companies.

This was a prelude to nationalization of General of General Insurance Business. With effect from 13th May, 1971 under the provisions of General Insurance (Emergency Provisions) Act, 1971 the Government of India took over the management of all General Insurance Companies operating in India whether they belonged to Indian or non-Indian shareholders.

Subsequently, the General Insurance (Emergency Provisions) Amendment Act, 1971 was passed withdrawing certain rights of the Directors and Members of the Companies, which they were enjoying under the Companies Act. General Insurance (Nationalization) Act, 1972 shortly followed and with effect from 2nf January, 1973 the provisions of the Act became effective.

The functions of the Corporation are enumerated in Section18 of the Act, some of are as follows:

Functions of Corporation –

(1) The functions of the Corporation shall include:-

(a) The carrying on of any part of the general insurance business, if it thinks it desirable to do so;

(b) Aiding, assisting and advising the acquiring companies in the matter of setting up of standards of conduct and sound practice in general insurance business and in the matter of rendering efficient services to holders of policies of general insurance;

(c) Advising the acquiring companies in the matter of the controlling their expenses including the payment of commission and other expenses.

(d) Advising the acquiring companies in the matter of the investment of their funds;

(e) Issuing directions to acquiring companies in relation to the conduct of general insurance business.

(2) In issuing any directions under sub-section (1), the Cooperation shall keep in mind the desirability of encouraging composition amongst the acquiring companies as far as possible in order to render their services more efficient."

Functions of acquiring companies:-

(1) Subject to the rules, if any, made by the Central Government in this behalf and to its memorandum and articles of association, it shall be the duty of every acquiring company to carry on general insurance business.

(2) Each acquiring company shall so function under this Act as to secure that general insurance business is developed to the best of the community.

(3) In the discharge of any of its functions, each acquiring company shall act so far as may be on business principles and where any directions have been issued by the Corporation shall be guided by such directions.

(4) For the removal of doubts it is hereby declared that the Corporations and any acquiring company may, subject to the rules, if any, made by the Central Government in this behalf, "enter into such contracts of reinsurance treaties as it may think fit for the protection of its interests".

Under Sec. 35, The Central Government may by notification specify the application of the provision of the Insurance Act with such modifications as is deemed necessary to the Corporation and the acquiring companies. The Central Government is also empowered to make rules to carry out the provisions of the Act and such rules may provide for:

(a) Manner in which the profits and other moneys received by the Corporation may be dealt with'

(b) The conditions subject to which the Corporation and the acquiring companies shall carry on general insurance business;

(c) The terms and conditions subject to which any re-insurance contract or treaties may be entered into;

(d) Form and manner in which any notice or application may be made to the Central Government;

(e) The reports which may be called for by the Central Government from the Corporation and acquiring companies; and

(f) Any other matter which is required to be or may be prescribed.

THE INSURANCE ACT, 1938

Earlier to the Insurance Act, 1938, the insurance business was carried by the insurance companies in accordance with the principles of the Company Law, 1913. When the business started growing, the need for an independent law to regulate the insurance business was noticed and a separate Act, the Insurance Act, 1938 was legislated.

The Act was used for all purposes relating to both life and general insurance businesses and their regulations. With regards to general insurance, this Act is being used to regulate the marine insurance, fire insurance and other insurances. Further growth of business has made it complex and more legal provisions were required to regulate it. The Marine Insurance Act, 1963, Public Liability Insurance Act, 1991, Insurance Regulatory and Development Authority Act, 1999 and regulations made b... IRDA are some of the legislations that govern the insurance business.

Short title, extent and commencement.

1. (1)) This Act may be called Insurance Act, 1938.

(2) It extends to the whole of India.

(3) It shall come into force on such date3 as the Central Government may, by Notification in the Official Gazette, appoint in this behalf.

Definitions.

2. In this Act, unless there is anything repugnant in the subject or context,-

(1) "Authority" means the Insurance Regulatory and Development Authority established under sub-section (1) of section 3 of the Insurance Regulatory and Development Authority Act, 1999;

(2) "Policy-holder" includes a person to whom the whole of the interest of the policy-holder in the policy is assigned once and for all, but does not include an assignee thereof whose interest in the policy is infeasible or is for the time being subject to any condition;

(3) "Approved securities," means-

(i) Government securities and other securities charged on the revenue of the Central Government or of the Government of a State or guaranteed fully as regards principal and interest by the Central Government or the Government of any State;

(ii) debentures or other securities for money issued under the authority of any Central Act or Act of a State Legislature by or on behalf of a port trust or municipal corporation or city improvement trust in any Presidency-town;

(iii) shares of a corporation established by law and guaranteed fully by the Central Government or the Government of a State as to the repayment of the principal and the payment of the divided;

(iv) securities issued or guaranteed fully as regards principal and interest by the Government of any Part B State and specified as approved securities for the purposes of this Act by the Central Government by notification in the Official Gazette; and

(4)"Auditor" means a person qualified under the Chartered Accountants Act, 1949 (38 of 1949), to act as an auditor of companies;

(4A)"Banking company" and "company" shall have the meanings respectively assigned in them in clauses (c) and (d) of sub-section (1) of Section 5 of the Banking Companies Act, 1949 (10 of 1949);

(5) "Certified" in relation to any copy or translation of a document required to be furnished by or on behalf of an insurer or a provident society as defined in Part III means certified by a principal officer of 6Esuch insurer or provident society to be a true copy or a correct translation, as the case may be;

(5A) "Chief agent" means a person who, not being a salaried employee of an insurer, in consideration of any commission-

(i) Performs any administrative and organizing functions for the insurer, and

(ii) Procures life insurance business for the insurer by employing or causing to be employed insurance agents on behalf of the insurer;

[(5-B) "Controller of Insurance" means the officer appointed by the Central Government under section 2B to exercise all the powers, discharge the functions and performs the duties of the Authority under this Act or the Life Insurance Corporation Act, 1956 (31 of 1956) or the General Insurance Business (Nationalization) Act, 1972 (57 of 1972) or the Insurance Regulatory and Development Authority Act, 1999;]

(6) "Court" means the principal Civil Court of original jurisdiction in a district and includes the High Court in exercise of its ordinary original civil jurisdiction;

(6A)"Fire insurance business" means the business of effecting, otherwise than incidentally to some other class of insurance business, contracts of insurance against loss by or incidental to fire or other occurrence customarily included among the risks insured against in fire insurance Policies;

(6B)"General insurance business" means fire, marine or miscellaneous insurance business, whether carried on singly or in combination with one or more of them;

(7)"Government security" means a Government security as defined in the Public Debt Act, 1944 (18 of 1944);

2[(7A) "Indian insurance company" means any insurer being a company-

(a) which is formed and registered under the Companies Act, 1956 (1 of 1956);

(b)in which the aggregate holdings of equity shares by a foreign company, either by itself or through its subsidiary companies or its nominees, do not exceed twenty-six percent paid-up equity capital of such Indian insurance company;

(c) whose sole purpose is to carry on life insurance business or general insurance business or re-insurance business.

(8) "Insurance company" means any insurer being a company, association or partnership which may be wound up under the Indian Companies Act, 1913 (7 of 1913), or to which the Indian Partnership Act, 1932 (9 of 1932), applies;

(9) "Insurer" means-

(a) any individual or unincorporated body of individuals or body corporate incorporated under the law of any country other than India, carrying on insurance business not being a person specified in sub-clause (c) of this clause which-

(i) carries on that business in India, or

(ii) has his or its principal place of business or is domiciled in India, or

(iii) with the object of obtaining insurance business, employs a representative, or maintains a place of business, in India;

(b) any body corporate [not being a person specified in sub-clause (c) of this clause] carrying on the business of insurance, which is a body corporate incorporated under any law for the time being in force in India; or stands to any such body corporate in the relation of a subsidiary company within the meaning of the Indian Companies Act, 1913 (7 of 1913), as defined by sub-section (2) of section 2 of that Act, and

(c) any person who in India has a standing contract with underwriters who are members of the Society of Lloyd's whereby such person is authorized within the terms of such contract to issue protection notes, cover notes, or other documents granting insurance cover to others on behalf of the underwriters. But does not include a principal agent' chief agent, special agent' or an insurance agent or a provident society as defined in Part III;

(10) "Insurance agent" means an insurance agent licensed under Sec. 42 who receives agrees to receive payment by way of

commission or other remuneration in consideration of his soliciting or procuring insurance business including business relating to the continuance, renewal or revival of policies of insurance;

(10A)"investment company" means a company whose principal business is the acquisition of shares, stocks debentures or other securities;

(10B) "Intermediary or insurance intermediary" shall have the meaning assigned to it in clause (f) of sub-section 2 of the Insurance Regulatory and Development Authority Act, 1999 (41 of 1999)

(11) "Life insurance business" means the business of effecting contracts of insurance upon human life, including any contract whereby the payment of money is assured on death (except death by accident only) or the happening of any

(12) "Manager" and "officer" have the meanings assigned to those expressions in clauses (9) and (11), respectively of Section 2 of the Indian Companies Act, 1913 (7 of 1913);

(13) "Managing agent" means a person, firm or company entitled to the management of the whole affairs of a company by virtue of an agreement with the company, and under the control and direction of the directors except to the extent, if any, otherwise provided for in the agreement, and includes any person, firm or company occupying such position by whatever name called.

Explanation.—If a person occupying the position of managing agent calls himself manager or managing director, he shall nevertheless be regarded as managing agent for the purposes of Sec. 32 of this Act;

(13A)"marine insurance business" means the business of effecting contracts of insurance upon vessels of any description, including cargoes, freights and other interests which may be legally insured, in or in relation to such vessels, cargoes and freights, goods, wares, merchandise and property of whatever description insured for any transit, by land or water, or both, and whether or not including warehouse risks or similar risks in addition or as incidental to such transit, and includes any other risks customarily included among the risks insured against in marine insurance policies;

(13B)"miscellaneous insurance business" means the business of effecting contracts of insurance which is not principally or wholly of any kind or kinds included in clause (6A), (11) and (13A);

(14) "Prescribed" means prescribed by rules made under this Act; and

(15) "Principal agent" means a person who, not being a salaried employee of an insurer, in consideration of any commission,—

(i) Performs any administrative and organizing functions for the insurer; and

(ii) Procures general insurance business whether wholly or in part by employing or causing to be employed insurance agents on behalf of the

(16) "Private company" and "public company" have the meanings respectively assigned to them in Clauses (13) and (13-A) of Sec. 2 of the Indian Companies Act, 1913 (7 of 1913);

(17) "Special agent" means a person who, not being a salaried employee of an insurer, in consideration of any commission, procures life insurance business for the insurer whether wholly or in part by employing or causing to be employed insurance agents on behalf of the insurer, but does not include a chief agent.

Appointment of Authority of Insurance.

(1) If at any time, the Authority is superseded under sub-section (1) of section19 of the Insurance Regulatory and Development Authority Act, 1999, the Central Government may, by notification in the Official Gazette, appoint a person to be the Controller of Insurance till such time the Authority is reconstituted under subsection (3) of section 19 of that Act.

(2) In making any appointment under this section, the Central Government shall have due regard to the following considerations, namely, whether the person to be appointed has had experience in industrial, commercial or insurance matter and whether such person has actuarial qualifications. Requirements as to capital.

No insurer carrying on the business of life insurance, general insurance or re58 insurance in India on or after the commencement of the Insurance Regulatory and Development authority Act, 199, shall be registered unless he has,-

(i) a paid-up equity capital of rupees one hundred crores, in case of a person carrying on the business of life insurance or general insurance; or

(ii) a paid-up equity capital of rupees two hundred crores, in case of a person carrying on exclusively the business as a reinsurer: Provided that in determining the paid-up equity capital specified under clause (i) or clause (ii), the deposit to be made under section 7 and any preliminary expenses incurred in the formation and registration of the company shall be excluded:

Provided further that an insurer carrying on business of life insurance, general insurance or re-insurance in India before the commencement of the Insurance Regulatory and Development Authority Act, 1999 and who is required to be registered under this Act, shall have a paid-up equity capital in accordance with clause (i) and clause (ii), as the case may be, within sex months of the commencement of that Act.

Deposits

Every insurer shall, in respect of the insurance business carried on by him in India, deposit and keep deposited with the Reserve Bank of India in one of the offices in India of the Bank for and on behalf of the Central Government the amount hereafter specified, either in cash or in approved securities estimated at the market value of the securities on the day of deposit, or partly in cash and partly in approved securities so estimated:-

(a) in the case of life insurance business, a sum equivalent to one per cent of his total gross premium written direct in India in any financial year commencing after the 31st day of March, 2000, not exceeding rupees ten crores;

(b) in the case of general insurance business, a sum equivalent to three per cent of his total gross premium written in India, in any financial year commencing after the 31st day of March, 2000, not exceeding rupees ten crores;

(c) in the case of re-insurance business, a sum of rupees twenty crores Provided that, where the business done or to be done is marine insurance only and relates exclusively to country craft or its cargo or both, the amount to be deposited under this sub-section shall be one hundred thousand rupees only: Provided further that in respect of an insurer not having a share capital and carrying on only such insurance business as in the opinion of the Central Government is not carried on ordinarily by insurers under separate policies, the Central Government may, by notification under Official Gazette, order that the provisions of this sub-section shall apply to such insurer with the modification that instead of sum of rupees twenty lakhs or rupees ten lakhs, as the case may be, the deposit to be made by such insurer shall be such amount, being not less than one hundred and fifty thousand rupees, as may be specified in the said order.

Audit

The balance-sheet, profit and loss account, revenue account and profit and loss appropriation account of every insurer, in the case of an insurer specified in sub-clause (a)(ii) or sub-clause (b) of clause (9) of section 2 in respect of all insurance business transacted by him, and in the case of any other insurer in respect of the insurance business transacted by him in India, shall, unless they are subject to audit under the Indian Companies Act, 1913 (7 of 1913), be audited annually by an auditor, and the auditor shall in the audit of all such accounts have the powers of, exercise the functions vested in, and discharge the duties and be subject to the liabilities and penalties imposed on, auditors of companies by section 145 of the Indian Companies Act, 1913.

This Act not to apply to preparation of account, etc., for periods prior to this Act coming into force.

Nothing in this Act shall apply to the preparation of accounts by an insurer and the audit and submission thereof in respect of any accounting year which has expired prior to the commencement of this Act, and notwithstanding the other provisions of this Act, such accounts shall be prepared, audited and submitted in accordance with the law in force immediately before the commencement of this Act.

Investment of Assets

(1) Every insurer shall invest and at all times keep invested assets equivalent to not less than the sum of-

(a) the amount of his liabilities to holders of life insurance policies in India on account of matured claims, and

(b) the amount required to meet the liability on policies of life insurance maturing for payment in India, less-

(i) the amount of premiums which have fallen due to the insurer on such policies but have not been paid and the days of grace for payment of which have not expired, and

(ii) any amount due to the insurer for loans granted on and within the surrender values of policies of life insurance maturing for payment in India issued by him or by an insurer whose business he has acquired and in respect of which he has assumed liability, in the manner following, namely, twenty-five per cent of the said sum in Government securities, a further sum equal to not less than twenty-five per cent of the said sum in Government securities or other approved securities and the balance in any of the approved investments specified in sub-section (1) of section 27A or, subject to the limitations, conditions and restrictions specified in sub-section (2) of that section, in any over investment.

(2) For the purposes of subsection (1),—

(a) the amount of any deposit made under section 7 or section 98 by the insurer in respect of his life insurance business shall be deemed to be assets invested or kept invested Government securities;

(b) The securities of, or guaranteed as to principal and interest by, the Government of the United Kingdom shall be regarded as approved securities other than Government securities for a period of four years from the commencement of the Insurance (Amendment) Act, 1950 (47 of 1950), in the manner and to the extent hereinafter specified, namely:—

(i) during the first year, to the extent of twenty-five per cent in value of the sum referred to in sub-section (1);

(ii) during the second year, to the extent of eighteen and three fourths per cent in value of the said sum;

(iii) during the third year, to the extent of twelve and a half per cent in value of the said sum; and

(iv) during the fourth year, to the extent of six and a quarter per cent in value of the said sum: Provided that, if the Authority so directs in any case, the securities specified in clause (b) shall be regarded as approved securities other than Government securities for a longer period than four years, but not exceeding six years in all and the manner in which and the extent to which the securities shall be so regarded shall be as specified in the direction;

(c) Any prescribed assets shall, subject to such conditions, if any, as may be prescribed, be deemed to be assets invested or kept invested in approved investments specified in sub-section (1) of section 27A.

(3) In computing the assets referred to in subsection (1),—

(a) any investment made with reference to any currency other than the Indian rupee which is in excess of the amount required to meet the liabilities of the insurer in India with reference to that currency, to the extent of such excess; and

(b) any investment made in the purchase of any immoveable property outside India or on the security of any such property, shall not be taken into account: Provided that nothing contained in this sub-section shall affect the operation of sub-section (2): Provided further that the Authority may, either generally or in any particular case, direct that any investment, whether made before or after the commencement of the Insurance (Amendment) Act, 1950 (47 of 1950), and whether made in or outside India, shall, subject to such conditions as may be imposed, be taken into account, in such manner as may be specified in computing the assets referred to in sub-section (1) and where any direction has been issued under this proviso copies thereof shall be laid before Parliament as soon as may be after it is issued.

(4) Where an insurer has accepted reassurance in respect of any policies of life insurance issued by another insurer and maturing for payment in India or has ceded reassurance to another insurer in respect of any such policies issued by himself, the sum referred to in subsection (1) shall be increased by the amount of the liability involved in such acceptance and decreased by the amount of the liability involved in such cession.

(5) The Government securities and other approved securities in which assets are under sub-section (1) to be invested and kept invested shall be held by the insurer free of any encumbrance, charge, hypothecation or lien.

(6) The assets required by this section to be held invested by an insurer incorporated or domiciled outside India shall, except to the extent of any part thereof which consists of foreign assets held outside India, be held in India and all such assets shall be held in trust for the discharge of the liabilities of the nature referred to in sub-section (1) and shall be vested in trustees resident in India and approved by the Authority, and the instrument of trust under this sub-section shall be executed by the insurer with the approval of the Authority and shall define the manner in which alone the subject-matter of the trust shall be dealt with.

Explanation.—This sub-section shall apply to an insurer-incorporated India whose share capital to the extent of one-third is owned by, or the members of whose governing body to the extent of one-third consists of, members domiciled elsewhere than in India.

Power to Appoint Staff

The Authority may appoint such staff, and at such places as it or he may consider necessary, for the scrutiny of the returns, statements and information furnished by insurers under this Act and generally to ensure the efficient performance of the functions of the Authority under this Act.

Registration of principal agents, chief agents and special agents

(1) The Authority or an officer authorized by it in this behalf shall in the prescribed manner and on payment of the prescribed fee, which shall not be more than twenty-five rupees for a principal agent or a chief agent and ten rupees for a special agent, register any person who makes an application to him in the prescribed manner if,—

(a) in the case of an individual, he does not suffer from any of the disqualifications mentioned in sub-section (4) of Section 42, or

(b) in the case of a company or firm, any of its directors or partners does not suffer from any of the said disqualifications, and a certificate to Act as a principal agent, chief agent or special agent, as the case may be, for the purpose of procuring insurance business shall be issued to him.

(2) A certificate issued under this section shall entitle the holder thereof to act as a principal agent, chief agent, or special agent, as the case may be, for any insurer.

(3) A certificate issued under this section shall remain in force for a period of twelve months only from the date of issue, but shall, on application made on this behalf, be renewed from year to year on production of a certificate from the insurer concerned that the provisions of clauses (2) and (3) of Part A of the Sixth Schedule in the case of a principal agent, the provisions of clauses (2) and (4) of Part B of the said Schedule in the case of a chief agent, and the provisions of clauses (2) and (3) of Part C of the said Schedule in the case of a special agent, have been complied with, and on payment of the prescribed fee, which shall not be more than twenty-five rupees, in the case of a principal agent

or a chief agent, and ten rupees in the case of a special agent, and an additional fee of the prescribed amount not exceeding five rupees by way of penalty, in cases where the application for renewal of the certificate does not reach the issuing authority before the date on which the certificate ceases to remain in force: Provided that, where the applicant is an individual, he does not suffer from any of the disqualifications mentioned in clauses (b) to (d) of sub-section (4) of section 42 and where the applicant is a company or a firm, any of its directors or partners does not suffer from any of the said disqualifications.

(4) Where it is found that the principal agent, chief agent or special agent being an individual is, or being a company or firm contains a director or partner who is suffering from any of the disqualifications mentioned in subsection (4) of section 42, without prejudice to any other penalty to which he may be liable, the Authority shall, and where a principal agent, chief agent or special agent has contravened any of the provisions of this Act may cancel the certificate issued under this section to such principal agent, chief agent or special agent.

(5) The authority which issued any certificate under this section may issue a duplicate certificate to replace a certificate lost, destroyed or mutilated on payment of the prescribed fee, which shall not be more than two rupees.

(6) Any person who acts as a principal agent, chief agent or special agent, without holding a certificate issued under this section to act as such, shall be punishable with fine which may extend to five hundred rupees, and any insurer or any person acting on behalf of an insurer, who appoints as a principal agent, chief agent or special agent any person not entitled to act as such or transacts any insurance business in India through any such person, shall be punishable with fine which may extend to one thousand rupees.

(7) Where the person contravening sub-section (6) is a company or a firm, then, without prejudice to any other proceedings which may be taken against the company or

firm, every director, manager, secretary or any other officer of the company, and every partner of the firm who is knowingly a party to such contravention shall be punishable with fine which may extend to five hundred rupees.

(8) The provisions of sub-sections (6) and (7) shall not take effect until the expiry of six months from the commencement of the Insurance (Amendment) Act, 1950.

(9) No insurer shall, on or after the commencement of the Insurance (Amendment) Act, 2002, appointment or transacts any insurance business in India through any principal agent, chief agent or special agent.

Regulation of Employment of Principal Agents

(1) No insurer shall, after the expiration of seven years from the commencement of the Insurance (Amendment) Act, 1950, appoint, or transact any insurance business in India, through a principal agent.

(2) Every contract between an insurer and a principal agent shall be in writing and the terms contained in Part A of the Sixth Schedule shall be deemed to be incorporated in, and form part of, every such contract.

(3) No insurer shall, after the commencement of the Insurance (Amendment) Act, 1950 (47 of 1950), appoint any person as a principal agent except in a presidency-town unless the appointment is by way of renewal of any contract subsisting at such commencement.

(4) Within sixty days of the commencement of the Insurance (Amendment) Act, 1950 (47 of 1950), every principal agent shall file with the insurer concerned a full list of insurance agents employed by him indicating the terms of the contract between the principal agent and each of such insurance agents, and, if any principal agent fails to file such a list within the period specified, any commission payable to such principal agent on premiums received from the date of expiry of the said period of sixty days until the date of the filing of the said list shall, notwithstanding anything in any contract to the contrary, cease to be so payable.

(5) A certified copy of every contract as is referred to in sub-section (2) shall be furnished by the insurer to the Authority within thirty days of his entering into such contract, and intimation of any change in any such contract shall be furnished by the insurer with full particulars thereof to the Authority within thirty days of the making of any such change.

(6) If the commission due to any insurance agent in respect of any general insurance business procured by such agent is not paid by the principal agent for any reason, the insurer may pay the insurance agent the commission so due and recover the amount so paid from the principal agent concerned.

(7) Every contract as is referred to in sub-section (2), subsisting at the commencement of the Insurance (Amendment) Act, 1950 (47 of 1950), shall, with respect to terms regarding remuneration, be deemed to have been so altered as to be in accordance with the provisions of sub-section (4) of section 40A.

(8) If any dispute arises as to whether a person is or was a principal agent the matter shall be referred to the Authority, whose decision shall be final.

(9) Every insurer shall maintain a register in which the name and address of every principal agent appointed by him, the date of such appointment and the date, if any, on which the appointment ceased shall be entered.

Commission, Brokerage or Fee Payable to Intermediary or Insurance Intermediary

(1) No intermediary or insurance intermediary shall be paid or contract to be paid by way of commission, fee or as remuneration in any form, an amount exceeding thirty per cent of the premium payable as may be specified by the regulations made by the Authority, in respect of any policy or policies effected through him: Provided that the Authority may specify different amounts payable by way of commission, fee or as remuneration to an intermediary or insurance intermediary or different classes of business of insurance.

(2) Without prejudice to the provisions contained in this Act, the Authority may, by the regulations made in this behalf, specify the requirements of capital, form of business and other conditions to act as an intermediary or insurance intermediary.

Register of Insurance Agents

Every insurer and every person who acting on behalf of an insurer employs insurance agents shall maintain a register showing the name and address of every insurance agent appointed by him and the date on which his appointment began and the date, if any, on which his appointment ceased.

IRDA ACT 1999

The Insurance Act, 1938 had provided for setting up of the Controller of Insurance to act as a strong and powerful supervisory and regulatory authority for insurance. Post nationalization, the role of Controller of Insurance diminished considerably in significance since the insurance companies were owned by the Government.

With the opening up of the insurance industry to the private sector, the need for a strong, independent and autonomous Insurance Regulatory Authority was felt. As the enacting of legislation would have taken time, the then Government constituted through a Government resolution an Interim Insurance Regulatory Authority pending the enactment of a comprehensive legislation. The Insurance Regulatory and Development Authority Act, 1999 is an act to provide for the establishment of an Authority to protect the interests of holders of insurance policies, to regulate, promote and ensure orderly growth of the insurance industry and for matters connected therewith or incidental thereto and further to amend the Insurance Act, 1938, the Life Insurance Corporation Act, 1956 and the General insurance Business (Nationalization) Act, 1972 to end the monopoly of the Life Insurance Corporation of India (for life insurance business) and General Insurance Corporation and its subsidiaries (for general insurance business).

Extent and Commencement

- This Act may be called the Insurance Regulatory and Development Authority Act, 1999.

- The act extends to the whole of India and will come into force on such date as the Central Government may, by notification in the Official Gazette specify. Different dates may be appointed for different provisions of this Act.
- The Act has defined certain terms, some of the most important ones are as follows:-
- Appointed day means the date on which the Authority is established under the act.
- Authority means the established under this Act.

With effect from such date as the Central Government may, by notification, appoint the Insurance Regulatory and Develop is to be constituted. The Authority shall be a body corporate, having perpetual succession and a common seal with power, subject to the provisions of this Act, to acquire, hold and dispose of property, and to contract and can be sue or be sued in its own name. The head office of the Authority shall be at such place as the Central Government may decide from time to time and it may establish offices at other places in India.

Composition of Authority

The Authority shall consist of the following members, namely

(a) a Chairperson;

(b) not more than five whole-time members;

(c) not more than four part-time members, to be appointed by the Central Government from amongst persons of ability, integrity and standing who have knowledge or experience in life insurance, general insurance, actuarial science, finance, economics, law, accountancy, administration or any other discipline which would, in the opinion of the Central Government, be useful to the Authority:

The Central Government while appointing the Chairperson and the whole-time members must ensure that at least one person each is a person having knowledge or experience in life insurance, general insurance or actuarial science respectively. Tenure of office of Chairperson and other members The Chairperson and every other whole-time member shall hold office for a term of five years from the date on which he enters upon his office and shall be eligible for reappointment: However, no person shall hold office as such Chairperson after he has attained the age of sixty-five years and no person shall hold office as such whole-time member after he has attained the age of sixty-two years.

A part-time member shall hold office for a term not exceeding five years from the date on which he enters upon his office.

A member may:-

(a) relinquish his office by giving in writing to the Central Government notice of not less than three months; or be removed from his office in accordance with the following provisions.

Removal from Office

The Central Government may remove from office any member who:-

(a) is, or at any time has been, adjudged as insolvent;

(b) has become physically or mentally incapable of acting as a member;

(c) has been convicted of any offence which, in the opinion of the Central Government, involves moral turpitude;

(d) has acquired such financial or other interest as is likely to affect prejudicially his functions as a member;

(e) has so abused his position as to render his continuation in office detrimental to the public interest.

No such member shall be removed under clause (d) or clause (e) unless he has been given a reasonable opportunity of being heard in the matter. Salary and allowances of Chairperson and members

The salary and allowances payable to, and other terms and conditions of service of, the members other than part-time members shall be such as may be prescribed.

The part-time members shall receive such allowances as may be prescribed. The salary, allowances and other conditions of service of a member shall not be varied to his disadvantage after appointment.

Bar on Future Employment of Members

The Chairperson and the whole-time members shall not, for a period of two years from the date on which they cease to hold office as such, except with the previous approval of the Central Government, accept:-

(a) any employment either under the Central Government or under any State Government; or

(b) any appointment in any company in the Insurance sector.

Administrative powers of Chairperson

The Chairperson shall have the powers of general superintendence and direction in respect of all administrative matters of the Authority.

Meeting of Authority

The Authority shall meet at such times and places, and shall observe such rules and procedures in regard to transaction of business at its meetings (including quorum at such meetings) as may be determined by regulations.

The Chairperson, or if for any reason he is unable to attend a meeting of the Authority, any other member chosen by the members present from amongst themselves at the meeting shall preside at the meeting. All questions which come up before any meeting of the Authority shall be decided by a majority vote of the members present and voting, and in the event of equality of votes, the Chairperson, or in his absence, the person presiding shall have a second or casting vote. The Authority may make regulations for the transaction of business at its meetings.

Vacancies, etc., not to Invalidate Proceedings of Authority

No Act or proceeding of the Authority shall be invalid merely by reason of:-

(a) any vacancy in, or any defect in the constitution of, the Authority;

(b) any defect in the appointment of a person acting as a member of the Authority;

(c) any irregularity in the procedure of the Authority not affecting the merits of the case.

Officers and Employees of Authority

The Authority may appoint officers and such other employees, as it considers necessary for the efficient discharge of its functions under this Act. The terms and other conditions of service of officers and other employees of the Authority shall be governed by regulations made under this Act.

Transfer of Assets, Liabilities, etc, of the Interim Insurance Regulatory

Authority will be transferred to the Authority on the appointed day.

All suits and other legal proceedings instituted or which could have been instituted by or against the Interim Insurance Regulatory Authority immediately before that day may be continued or may be instituted by or against the Authority.

Duties, Powers and Functions of Authority

Subject to the provisions of this Act and any other law for the time being in force, the Authority has the duty to regulate, promote and ensure orderly growth of the insurance business and re-insurance business. The powers and functions of the Authority include:-

(a) to issue to the applicant a certificate of registration, to renew, modify, withdraw, suspend or cancel such registration

(b) protection of the interests of the policy-holders in matters concerning assigning of policy, nomination by policy-holders, insurable interest, settlement of insurance claim, surrender value of policy, and other terms and conditions of contracts of insurance

(c) specifying requisite qualifications code of conduct and practical training for intermediary or insurance intermediaries and agents

(d) specifying the code of conduct for surveyors and loss assessors

(e) promoting efficiency in the conduct of insurance business

(f) promoting and regulating professional organizations connected with the insurance and reinsurance business

(g) levying fees and other charges for carrying out the purposes of this Act

(h) calling for information from, undertaking inspection of, conducting enquiries and investigations including audit of the insurers, intermediaries, insurance intermediaries and other organizations connected with the insurance business

(i) control and regulation of the rates, advantages, terms and conditions that may be offered by insurers in respect of general insurance business not so controlled and regulated by the Tariff Advisory Committee under section 64U of the Insurance Act, 1938

(j) prescribing the form and manner in which books of account shall be maintained and statement of accounts will be rendered by insurers and other insurance intermediaries

(k) Regulating investment of funds by insurance companies

(l) regulating maintenance of margin of solvency

(m) adjudication of disputes between insurers and intermediaries or insurance intermediaries

(n) supervising the functioning of the Tariff Advisory Committee

(o) specifying the percentage of premium income of the insurer to finance schemes for promoting and regulating professional organizations

(p) specifying the percentage of life insurance business and general insurance business to be undertaken by the insurer in the rural or social sector

(q) exercising such other powers as may be prescribed

Finance, Accounts and Audit

Grants by Central Government

The Central Government may, after due appropriation made by the Parliament by law in this behalf, make to the Authority grants of such sums of money as the Government may think fit for being utilized for the purposes of this Act.

Fund

A Fund to be called "The Insurance Regulatory and Development Authority Fund" is to be established and the following sums will be credited thereto:-

(a) all Government grants, fees and charges received by the Authority

(b) all sums received by the Authority from such other source as may be decided upon by the Central Government

(c) the percentage of prescribed income received from the insurer.

The Fund shall be applied for meeting the following expenses:-

(a) the salaries, allowances and other remuneration of the members, officers and other employees of the Authority

(b) the other expenses of the Authority in connection with the discharge of its functions and for the purposes of this Act.

Accounts and Audit

The Authority shall maintain proper accounts and other relevant records and prepare an annual statement of accounts in such form as may be prescribed by the Central Government in consultation with the Comptroller and Auditor General of India. The accounts of the Authority shall be audited by the Comptroller and Auditor General of India at such intervals as may be specified by him and any expenditure incurred in connection with such audit shall be payable by the Authority to the Comptroller and Auditor General of India. The Comptroller and Auditor-General of India and other person appointed by him in connection with the audit of the accounts of the Authority shall have the same rights and privileges and authority in connection with such audit as the Comptroller and Auditor General generally has in connection with the audit of the Government accounts and, in particular, shall have the right to demand the production of books, accounts, connected vouchers and other documents and papers and to inspect any of the officers of the Authority. The accounts of the Authority as certified by the Comptroller and Auditor General of India or any other person appointed by him in this behalf together with the audit report thereon shall be forwarded annually to the Central

Government and that Government shall cause the same to be laid before each House of Parliament.

Powers of Central Government

The Authority shall, in exercise of its powers or the performance of its functions under this Act, be bound by such directions on questions of policy, other than those relating to technical and administrative matters, as the Central Government may give in writing to it from time to time However, Authority must, as far as practicable, be given an opportunity to express its views before any such direction is given. The decision of the Central Government, whether a question is one of policy or not, shall be final. Power of Central Government to supersede Authority If at any time the Central Government is of the opinion:-

(a) that, on account of circumstances beyond the control of the Authority, it is unable to discharge the functions or perform the duties imposed on it by or under the provisions of this Act: or

(b) that the Authority has persistently defaulted in complying with any direction given by the Central Government under this Act or in the discharge of the functions or performance of the duties imposed on it by or under the provisions of this Act and as a result of such default the financial position of the Authority or the administration of the Authority has suffered; or

(c) that circumstances exist which render in necessary in the public interest so to do, the Central Government may, by notification and for reasons to be specified therein, supersede the Authority for such period, not exceeding six months, as may be specified in the notification and appoint a person to be the Controller of Insurance. However, before issuing any such notification, the Central Government shall give a reasonable opportunity to the Authority to make representations against the proposed supersession and shall consider the representations, if any, of the Authority.

Upon the publication of such notification superseding the Authority:-

(a) the Chairperson and other members shall, as from the date of supersession, vacate their offices as such;

(b) all the powers, functions and duties which may, by or under the provisions of this Act, be exercised or discharged by or on behalf of the Authority shall, until the Authority is reconstituted, be exercised and discharged by the Controller of Insurance; and

(c) all properties owned or controlled by the Authority shall, until the Authority is reconstituted vest in the Central Government.

On or before the expiration of the period of supersession specified in such a notification, the Central Government shall reconstitute the Authority by a fresh appointment of its Chairperson and other members and in such case any person who had vacated his office under the notification shall not be deemed disqualified for reappointment.

The Central Government shall cause a copy of the notification issued and a full report of any action taken under this section and the circumstances leading to such action to be laid before each House of Parliament at the earliest.

Furnishing of Eeturns, etc., to the Central Government

The Authority must furnish to the Central Government at such time and in such form and manner as may be prescribed, or as the Central Government may direct, such returns and statements and such particulars in regard to any proposed or existing programme for the promotion and development of the insurance industry as the Central Government may, from time to time, require.

The Authority must, within nine months after the close of each financial year, submit to the Central Government a report giving a true and full account of its activities including the activities for promotion and development of the insurance business during the previous financial year. Copies of the reports must be laid, as soon as may be after they are received, before each House of Parliament. Chairperson, members, officers and employees of Authority to be public servants. The Chairperson, members, officers and other employees of the Authority shall be deemed, when acting or purporting to act in pursuance of any of the provisions of this Act, to be public servants within the meaning of section 21 of the Indian Penal Code.

Protection of Action taken in Good Faith

No suit, prosecution or other legal proceedings shall lie against the Central Government or any officer of the Central Government or any member, officer or other employee of the Authority for anything which is in good faith done or intended to be done under this Act or the rules or regulations made there under. However, nothing in this Act exempts any person from any suit or other proceedings which might, apart from this Act, be brought against him.

Delegation of Powers

The Authority may, by general or special order in writing, delegate to the Chairperson or any other member or officer of the Authority, subject to such conditions, if any, as may be specified in the order such of its powers and functions under this Act as it may deem necessary. The Authority may, by a general or special order in writing, also form Committees of the members and delegate to them the powers and functions of the Authority as may be specified by the regulations.

Power to make Rules

The Central Government may, by notification, make rules for carrying out the purposes of this Act. Such rules may provide for all or any of the following matters, namely:-

(a) the salary and allowances payable to and other conditions of service of the members other than part-time members

(b) the allowances to be paid to the part-time members

(c) such other powers that may be performed by the Authority

(d) the form of annual statement of accounts to be prepared by the Authority

(e) the time at, the form and the manner in which returns and statements and particulars are to be furnished to the Central Government

(f) the matters on which the Insurance Advisory Committee shall advise the authority

(g) any other matter which is to be, or may be, prescribed, or in respect of which provision is to be or may be made by rules.

Establishment of Insurance Advisory Committee

The Authority may, by notification, establish with effect from such date as it may specify in such notification, a Committee to be known as the Insurance Advisory Committee. The Insurance Advisory Committee shall consist of not more than twenty-five members excluding ex officio members to represent the interests of commerce, industry, transport, agriculture, consumer fora, surveyors, agents, intermediaries, organizations engaged in safety and loss prevention, research bodies and employees' association in the insurance sector.

The Chairperson and the members of the Authority shall be the ex officio Chairperson and ex officio members of the Insurance Advisory Committee. The objects of the Insurance Advisory committee shall be to advise the Authority on matters relating to the making of the regulations. The Insurance Advisory Committee may advise the Authority on such other matters as may be prescribed.

Capital Requirements

Requirement as to Capital

No insurer carrying on the business of life insurance, general insurance, or reinsurance in India on or after the commencement of the Insurance Regulatory and Development Authority Act, 1999, shall be registered unless he has:-

1. a paid-up equity capital of rupees one hundred crores, in case of a person carrying on the business of life insurance or general insurance; or
2. a paid-up equity capital of rupees two hundred crores, in case of a person carrying on exclusively the business as a reinsurer:

In determining the paid-up equity capital specified under clause (i) or clause (ii), the deposit to be made under section 7 and any preliminary expenses incurred in the formation and registration of the company shall be excluded: An insurer carrying on business of life insurance, general insurance or reinsurance in India before the commencement of the Insurance Regulatory and Development Authority Act, 1999 and who is required to be registered under this Act, shall have a paid-up equity capital in accordance with clause (i) and clause (ii), as the case may be, within six months of the commencement of that Act.

Where, the nominal value of the shares intended to be transferred by any individual, firm, group, constituents of a group, or body corporate under the same management, jointly or severally exceeds one per cent. Of paid up capital of the insurer, previous approval of the Authority must be obtained for the transfer. Explanation.-For the purpose of this sub-clause, the expressions "group" and "same management", shall have the same meanings respectively assigned to them in the Monopolies and Restrictive Trade Practices Act, 1969.

The following sections have been inserted:-

Provisions of investment of funds outside India.

No insurer shall directly or indirectly invest outside India, the funds of the policyholders.

Manner and Conditions of Investment

The Authority may, in the interests of the policyholders, specify by regulations made by the Authority, the time, manner and other conditions of investment of assets to be held by an insurer for the purposes of this Act.

The Authority may, after taking into account the nature of business and to protect the interests of the policyholders, issue to an insurer the directions relating to the time, manner, and other conditions of investment of assets to be held by him. However, no directions shall be issued unless the insurer concerned has been given a reasonable opportunity of being heard.

Insurance Business in Rural or Social Sector

Every insurer shall, after the commencement of the Insurance Regulatory and Development Authority Act, 1999, undertake such percentages of life insurance business and general insurance business in the rural or social sector, as may be specified, in the Official Gazette by the Authority, in this behalf.

Miscellaneous Provisions

Penalty for default in complying with, or act in contravention of, this Act. lf any person, who is required under this Act, or rules or regulations made there under,-

(a) to furnish any document, statement, account, return or report to the Authority, fail to furnish the same; or

(b) to comply with the directions, fails to comply with such directions;

(c) to maintain solvency margin, fails to maintain such solvency margin;

(d) to comply with the directions on the insurance treaties, fails to comply with sue directions on the insurance treaties, he shall be liable to a penalty not exceeding five lakhs rupees for each such failure and punishable with fine.

lf a person makes a statement, or furnishes any document, statement, account, return or report which is false and which he either knows or believes to be false or does not believe to be true,- (

(a) he shall be liable to a penalty not exceeding five lakhs rupees for each such failure; and

(b) he shall be punishable with imprisonment which may extend to three years or with fine for each such failure.

If any director, managing director, manager or to~ officer or employees of an insurer wrongfully obtains possession of any property or wrongfully applies to any purpose of the Act, he shall be liable to a penalty not exceeding two lakhs rupees for each such failure.

Offences by companies, Where any offence under this Act has been committed by a company, every person who, at the time the offence was committed, was in charge of, and was responsible to, the Company for the conduct of the business of the company as well as the company shall be deemed to be guilty of the offence and shall be liable to be proceeded against and punished accordingly: Nothing contained in this sub-section shall render any such person liable to any punishment, if he proves that the offence was committed without his knowledge or that he had exercised all due diligence to prevent the commission of such offence. Where any offence under this Act has been committed by a company and it is proved that the offence has been committed with the consent or connivance of, or is attributable to any neglect on the part of, any director, manager, secretary or other officer of the company, such director, manager, secretary or other officer shall be deemed to be guilty of that offence and shall be liable to be proceeded against and punished accordingly.

Explanation: For the purposes of this section,-

(a) "company" means any body corporate, and includes a firm, an association of person or a body of individuals whether incorporated or not; and

(b) "director", in relation to-

   (i) a firm means a partner in the firm;

   (ii) an association of persons or a body of individuals, means any-member controlling the affairs thereof.

Power of Authority to make regulations.

The Authority may, by notification in the Official Gazette, make regulations consistent with this Act and the rules made there under, to carry out the provisions of this Act.

AGENCY LAW

At times all of us act as principals and agents. If I my friend ask me to deposit his water bill, then he is acting as principal and I am as agent. Agency Law is contained in Chapter X {Secs182 to 238} of the Indian Contact Act 1872. "Agent" and "principal": An "agent" is a person employed to do any act for another, or to represent another in dealings with third persons. The person for whom such act is done, or represented, is called the "principal". {sec182}.

Who may employ agent: Any person who is of the age of majority according to the law to which he is subject, and who is of sound mind, may employ an agent. Who may be an agent: As between the principal and third persons, any person may become an agent, but no person who is not of the age of majority and sound mind can become an agent, so as to be responsible to the principal according to the provisions in that behalf herein contained.

Consideration not necessary: No consideration is necessary to create an agency. Agent's authority may be express or implied: The authority of an agent may be express or implied.

Definitions of express and implied authority: An authority is said to be express when it is given by words spoken or written. An authority is said to be implied when it is to be inferred from the circumstances of the case; and things spoken or written, or the ordinary course of dealing, may be accounted circumstances of the case.

Illustration

Aman owns a shop in Serampur, living himself in Calcutta, and visiting the shop occasionally. Bharat manages the shop, and he is in the habit of ordering goods from Chaman in the name of Aman for the purposes of the shop, and of paying for them out of Aman's funds with Aman's knowledge. Bharat has an implied authority from Aman to order goods from Chaman in the name of Aman for the purpose of the shop.

Extent of agent's authority: An agent, having an authority to do an act, has authority to do every lawful thing, which is necessary in order to do such act. An agent having an authority to carry on a business has authority to do every lawful thing necessary for the purpose, or usually done in the course, of conducting such business.

Illustrations

(a) A is employed by B, residing in London, to recover at Bombay a debt due to B. A may adopt any legal process necessary for the purpose of recovering the debt, and may give a valid discharge for the same.

(b) A constitutes B his agent to carry on his business of a shipbuilder. B may purchase timber and other materials, and hire workmen, for the purpose of carrying on the business.

Agent's Authority in an Emergency: An agent has authority, in an emergency, to do all such acts for the purpose of protecting his principal from loss and would be done by a person or ordinary prudence, in his own case, under similar circumstances.

SUB AGENT

When Agent cannot Delegate

An agent cannot lawfully employ another to perform acts, which he has expressly, or impliedly undertaken to perform personally, unless by the ordinary custom of trade a sub-agent may, or, from the nature of agency, a sub-agent must, be employed.

"Sub-agent" Defined

A "sub-agent" is a person employed by, and acting under the control of, the original agent in the business of the agency.

Representation of Principal by Sub-agent Properly Appointed

Where a sub-agent is properly appointed, the principal is, so far as regards third persons, represented by the sub-agent, and is bound by and responsible for his acts, as if he were an agent originally appointed by the principal. Agent's responsibility for sub-agents: The agent is responsible to the principal for the acts of the sub-agent.

Sub-agent's responsibility: The sub-agent is responsible for his acts to the agent, but not to the principal, except in case of fraud or willful wrong.

Agent's Responsibility for Sub-agent Appointed without Authority

Where an agent, without having authority to do so, has appointed a person to act as a sub-agent, the agent stands towards such person in the relation of a principal to an agent, and is responsible for his acts both to the principal and to third person; the principal is not represented, by or responsible for the acts of the person so employed, nor is that person responsible to the principal. Relation between principal and person duly appointed by agent to act in business of agency When an agent, holding an express or implied authority to name another person to act for the principal in the business of the agency, has named another person accordingly, such person is not a sub-agent, but an agent of the principal for such part of the business of the agency as is entrusted to him.

Agent's Duty in Naming such Person

In selecting such agent for his principal, an agent is bound to exercise the same amount of discretion as a man of ordinary prudence would exercise in his own case; and, if he does this, he is not responsible to the principal for the acts of negligence of the agent so selected.

Illustrations

A instructs B, a merchant, to buy a ship for him. B employs a ship-surveyor of good reputation to choose a ship for A. The surveyor makes the choice negligently and the ship turns out to be unseaworthy and is lost. B is not, but the surveyor is, responsible to A. Right of person as to acts done for him without his authority-effect of ratification

Where acts are done by one person on behalf of another, but without his knowledge or authority, he may elect to ratify or to disown such acts. If he ratifies them, the same effects will follow as if they had been performed by his authority. Ratification may be expressed or implied

Ratification may be expressed or may be implied in the conduct of the person on whose behalf the acts are done.

Illustrations

(a) A, without authority, buys goods, for B. Afterwards B sells them to C on his own account; B's conduct implies a ratification of the purchase made for him by A.

(b) A, without B's authority, lends B's money to C. Afterwards B accepts interest on the money from C. B's conduct implies a ratification of the loan. Knowledge requisite for valid ratification

No valid ratification can be made by a person whose knowledge of the facts of the case is materially defective.

Effect of ratifying unauthorized act forming part of a transaction

A person ratifying any unauthorized act done on his behalf ratifies the whole of the transaction of which such act formed a part.

Ratification of Unauthorized act cannot Injure Third Person

An act done by one person on behalf of another, without such other person's authority, which, if done with authority would have the effect of subjecting a third person to damages, or of terminating any right to interest of a third person cannot, by ratification, be made to have such effect.

REVOCATION OF AUTHORITY

Termination of Agency

An agency is terminated by the principal revoking his authority, or by the agent renouncing the business of the agency; or by the business of the agency being completed; or by either the principal or agent dying or becoming of unsound mind; or by the principal being adjudicated an insolvent under the provisions of any Act for the time being in force for the relief of insolvent debtors. Termination of agency, where agent has an interest in subject-matter Where the agent has himself an interest in the property, which forms the subject matter of the agency, the agency cannot, in the absence of an express contract, be terminated to the prejudice of such interest.

Illustration

A, gives authority to B to sell A's land, and to pay himself, out of the proceeds, the debts due to him from A.A cannot revoke this authority, nor can it be terminated by his insanity or death.

When principal may revoke agent's authority.

The principal may, save as is otherwise provided by the last preceding section, revoke the authority given to his agent at any time before the authority has been exercised, so as to bind the principal.

Revocation where authority has been partly exercised.

The principal cannot revoke the authority given to his agent after the authority has been partly exercised; so far as regards such acts and obligations as arise from acts already done in the agency.

Compensation for revocation by principal, or renunciation by agent.

Where there is an express or implied contract that the agency should be continued for any period of time, the principal must make compensation to the agent, or the agent to the principal, as the case may be, for any previous revocation or renunciation of the agency without sufficient cause.

Notice of revocation or renunciation.

Reasonable notice must be given of such revocation or renunciation, otherwise the damage thereby resulting to the principal or the agent, as the case may be, must be made good to the one by the other.

Revocation and renunciation may be expressed or implied.

Revocation or renunciation may be expressed or may be implied in the conduct of that principal or agent respectively.

Illustration

A empowers B to let A's house. Afterwards A lets it himself. This is an implied revocation of B's authority.

When termination of agent's authority takes effect as to agent, and as to third persons

The termination of the authority of an agent does not, so far as regards the agent, take effect before it becomes known to him, or, so far as regards third persons, before it becomes known to them.

Agent's duty on termination of agency by principal's death or insanity When an agency is terminated by the principal dying or becoming of unsound mind, the agent is bound to take on behalf of the representative, of his late principal, all reasonable steps for the protection and reservation of the interests entrusted to him.

Termination of Sub-agent's Authority

The termination of the authority of an agent causes the termination (subject to the rules herein contained regarding the termination of an agent's authority) of the authority of all sub-agents appointed by him.

AGENT'S DUTY TO PRINCIPAL

Agent's Duty in Conducting Principal's Business

An agent is bound to conduct the business of his principal according to the directions given by the principal, or in the absence of any such directions according to the customs, which prevails in doing business of the same kind at the place where the agent conducts such business. When the agent acts otherwise, if any loss be sustained, he must make it good to his principal and if any profit accrues, he must account for it.

Skill and Diligence required from Agent

An agent is bound to conduct the business of the agency with as much skill as is generally possessed by person engaged in similar business unless the principal has notice of his want of skill.

The agent is always bound to act with reasonable diligence, and to use such skill as he possesses; and to make compensation to his principal in respect of the direct consequences of his own neglect, want of skill, or misconduct, but not in respect of loss or damage which are indirectly or remotely caused by such neglect, want of skill, or misconduct.

Agent's Accounts

An agent is bound to render proper accounts to his principal on demand. Agent's, duty to communicate with principal

It is the duty of an agent in case of difficulty, to use all reasonable diligence in communicating with his principal, and in seeking to obtain his instructions. Right of principal when agent deals, on his own account, in business of agency without principal's consent

If an agent deals on his own account in the business of the agency, without first obtaining the consent of his principal and acquainting him with all material circumstances, which have come to his own knowledge on the subject, the principal may

Repudiate the transaction, if the case shows, either that any material fact has been dishonestly concealed from him by the agent, or that the dealings of the agent have been disadvantageous to him.

Illustrations

(a) A direct B to sell A's estate. B buys the estate for himself in the name of C. A, on discovering that B has bought the estate for himself, may repudiate the sale, if he can show that B has dishonestly concealed any material fact, or that the seals has been disadvantageous to him.

(b) A directs B to sell A's estate. B, on looking over the estate before selling it, finds a mine on the estate which is unknown to A. B informs A that he wished to buy the estate for himself but conceals the discovery of the mine. A allows B to buy, in ignorance of the existence of the mine. A, on discovering that B knew of the mine at the time he bought the estate, may either repudiate or adopt the sale at his option.

Principal's right to benefit gained by agent dealing on his own account in business of agency

If an agent, without the knowledge of his principal, deals in the business of the agency on his own account instead of on account to his principal, the principal is entitled to claim from the agent any benefit which may have resulted to him from the transaction.

Agent's right of retainer out of sums received on principal's account An agent may retain, out of any sums received on account of the principal in the business of the agency, all moneys due to himself in respect of advances made or expenses properly incurred by him in conducting such business, and also such remuneration as may be payable to him for acting as agent.

Agent's Duty to Pay sums received for Principal

Subject to such deductions, the agent is bound to pay to his principal all sums received on his account.

When agent's remuneration becomes due.

In the absence of any special contract, payment for the performance of any act is not due to the agent until the completion of such act; but an agent may detain moneys received by him on account of goods sold, although the whole of the goods consigned to him for sale may not have been sold, or although the sale may not be actually complete.

Agent not entitled to remuneration for business misconduct.

An agent, who is guilty of misconduct in the business of the agency, is not entitled to any remuneration in respect of that part of the business, which he has misconducted.

Illustrations

A employs B to recover 1,000 rupees from C. Through B's misconduct the money is not recovered. B is entitled to no remuneration for his services and must make good the loss.

Agent's Lien on Principal's Property

In the absence of any contract to the contrary, an agent is entitled to retain goods, papers, and other property, whether movable or immovable of the principal received by him, until the amount due to himself for commission, disbursements and services in respect of the same has been paid or accounted for to him.

PRINCIPAL'S DUTY TO AGENT

Agent to be indemnified against consequences of lawful acts The employer of an agent is bound to indemnify him against the consequences of all lawful acts done by such agent in exercise of the authority conferred upon him. Agent to be indemnified against consequences of acts done in good faith Where one person employs another to do an act, and the agent does the act in good faith, the employer is liable to indemnify the agent against the consequences of that act, though it may cause an injury to the rights of third persons. Non-liability of employer of agent to do a criminal act Where one person employees another to do an act which is criminal, the employer is not liable to the agent, either upon an express or an implied promise to indemnify him against the consequences of that Act.

Illustrations

A employs B to beat C, and agrees to indemnify him against all consequences of the act. B thereupon beats C, and has to pay damages to C for so doing. A is not liable to indemnify B for those damages. Compensation to agent for injury caused by principal's neglect. The principal must make compensation to his agent in respect of injury caused to such agent by the principal's neglect or want of skill.

Illustration

A employs B as a bricklayer in building a house, and put up the scaffolding himself. The scaffolding is unskillfully put up, and B is in consequence hurt. A must make compensation to B.

EFFECT OF AGENCY ON CONTRACTS WITH THIRD PERSONS

Enforcement and Consequences of Agent's Contract

Contracts entered into through an agent, and obligations arising from acts done by an agent, may be enforced in the same manner, and will have the same legal consequences as if the contracts had been entered into the acts done by the principal in person.

Illustrations

(a) A buys goods from B, knowing that he is an agent for their sale, but not knowing who the principal is. B's principal is the person entitled to claim from A the price of the goods, and A cannot, in a suit by the principal, set-off against that claim a debt due to himself from B.

(b) A, being B's agent; with authority to receive money on his behalf, receives from C a sum of money due to B. C is discharged of his obligation to pay the sum in question to B.

Principal how far Bound, when Agent exceeds Authority

When an agent does more than he is authorized to do, and when the part of what he does, which is within his authority, can be separated from the part, which is beyond his authority, so much only of what he does as is within his authority is binding as between him and his principal.

Principal not bound when excess of agent's authority is not separable Where an agent does more than he is authorized to do, and what he does beyond the scope of his authority cannot be separated from what is within it, the principal is not bound to recognize the transaction.

Illustration

A authorizes B to buy 500 sheep for him. B buys 500 sheep and 200 lambs for a sum of 6,000 rupees. A may repudiate the whole transaction.

Consequences of Notice given to Agent

Any notice given to or information obtained by the agent, provided it be given or obtained in the course of the business transacted by him for the principal, shall, as between the principal and third parties, have the same legal consequences as if it had been given to or obtained by the principal.

Illustrations

A is employed by B to buy from C goods of which C is the apparent owner. A was, before he was so employed a servant of C, and then learnt that the goods really belonged to D, but B is ignorant of that fact. In spite of the knowledge of his agent, B may set-off against the price of the goods a debt owing to him from C.

Agent cannot personally enforce, nor be bound by, contracts on behalf of principal

In the absence of any contract to that effect an agent cannot personally enforce contracts entered into by him on behalf of his principal, nor is he personally bound by them.

Presumption of contract to the contrary: Such a contract shall be presumed to exit in the following cases-

(1) Where the contract is made by an agent for the sale or purchase of goods for a merchant resident abroad;

(2) Where agent does not disclose the name of his principal;

(3) Where the principal, though disclosed, cannot be sued.

Right of Parties to a Contract made by Agent not Disclosed

If an agent makes a contract with a person who neither, knows nor has reason to suspect, that he is an agent, his principal may require the performance of the contract; but the other contracting party has, as against the principal, the same right as he would have had as against if the agent had been the principal. If the principal discloses himself before the contract is completed, the other contracting party may refuse to fulfill the contract, if he can show that, if he had known who was the principal in the contract, or if he had known that the agent was not a principal, he would not have entered into the contract.

Performance of Contract with Agent Supposed to be Principal

Where one man makes a contract with another, neither knowing nor having reasonable ground to suspect that the other is an agent, the principal, if he requires the performance of the contract, can only obtain such performance subject to the right and obligations subsisting between the agent and the other party of the contract. Liability of principal inducing belief that agent's unauthorized acts were authorized.

When an agent has, without authority, done acts or incurred obligations to third person on behalf of his principal, the principal is bound by such acts or obligations, if he has by his word or conduct induced such third person to believe that such acts and obligations were within the scope of the agent's authority.

Illustrations

(a) A consigns goods to B for sale, and gives him instructions not to sell under a fixed price. C, being ignorant of B's instruction, enters into a contract with B to buy the goods at a price lower than the reserved price. A is bound by the contract

(b) A entrusts B with negotiable instruments endorsed in blank. B sells them to C in violation of private order from A. The sale is good.

Effect, on agreement, of misrepresentation or fraud by agent.

Misrepresentation made or fraud committed, by agent acting in the course of their business for their principals, have the same effect on agreements made by such agents as if such misrepresentations of frauds had been made or committed by the principals; but misrepresentations made, or frauds committed, by agents, in matters which do not affect their authority, do not affect their principals

Illustrations

(a) A, being B's agent for the sale of goods, induces C to buy them by a misrepresentation, which he was not authorized by B to make. The contract is voidable, as between B and C, at the option of C.

(c) A, the captain of B's ship, signs bills of lading without having received on board the goods mentioned therein. The bills of lading are void as between B and the pretended consignor.

CONSUMER PROTECTION ACT, 1986

The Consumer Protection Act was passed by the Parliament in 1986 and it came into force from 1987. Its purposes to protect consumers against defective goods, unsatisfactory services, unfair trade practices, etc. The Act provides for three-tier machinery consisting of District Forum, State Commission and National Commission. It also provides for the formation protection councils in every state. The consumers can file their complaints at the appropriate forum for quick redressal. The complaint may relate to defective refrigerator or TV set, nonfunctional telephone, lack of due cares in medical treatment and so on. Any service or product given free of charge is not covered by the Act.

Definitions of Important Terms

Before studying the provisions of the CPA, it is necessary to understand the terms used in the Act. Let us understand some of the more important definitions. Complainant means:-

1. A consumer; or
2. Any voluntary consumer association registered under the Companies Act, 1956 or under any other law for the time being in force; or
3. The Central Government or any State Government, who or which makes a complaint; or
4. One or more consumers where there are numerous consumers having the same interest

Complaint means any allegation in writing made by a complainant that:-

1. an unfair trade practice or a restricted trade practice has been adopted by any trader
2. the goods bought by him or agreed to be bought by him suffer from one more defects
3. the services hired or availed of or agreed to be hired or availed of by him suffer from deficiency in any respect
4. the trader has charged for the goods mentioned in the complaint a price excess of the price fixed by or under any law for the time being in force or displayed on the goods or any package containing such goods.

5. goods which will be hazardous to life and safety when used, are being offered for sale to the public in contravention of the provisions of any law for the time being in force, requiring traders to display information in regard to the contents, manner and effect of use of such goods; with a view to obtaining any relief provided by law under the CPA.

Consumer means any person who:-

1. buys any goods for a consideration which has been paid or promised or partly paid and partly promised, or under any system of deferred payment (for example hire purchase or installment sales) and includes any other user of such goods when such use is made with the approval of the buyer, but does not include a person who obtains such goods for resale or for any commercial purpose; or
2. hires or avails of any services for a consideration which has been paid or promised, or partly paid and partly promised, or under any system of deferred payment and includes any beneficiary of such services when such services are availed of with the approval of the first mentioned person For the purposes of this definition "commercial purpose" does not include use by a consumer of goods bought and used by him exclusively for the purpose of earning his livelihood by means of self-employment.

Goods mean goods as defined in the Sale of Goods Act, 1930. Under that act, goods means every kind of movable property other than actionable claims and money and includes stocks and shares, growing crops, grass and things attached to or forming part of the land which are agreed to be severed before sale or under the contract of sale. Service is defined to mean service of any description which is made available to potential users and includes the provision of facilities in connection with banking, financing, insurance, transport, processing, supply of electrical or other energy, board or lodging or both, housing construction, entertainment, amusement or the purveying of news or other information but does not include the rendering of any service free of charge or under a contract of personal service.

Consumer dispute means dispute where the person against whom a complaint has been made, denies or disputes the allegation contained in the complaint. Restrictive Trade Practice means any trade practice which requires a consumer to buy, hire, or avail of any good or as the.case may be, services as a condition precedent for buying, hiring or availing of any other goods or services.

Unfair Trade Practice means unfair trade practice as defined under the Monopolies and Restrictive Trade Practices Act. The MRPT act has defined certain practices to be unfair trade practices.

Defect means any fault, imperfection or shortcoming in the quality, quantity, potency, purity or standard which is required to be maintained by or under any law for the time being in force or under any contract, express or implied, or as is claimed by the trade in any manner whatsoever in relation to any goods.

Deficiency means any fault, imperfection or shortcoming or inadequacy in the quality, nature and manner of performance which is required to be maintained by or under any law for the time being in force or has been undertaken to be performed by a person in pursuance of a contract or otherwise in relation to any service. A consumer is a user of goods and services. Any person paying for goods and services, which he uses, is entitled to expect that the goods and services be of a nature and quality promised to him by the seller.

The earlier principle of "Caveat Emptor" or "let the buyer beware" which was prevalent has given way to the principle of "Consumer is King". The origins of this principle lie in the fact that in today's mass production economy where there is little contact between the producer and consumer, often sellers make exaggerated claims and advertisements, which they do not intend to fulfill. This leaves the consumer in a difficult position with very few avenues for redressal. The onset on intense competition also made producers aware of the benefits of customer satisfaction and hence by and large, the principle of "consumer is king" is now accepted.

Objects of the Consumer Protection Act, 1986

The preamble to the Act states that the Act is legislated to provide for better protection of the interests of consumers and for that purpose to make provision for the establishment of consumer councils and other authorities for the settlement of consumer's disputes and for matters connected therewith. The CPA extends to the whole of India except the State of Jammu and Kashmir and applies to all goods and services unless otherwise notified by the Central Government. The basic rights of consumers as per the Consumer Protection Act (CPA) are:

1. Right to safety.
2. Right to be informed.
3. Right to choose
4. Right to representation (or to be heard).
5. Right to seek redressal.
6. Right to consumer education.

1. Right to Safety It is the consumer right to be protected against goods and services which is hazardous to health or life.
2. Right to be Informed The consumer has the right to be informed about the quality, quantity, purity, standard and price of goods he intends to purchase. Therefore, the manufacture must mention complete information about the product, its ingredients, date of manufacture, price, precaution of use, etc. on the label and package of the product.
3. Right to Choose The consumer should be assured of freedom to choose from a variety of products at competitive prices. Every consumer wants to buy a product on his free will. There should be free competition in the market so that the consumer may make the right choice in satisfying his needs.
4. Right to Representation (or to be Heard) The consumer has a right to register dissatisfaction with any product and get his complaint heard. Most of the reputed firms have set up consumer service cells to listen to the consumer's complaint and take appropriate steps to redress their grievances.
5. Right to Seek Redressal. It is the right to seek redressal against any defect in goods or unfair trade suffered by the

consumer. If the quality and performance of a product falls short of seller's claims, the consumer has a right to certain remedies. The Consumer Protection Act requires that the product must be repaired, replaced or taken back by the seller as provided under the contract between the buyer and the seller.

6. Right to Consumer Education. It means right of acquiring knowledge and being a well-informed consumer throughout his life. He should also be made aware of his rights and the remedies available through publicity in the mass media.

Consumer Responsibilities

(i) To provide adequate information to the seller The consumer has the responsibility to provide adequate information about his needs and expectation to the sellers.

(ii) To exercise caution in purchasing The consumer must try to get full information on the quality, design, utility, quantity, price, etc. of the product before purchasing it.

(iii) To insist on cash memo or receipt The consumer must get a cash memo or receipt as a proof of purchase of goods from the seller. This would help him in making a complaint to the seller in case of any defect in the goods.

(iv) To file complaint against genuine grievance The consumer must file a complaint with the seller or manufacturer about any defects or shortcoming in the products and services.

(v) To be quality conscious The consumer should never compromise on the quality of goods. While making purchases, the consumers must look for standard quality certification marks such as ISI, Agmark, Woolmark, FPO, etc. For example, electric iron must carry ISI mark.

Redressal Machinery under the Act

Consumer Protection Councils

The interests of consumers are enforced through various authorities set up under the CPA. The CPA provides for the setting up of the Central Consumer Protection Council, the State Consumer Protection Council and the District Forum.

Central Consumer Protection Council

The Central Government has set up the Central Consumer Protection Council, which consists of the following members:-

(a) The Minister in charge of Consumer Affairs in the Central Government who is its Chairman, and

(b) Other official and non-official members representing varied interests

The Central council consists of 150 members and its term is 3 years. The Council meets as and when necessary but at least one meeting is held in a year.

State Consumer Protection Council

The State Council consists of:-

(a) The Minister in charge of Consumer Affairs in the State Government who is its Chairman, and

(b) Other official and non-official members representing varied interests The State Council meets as and when necessary but not less than two meetings must be held every year.

Redressal Machinery under the Act

The CPA provides for a 3-tier approach in resolving consumer disputes. The District Forum has jurisdiction to entertain complaints where the value of goods / services complained against and the compensation claimed is less than Rs. 20 lakhs, the State Commission for claims exceeding Rs. 20 lakhs but not exceeding Rs. 1crore and the National Commission for claims exceeding Rs.1 crore.

District Forum

Under the CPA, the State Government has to set up a district Forum in each district of the State. The government may establish more than one District Forum in a district if it deems fit. Each District Forum consists of:-

(a) A person who is, or who has been, or is qualified to be, a District Judge who shall be its President

(b) Two other members who shall be persons of ability, integrity and standing and have adequate knowledge or experience of or have shown capacity in dealing with problems relating to economics, law, commerce, accountancy, industry, public affairs or administration, one of whom shall be a woman.

Appointments to the State Commission shall be made by the State Government on the recommendation of a Selection Committee consisting of the President of the State Committee, the Secretary-Law Department of the State and the secretary in charge of Consumer Affairs Every member of the District Forum holds office for 5 years or up to the age of 65 years, whichever is earlier and is not eligible for re-appointment. A member may resign by giving notice in writing to the State Government whereupon the vacancy will be filled up by the State Government.

The District Forum can entertain complaints where the value of goods or services and the compensation, if any, claimed is less than rupees twenty lakhs. However, in addition to jurisdiction over consumer goods services valued upto Rs.20 lakhs, the District Forum also may pass orders against traders indulging in unfair trade practices, sale of defective goods or render deficient services provided the turnover of goods or value of services does not exceed rupees twenty lakhs. A complaint shall be instituted in the District Forum within the local limits of whose jurisdiction

(a) The opposite party or the defendant actually and voluntarily resides or carries on business or has a branch office or personally works for gain at the time of institution of the complaint; or

(b) Any one of the opposite parties (where there are more than one) actually and voluntarily resides or carries on business or has a branch office or personally works for gain, at the time of institution of the complaint provided that the other opposite party/parties acquiescence in such institution or the permission of the Forum is obtained in respect of such opposite parties; or

(c) The cause of action arises, wholly or in part.

State Commission

The Act provides for the establishment of the State Consumer Disputes Redressal Commission by the State Government in the State by notification. Each State Commission shall consist of:-

(a) A person who is or has been a judge of a High Court appointed by State Government (in consultation with the Chief Justice of the High Court) who shall be its President;

(b) Two other members who shall be persons of ability, integrity, and standing and have adequate knowledge or experience of, or have shown capacity in dealing with, problems relating to economics, law, commerce, accountancy, industry, public affairs or administration, one of whom must be a woman.

Every appointment made under this is made by the State Government on the recommendation of a Selection Committee consisting of the President of the State Commission, Secretary-Law Department of the State and Secretary in charge of Consumer Affairs in the State.

Every member of the District Forum holds office for 5 years or upto the age of 65 years, whichever is earlier and is not eligible for re-appointment. A member may resign by giving notice in writing to the State Government whereupon the vacancy will be filled up by the State Government.

The State Commission can entertain complaints where the value of goods or services and the compensation, if any, exceeds Rs. 20 lakhs but does not exceed Rs. 1crore.

The State Commission also has the jurisdiction to entertain appeal against the orders of any District Forum within the State The State Commission also has the power to call for the records and appropriate orders in any consumer dispute which is pending before or has been decided by any District Forum within the State if it appears that such District Forum has exercised any power not vested in it by law or has failed to exercise a power rightfully vested in it by law or has acted illegally or with material irregularity.

National Commission

The Central Government provides for the establishment of the National Consumer Disputes Redressal Commission The National Commission shall consist of:-

(a) A person who is or has been a judge of the Supreme Court, to be appoint by the Central Government (in consultation with the Chief Justice of India) who be its President;

(b) Four other members who shall be persons of ability, integrity and standing and have adequate knowledge or experience of, or have shown capacity in dealing with, problems relating to economics, law, commerce, accountancy, industry, public affairs or administration, one of whom shall be a woman

Appointments shall be by the Central Government on the recommendation of a Selection Committee consisting of a Judge of the Supreme Court to be nominated by the Chief Justice of India, the Secretary in the Department of Legal Affairs and the Secretary in charge of Consumer Affairs in the Government of India. Every member of the National Commission shall hold office for a term of five years or upto seventy years of age, whichever is earlier and shall not be eligible for reappointment.

The National Commission shall have jurisdiction:-

a. to entertain complaints where the value of the goods or services and the compensation, if any, claimed exceeds rupees one crores:
b. to entertain appeals against the orders of any State Commission; and
c. to call for the records and pass appropriate orders in any consumer dispute which is pending before, or has been decided by any State Commission where it appears to the National Commission that such Commission has exercised a jurisdiction not vested in it by law, or has failed to exercise a jurisdiction so vested, or has acted in the exercise of its jurisdiction illegally or with material irregularity.

Complaints may be filed with the District Forum by:-

1. The consumer to whom such goods are sold or delivered or agreed to be sold or delivered or such service provided or agreed to be provided
2. Any recognized consumer association, whether the consumer to whom goods sold or delivered or agreed to be sold or delivered or service provided or agreed to be provided, is a member of such association or not
3. One or more consumers, where there are numerous consumers having the same interest with the permission

of the District Forum, on behalf of or for the benefit of, all consumers so interested

4. The Central or the State Government.

On receipt of a complaint, a copy of the complaint is to be referred to the opposite party, directing him to give his version of the case within 30 days. This period may be extended by another 15 days. If the opposite party admits the allegations contained in the complaint, the complaint will be decided on the basis of materials on the record. Where the opposite party denies or disputes the allegations or omits or fails to take any action to represent his case within the time provided, the dispute will be settled in the following manner:-

In case of dispute relating to any goods: Where the complaint alleges a defect in the goods which cannot be determined without proper analysis or test of the goods, a sample of the goods shall be obtained from the complainant, sealed and authenticated in the manner prescribed for referring to the appropriate laboratory for the purpose of any analysis or test whichever may be necessary, so as to find out whether such goods suffer from any other defect. The appropriate laboratory' would be required to report its finding to the referring authority, i.e. the District Forum or the State Commission within a period of forty-five days from the receipt of the reference or within such extended period as may be granted by these agencies.

Limitation Period for Filing of Complaint

The District Forum, the State Commission, or the National Commission shall not admit a complaint unless it is filed within two years from the date on which the cause of action has arisen. However, where the complainant satisfies the District Forum / State Commission, that he had sufficient cause for not filing the complaint within two years, such complaint may be entertained by it after recording the reasons for condoning the delay.

Powers of the Redressal Agencies

The District Forum, State Commission and the National Commission are vested with the powers of a civil court under the Code of Civil Procedure while trying a suit in respect of the following matters:-

1. The summoning and enforcing attendance of any defendant or witness examining the witness on oath;
2. The discovery and production of any document or other material producible as evidence;
3. The reception of evidence on affidavits:
4. The requisitioning of the report of the concerned analysis or test from the appropriate laboratory or from any other relevant source:
5. Issuing of any commission for the examination of any witness; and
6. Any other matter which may be prescribed.

Under the Consumer Protection Rules, 1987, the District Forum, Commission and the National Commission have the power to require any person:-

(i) To produce before, and allow to be examined by an officer of any authorities, such books of accounts, documents or commodities as may be required and to keep such book, documents etc. under its custody for the purposes of the Act;

(ii) To furnish such information which may be required for the purposes to any officer so specified.

They have the power to:-

(i) To pass written orders authorizing any officer to exercise power of entry and search of any premises where these books, papers, commodities, or documents are kept if there is any ground to believe that these may be destroyed, altered, falsified or secreted. Such authorized officer may also seize books, papers, documents or commodities if they are required for the purposes of the Act, provided the seizure is communicated to the District Forum / State Commission / National commission within 72 hours. On examination of such documents or commodities, the agency concerned may order the retention thereof or may return it to the party concerned.

(ii) to issue remedial orders to the opposite party.

(iii) to dismiss frivolous and vexatious complaints and to order the complainant to make payment of costs, not exceeding Rs. 10,000 to the opposite party.

Remedies Granted under the Act

The District Forum / State Commission / National Commission may pass one or more of the following orders to grant relief to the aggrieved consumer:-

1. To remove the defects pointed out by the appropriate laboratory from goods in question;
2. To replace the goods with new goods of similar description, which shall be free from any defect;
3. To return to the complainant the price, or, as the case may be, the charges paid by the complainant;
4. To pay such amount as may be awarded by it as compensation to the consumer for any loss or injury suffered by the consumer due to negligence of the opposite party;
5. To remove the defects or deficiencies in the services in question;
6. To discontinue the unfair trade practice or the restrictive trade practice or not to repeat them;
7. Not to offer the hazardous goods for sale:
8. To withdraw the hazardous goods from being offered for sale:
9. To provide for adequate costs to parties.

Appeals

Any person aggrieved by an order made by the Forum may prefer an appeal to the State Commission in the prescribed form and manner. Similarly, any person aggrieved by any original order of the State Commission may prefer an appeal to the National Commission in the prescribed form and manner. Any person aggrieved by any original order of the National Commission may prefer an appeal to the Supreme Court.

All such appeals are to be made within thirty days from the date of the order provided that the concerned Appellate authority may entertain an appeal after the said period of thirty days if it is satisfied that there was sufficient cause for not filling it within that period. The period of 30 days is to be computed from the date of receipt of the order by the appellant.

Where no appeal has been preferred against any of the orders of the authorities, such orders would be final. The District Forum, State Commission or National Commission may enforce respective orders as if it was a decree or order made by a Court and in the event of their inability to execute the same; they may send the order to the Court for execution by it as if it were a Court decree or order.

Penalties

Failure or omission by a trader or other person against whom a complaint is made or the complainant to comply with any order of the State Commission or the National Commission shall be punishable with imprisonment for a term which shall not be less than one month but which may extend to 3 years, or with fine of not less than Rs. 2,000 but which may to Rs. 10000 or with both.

However, if it is satisfied that the circumstances of any case so requires, then the District Forum or the State Commission or the National Commission may impose a lower fine or a shorter term of imprisonment.

SUMMARY

During the mushrooming of insurance companies many financially unsound concerns were also floated which failed miserably. The Insurance Act 1938 was the first legislation governing not only life insurance but also non-life insurance to provide strict state control over insurance business. The demand for nationalization of life insurance industry was made repeatedly in the past but it gathered momentum in 1944 when a bill to amend the Life Insurance Act 1938 was introduced in the Legislative Assembly. However, it was much later on the 19th of January, 1956, that life insurance in India was nationalized. About 154 Indian insurance companies, 16 non-Indian companies and 75 provident were operating in India at the time of nationalization. Nationalization was accomplished in two stages; initially the management of the companies was taken over by means of an Ordinance, and later, the ownership too by means of a comprehensive bill. The Parliament of India passed the Life Insurance Corporation Act on the 19th of June 1956, and the Life Insurance Corporation of India was created on 1st September,

1956, with the objective of spreading life insurance much more widely and in particular to the rural areas with a view to reach all insurable persons in the country, providing them adequate financial cover at a reasonable cost.

The IRDA Bill provides for the establishment of an authority to protect the interests of the holders of insurance policies, to regulate, promote and insure orderly growth of the insurance industry and amend the Insurance Act, 1938, the Life Insurance Act, 1956 and the General Insurance Business (Nationalization) Act, 1972. The bill allows foreign equity stake in domestic private insurance companies to a maximum of 26 per cent of the total paid-up capital and seeks to provide statutory status to the insurance regulator. The insurance business in India is pegged at $ 6.6 Billion whereas industry leaders feel privatization will increase it to $ 40 Billion within next 3-5 years.

GLOSSARY

Annuity It is a scheme where under certain amount is paid at yearly/half yearly/quarterly/monthly intervals.

Grace Period A specified period after a premium payment is due, in which the policyholder may make such payment, and during which the protection of the policy continues

Insurable Interest A condition in which the person applying for insurance and the person who is to receive the policy benefit will suffer an emotional or financial loss, if any untouched event occurs. Without insurable interest, an insurance contract is invalid.

Insured The person whose life is covered by a policy of insurance.

Policy Is the legal document that has the conditions of the insurance contract Premium Notice: Notice of a premium due, sent out by the company or one of its agencies to an insured. Synonym for "Renewal Notice".

Surrender Value Surrender value is the amount payable to the policy holder on his surrendering his right under a policy and terminating the contract of insurance.

Term Life Insurance A form of life insurance, which provides coverage for a specified period of time and does not build cash value.

Term: Term is the period for which insurance coverage is given.

Void Contract A contract obtained by fraud is a void contract. It is not a contract at all. Under this there cannot be any action as no rights or obligations are cast on the parties to the contract.

Voidable Contract A contract, which is valid until it is treated as void by the aggrieved party, is a voidable contract. Obviously in such an event the insurer would be the aggrieved party and has the option to repudiate liability.

Underwriting The process of selecting risks for insurance and determining in what amounts and on what terms the insurance company will accept the risk. Balance Sheet Provides a snapshot of a company's financial condition at one point in time. It shows assets, including investments and reinsurance, and liabilities, such as loss reserves to pay claims in the future, as of a certain date. It also states a company's equity, known as policyholder surplus. Changes in that surplus are one indicator of an insurer's financial standing.

Bond A security that obligates the issuer to pay interest at specified intervals and to repay the principal amount of the loan at maturity. In insurance, a form of surety ship. Bonds of various types guarantee a payment or a reimbursement for financial losses resulting from dishonesty, failure to perform and other acts Indemnify Provide financial compensation for losses.

Capital Markets The markets in which equities and debt are traded.

Insolvency Insurer's inability to pay debts.

Capital Shareholder's equity (for publicly-traded insurance companies) and retained earnings (for mutual insurance companies).

6

LIFE INSURANCE: A CONTRACT OF LIFE

INTRODUCTION

As Discussed before, Insurance is a contract in writing under which insurer agrees in return for a consideration (premium) to indemnify the insured against the loss suffered on account of an uncertain future event. Life insurance is a contract for payment of a sum of money to the person assured on the occurrence of the event insured by the contract.

OBJECTIVES

After going through this unit you should be able to:

- Develop an understanding of life insurance basics and its importance
- Understand various types of life insurance policies offered by insurance companies
- Mention the suitability of various life insurance policies to different persons with variety of needs.
- Know various documents prepared by insurance company for a life insurance contract.
- Explain the procedure to handle death claims and maturity claims.
- Understand pricing objectives and elements of life insurance.
- Understand procedure of underwriting of new business

CONCEPT, DOCUMENTATION & CLAIM SETTLEMENT

Meaning and Importance Concept of Life Insurance: Life insurance is a contract under which the insurer (Insurance

Company) in consideration of a premium paid undertakes to pay a fixed sum of money on the death of the insured or on the expiry of a specified period of time whichever is earlier. In case of life insurance, the payment for life insurance policy is certain. The event insured against is sure to happen only the time of its happening is not known. So life insurance is known as 'Life Assurance'. The subject matter of insurance is life of human being. Life insurance provides risk coverage to the life of a person. On death of the person insurance offers protection against loss of income and compensate the titleholders of the policy.

BASIC PRINCIPLES OF LIFE INSURANCE CONTRACT.

Insurable Interest

The insured must have insurable interest in the life assured. In absence of insurable interest, Contract of insurance is void. Insurable interest must be present at the time of entering into contract with insurance company for life insurance. It is not necessary that the assured should have insurable interest at the time of maturity also.

Insurable interest exists in the following cases:

(a) A person has an unlimited insurable interest in his/her own life.

(b) A person has an insurable interest in the life of his/her spouse.

(c) A father has an insurable interest in the life of his son or daughter on whom he is dependent. Likewise a son may have insurable interest in life of his parents.

(d) A creditor has an insurable interest in the life of the debtor, to the extent of the debt.

(e) A servant employed for a specified period has insurable interest in the life of his employer.

Utmost good Faith

The contract of life insurance is a contract of utmost good faith. The insured should be open and truthful and should not conceal any material fact in giving information to the insurance company, while entering into a contract with insurance company.

Misrepresentation or concealment of any fact will entitle the insurer to repudiate the contract if he wishes to do so.

Not a Contract of Indemnity

The life insurance contract is not a contract of indemnity. A Contract of life insurance is not a contract of indemnity. The loss of life cannot be compensated and only a fixed sum of money is paid in the event of death of the insured. So, the life insurance contract is not a contract of indemnity. The loss resulting from the death of life assured cannot be calculated in terms of money.

IMPORTANCE OF LIFE INSURANCE.

Life Insurance is of great importance to individuals, groups, business community and general public. Some of the main benefits of life insurance are given below.

Protection against untimely Death

Life insurance provides protection to the dependents of the life insured and the family of the assured in case of his untimely death. The dependents or family members get a fixed sum of money in case of death of the assured.

Saving for Old Age

After retirement the earning capacity of a person reduces. Life insurance enables a person to enjoy peace of mind and a sense of security in his/her old age.

Promotion of Savings

Life insurance encourages people to save money compulsorily. When a life policy is taken, the assured is to pay premiums regularly to keep the policy in force and he cannot get back the premiums, only surrender value can be returned to him. In case of surrender of policy, the policyholder gets the surrendered value only after the expiry of duration of the policy.

Initiates Investments

Life Insurance Corporation encourages and mobilizes the public savings and channelises the same in various investments for the economic development of the country. Life insurance is an important tool for the mobilization and investment of small savings.

Credit Worthiness

Life insurance policy can be used as a security to raise loans. It improves the credit worthiness of business.

Social Security

Life insurance is important for the society as a whole also. Life insurance enables a person to provide for education and marriage of children and for construction of house. It helps a person to make financial base for future.

Tax Benefit

Under the Income Tax Act, premium paid is allowed as a deduction from the total income under section 80C.

Types of Life Insurance Policies

Life insurance policies can be grouped into the following categories:

TERM POLICY

In case of Term assurance plans, insurance company promises the insured for a nominal premium to pay the face value mentioned in the policy in case he is no longer alive during the term of the policy. Term assurance policy has the following features:

- It provides a risk cover only for a prescribed period. Usually these policies are short-term plans and the term ranges from one year onwards. If the policyholder survives till the end of this period, the risk cover lapses and no insurance benefit payment is made to him.
- The amount of premium to be paid for these policies is lower than all other life insurance policies. As savings and reserves are not accumulated under this policy, it has no surrender value and loan or paid-up values are not allowed on these policies.
- This plan is most suitable for those who are initially unable to pay high premium
- when income is low as required for Whole Life or Endowment policies, but requires life cover for a high amount.

WHOLE LIFE POLICY

This policy runs for the whole life of the assured. The sum assured becomes payable to the legal heir only after the death of the assured. The whole life policy can be of three types.

(1) Ordinary whole life policy – In this case premium is payable periodically throughout the life of the assured.

(2) Limited payment whole life policy – In this case premium is payable for a specified period (Say 20 Years or 25 Years) Only.

(3) Single Premium whole life policy – In this type of policy the entire premium is payable in one single payment.

ENDOWMENT LIFE POLICY

In this policy the insurer agrees to pay the assured or his nominees a specified sum of money on his death or on the maturity of the policy which ever is earlier. The premium for endowment policy is comparatively higher than that of the whole life policy. The premium is payable till the maturity of the policy or until the death of the assured which ever is earlier. It provides protection to the family against the untimely death of the assured.

HEALTH INSURANCE SCHEMES

An individual is subject to uncertainty regarding his health. He may suffer from ailments, diseases, disability caused by stroke or accident, etc. For serious cases the person may have to be hospitalized and intensive medical care has to be provided which can be very expensive. It is here that medical insurance is helpful in reducing the financial burden.

These days the vulnerability to lifestyle diseases such as heart, cancer, neurotic, and pollution based, etc are on the increase. So it makes sense for an individual to go for medical insurance cover.

JOINT LIFE POLICY

This policy is taken on the lives of two or more persons simultaneously. Under this policy the sum assured becomes payable on the death of any one of those who have taken the joint life policy. The sum assured will be paid to the survivor(s). For example, a joint life policy may be taken on the lives of husband and wife, sum assured will be payable to the survivor on the death of the spouse.

WITH PROFIT AND WITHOUT PROFIT POLICY

Under with profit policy the assured is paid, in addition to the sum assured, a share in the profits of the insurer in the form of bonus. Without profit policy is a policy under which the assured does not get any share in the profits earned by the insurer and gets only the sum assured on the maturity of the policy. With profit and without profit policies are also known as participating and non –participating policies respectively.

DOUBLE ACCIDENT BENEFIT POLICY

This policy provides that if the insured person dies of any accident, his beneficiaries will get double the amount of the sum assured.

ANNUITY POLICY

Under this policy, the sum assured is payable not in one lump sum payment but in monthly, quarterly and half-yearly or yearly installments after the assured attains a certain age. This policy is useful to those who want to have a regular income after the expiry of a certain period e.g. after retirement. Annuity is paid so long as the assured survives. In annuity policy medical checkup is not required. Annuity is paid so long as the assured survives.

POLICIES FOR WOMEN

Women, now a days are free to take life assurance policies. However, some specially designed policies suit their needs in a unique manner; the synopsis of some these policies are as follows:

a. Jeevan Sathi is also known a Life Partner plan where the husband and wife are covered under this endowment policy, which gives the following benefits.
    i. On maturity, provided both are alive, full sum assured with bonus is paid.
    ii. On the death of one of the assured during the period of the policy, basic sum assured is paid to the surviving

partner, who is not required to pay any further premiums.

iii. The surviving partner remains covered for the full sum assured. If she/he dies, then the sum assured is paid to the nominee, but this is before the maturity date.

iv. The surviving partner will be paid sum assured with bonuses if he survives till the maturity date. Hence this policy gives a comprehensive family protection.

b. Jeevan Sukanya is highlighted by the following points.

i. Only female child aged between 1 to 12 years is covered in this plan.

ii. band is automatically covered under the policy after marriage.

iii. Risk of the child starts either after 2 years of taking the policy or not before the age of 7, whichever is early.

iv. Premium paying period is 20 years minus age at entry.

v. On surviving the age of 20, the life assured receives the sum assured as survival benefit and the policy continues to cover the life assured till maturity date when vested bonus will be paid only. If life assured dies before maturity, sum assured with bonuses will be paid.

GROUP INSURANCE

Group life insurance is a plan of insurance under which the lives of many persons are covered under one life insurance policy. However, the insurance on each life is independent of that on the other lives. Usually, in group insurance, the employer secures a group policy for the benefit of his employees. Insurer provides coverage for many people under single contract.

POLICIES FOR CHILDREN

Policies for children are meant for the various needs of the children such as education, marriage, security of life etc. Some of the major children policies are:

(1) Children's deferred assurances
(2) Marriage endowment and educational annuity plans
(3) Children endowment policy

MONEY BACK POLICY

In this case policy money is paid to the insured in a number of separate cash payments. Insurer gives periodic payments of survival benefit at fixed intervals during the term of policy as long as the policyholder is alive.

Documentation

The contract for the life insurance starts with the proposal made by the proposer in standard application form available with insurance company and then various other documents are prepared.

PROPOSAL FORMS

The proposal form is a standardized form. The proposal form is a type of an application form, which a proposer has to fill all the relevant details about the life to be assured. The agent has the proposal form with him provided by the insurer. There are different types of policies and so the different types of proposal forms are there. It has the entire details regarding the duration of the policy, type of plan, mode of payment, etc. A proposal form is to be to be completed by the proposer in his own handwriting and signed in the presence of the agent. The proposal form contains a declaration at the end, to ensure the authenticity of the information given.

Usually the proposal form contains the following information to be filled by the prospective insured:

1. Name of life assured
2. Address
3. Date of Birth
4. Occupation
5. Age
6. Name of the employer (if any)
7. Sum assured of the proposed policy

8. Number and age of the family members
9. Family medical history
10. Proposer's Medical history

Besides these there are other related forms regarding health, occupation, the agent's confidential report and many others. In addition there is a consent letter which shows the consent of the life assured to the imposition of some clause or extra premium, duly signed by the life assured.

FIRST PREMIUM RECEIPT

The agent provides the proposal form and other related documents and the underwriter examines the form and other documents and then determines the terms on which to accept the risk or reject the same.

The consent of the person assured is obtained in the form of payment of premium. After receiving the payment, the insurance company issues the First Premium Receipt, which acknowledges the proposal of the life-assured. It contains all particulars of the policy. It has the details of the next premium to be paid. The policy bond is sent within 45-50 days from the date of first premium receipt to the life assured. The First Premium Receipt is an important and powerful document on the basis of which the life-assured can ask the insurer to issue the policy bond, which is treated as Evidence of the Contract of Life assurance.

POLICY BOND

After issuing the First Premium Receipt, the next step is that of the insurer of sending the policy bond to the life-assured and this document is also known as Policy Contract, which is the ultimate evidence of the life-assured.

The Policy Contract contains all the terms and conditions of the contract between insurance company and the life assured, duly stamped as per the Indian Stamp Act. The policy is sent to the life assured by the insurer. The policy contract contains the details of the insurance such as duration of the policy, the type of policy, sum assured, premium amount and the date of maturity, extra premium, nominee, assignee etc.

ALTERATIONS AND ENDORSEMENTS

Endorsement is an authenticated noting on the back of Policy Contract and forms a part of the contract. In the case of lack of space, the endorsements can be put on a separated sheet of papers and attached to the policy. Endorsements are required because life assurance is a long-term contract and the life assured may want certain changes in the terms of contract. There are different type of alterations or modifications that can be made during the tenure of the policy such as changes regarding increase or reduction in the sum assured, mode of payment of premium, modification related on account of mistakes in the preparation of the policy by the insurer, modifications related to reduction in term, conversion from "Non-profit" to "With Profit" and similar other like change of name, plan-term and so on.

REMINDING NOTICE

It is basically information sent by the insurer to the policyholder, reminding the latter about the due date of a particular premium and the amount of premium. However it is not the duty of the insurance company (insurer) to do so. The insurer also informs the policyholder about the lapse of a policy if the premiums are not paid in time.

OTHER DOCUMENTS

Apart from other documents there are some other specialized documents, which are as follows:

i. Proposal on the lives of Non Resident Indians, which consists of some special questionnaire asking for relevant information.
ii. Partnership Insurance which consist of papers asking for the Profit & Loss account of the firm for the last three years, the insurance of the partner, the partnership deed and the deed of variation allowing the purchase of the assurance policy.

Settlement of Claims

The easy and timely settlement of a valid claim is an important function of an insurance company. The yardstick to judge insurance company's efficiency is as to how quick the claim settlement is. The speed, kindness and fairness with which an insurer handles claims show the maturity of the company and may lead to great satisfaction of the client. In every insurance company claim handling is of immense importance. It is the liability of the insurance company to honour valid and legal claims. At the same the company must identify the fraudulent and invalid claims. A claim may arise:

i) On death of Policyholder before the maturity date.

ii) On maturity, i.e. after expiry of the endowment period specified in the policy contract when the policy money becomes payable.

Certain features are common to all life insurance claims. These are:

1. Policy must be in force at the time of claims.
2. Insured must be covered by the policy.
3. Nothing was outstanding to the insurer at the time of claim.
4. Claim is covered by the policy.

DEATH CLAIMS

Intimation of Death

The death of the life assured has to be intimated in writing to the insurer. It can be done by the Assignee or nominee under the policy or from a person representing such Assignee or Nominee or when there is no nomination or assignment by a relative of the life assured, the employer, the agent or the development officer. Where policy is assigned to a creditor or a bank for valuable consideration, intimation of death may be received from such assignee. Sometimes, the office need not wait till the intimation of claim is received. The concerned agent, newspaper reports in case of accidents or air crashes, obituary columns may give information and claim action can be started. However, the identity of the deceased should be established carefully. The intimation of the death of the life assured by the claimant should contain the following particulars:

(1) his or her relationship with the deceased,

(2) the name of the policyholder,

(3) the number/s of the policy/policies,

(4) the date of death

(5) the cause of death and

(6) sum assured etc.

If any of these particulars are missing the claimant can be asked to furnish the same to the insurer. The intimation must satisfy two conditions (1) It must establish properly the identity of the deceased person as the life assured under the policy, (2) It must be from a concerned person.

Proof of Death and Other Documents

In case of claim by death, after the receiving the intimation of death the insurance company ensures that the insurance policy has been in force for the sum assured on the date of death and the intimation has been received from assignee, nominee or other claimant.

The following documents are required:

(i) Certificate of death.

(ii) Proof of age of the life assured (if not already given).

(iii) Deeds of assignment / reassignments.

(iv) Policy document.

(v) Form of discharge.

If the claim has accrued within three years from the beginning of the policy, the following additional requirements may be called for:

(i) Statement from the hospital if the deceased had been admitted to hospital.

(ii) Certificate of medical attendant of the deceased giving details of his/her last illness.

(iii) Certificate of cremation or burial to be given by a person of known character and responsibility present at the cremation or burial of the body of the deceased.

(iv) Certificate by employer if the deceased was an employee.

Proof of death and other documents to be submitted will depend upon the cause of death and circumstances of each case.

(1) In case of an air crash the certificate from the airline authorities would be necessary certifying that the assured was a passenger on the plane. In case of ship accident a certified extract from the logbook of the ship is required. In case of sudden cardiac arrest, murder the doctors' certificate may not be available.

(2) The insurance may waive strict evidence of title if the sum assured of the policy is small and there is no dispute among the survivors of the policy moneys.

(3) If the life assured had a death due to accident, suicide or unknown cause the police inquest report, panchanama, post mortem report, etc would be required.

If by any chance policy contract is lost, advertisement of the lost of policy is to be given. Payment can be made on the basis of an indemnity given by the policyholder.

If the deceased has taken out policies with more than one branch and the claimant has produced proof of death to any one of them and desires that the other branch or branches, may act on the same proof, his request should be complied with. The Branch requiring proof of death should directly call for the certified copies from the branch concerned.

Net Payable Amount of Claim

After receiving the required documents the company calculates the amount payable under the policy. For this purpose, a form is filled in which the particulars of the policy, assignment, nomination, bonus etc. should be entered by reference to the Policy Ledger Sheet.

If a loan exists under the policy, then the section dealing with loan is contacted to give the details of outstanding loan and interest amount, which is deducted from the gross policy amount to calculate net payable claim amount. The net amount of claim payable is calculated and is called payment voucher. In the case of 'in force' policy unpaid premiums if any due before the Assured's death with late fee where necessary and the premium falling due in the policy year current at the time of death should be deducted from the claim amount.

MATURITY CLAIMS

If the life insured survives to the full term, then basic sum assured is payable. This payment by the insurer to the insured on the date of maturity is called maturity payment. The amount payable at the time of the maturity includes a sum assured and bonus/incentives. The insurer sends in advance the intimation to the insured with a blank discharge form for filling various details in it. It is to be returned to the office along with

- Original Policy document
- Age proof if age is not already submitted
- Assignment /reassignment, if any..

Legally no claim is acceptable in respect for a lapsed policy or death of the Life assured happening within 3 years from the date of beginning of the policy. However, some concessions are given and payment of claims is made:

- If the Life assured had paid at least 3 years' premiums and thereafter if premiums have not been paid, the nominees/ life assured get proportionate paid up value.
- In the event of the death of' the Life assured within 3 years and the policy is under the lapsed position, nothing is payable.

PROCEDURE OF THE MATURITY CLAIMS

Settlement procedure for maturity claim is simple after receipt of completed and stamped discharge form from the person entitled to the policy money along with policy documents, claim amount will be paid by account payee cheque.

- If the life assured is reported to have died after the date of maturity but before the receipt is discharged, the claim is to be treated as the maturity claim and paid to the legal heirs. In this case death certificate and evidence of title is required.
- Where the assured is known to be mentally deranged, a certificate from the court of law under the Indian Lunacy Act appointing a person to act as guardian to manage the properties of the lunatic should be called.

ADDITIONAL BENEFITS APART FROM REGULAR CLAIMS

Double Accident Benefit: For claiming the benefits under the Double Accident Benefit the claimant has to produce the proof to the satisfaction of the Corporation that the accident is defined as per the policy conditions. Normally for claiming this benefit documents like FIR, Post-mortem Report are required.

Disability Benefit Claims include waiver of all premiums to be paid in future till the expiry of the policy of the life assured if a person is totally and permanently disabled and cannot earn any wage/compensation/profit as a result of the accident.

Presently, all over the country there are 12 centers where the Insurance Ombudsman has been appointed. They are part of grievance redressal machinery. They consider the complaints regarding disputes related to premiums, claims etc.

UNDER WRITING AND SERVICING

Underwriting of New Business

One of the most important functions of the New Business Department is to decide whether to accept, postpone or decline a risk and to determine the terms to be offered if the risk is to be accepted. This is called underwriting or selection of risk. The underwriter has to evaluate the hazards associated with the risk, which is being proposed.

The life insurance underwriting is concerned with mortality rate and risk, i.e., the risk that the life insured may die before the maturity of the policy. Mortality risk depends upon the life insured's health, family medical history, nature of work etc.

Underwriting is the insurance function that is responsible for assessing and classifying the degree of risk a proposer has and then deciding whether to accept or reject the risk.

UNDERWRITING PROCESS

The person willing to purchase the life insurance policy fills the proposal form. The proposal form along with the medical examiner's report and the other reports is checked and the risk associated with the case is calculated. After evaluation of risk, the insurer has following choices:

The insurance company may accept the proposal.

If a company decides to accept then the calculation regarding the premium to be charged from the proposer is to be made and terms and conditions are decided upon. The premium should be paid within a particular period specified by the insurer failing which the proposal stands cancelled.

The insurance company may reject the proposal

If the company decides not to accept the proposal then the proposer is informed accordingly. If the insurer decides to accept the proposal on special terms the proposer is informed accordingly.

The process of underwriting consists of following steps:

EVALUATION OF DOCUMENTS

1. The proposal papers will be complete when the proposal forms; medical examiner's report, agent's confidential report and personal statement are attached. In some cases medical examination may not be required. The question sin the proposal form must be answered with full honesty and no material fact should be concealed. The following particulars are generally required by the insurer:
    i) Age, Sex, Height and weight.
    ii) Occupation: The detailed information can be asked about the occupation if considered hazardous like aviation, electrical and chemical industry.
    iii) Other Policies: The number and amount of other policies of the proposer.
    iv) Premium to be paid and income of the proposer should be consistent, i.e., ensuring that proposer will not have any problem paying the premium of the policy.
    v) Date of Birth: The proposer who is either less than 20 years of age or more than 50 years of age should give satisfactory proof of age.
    vi) Risky habits of the proposer (Car racing etc)
    vii) Alcohol intake (Excessive intake of alcohol may affect the death probability of the proposer)
    viii) Frequency of foreign travel

ix) Marital status and number of children of proposer
x) Medical examiner's report

CLASSIFICATION AND REVIEW OF RISK

Once all of the information is available, underwriter from insurance company evaluates the data. At this evaluation, the underwriter wants to classify the risk attached to the proposal. If the risk is more than what the insurance company is willing to bear for that proposal, the application is rejected by the underwriter. If the risk attached to the proposal is within the limits acceptable to the company, the proposal is accepted. Then the underwriter decides the category in which the risk falls and premium to be paid is calculated accordingly. In the underwriting process, the life insurance agent gives the details of information required by the underwriter.

ENTERING THE PROPOSAL IN PROPOSAL REGISTER

When the proposal is consistent with the rules and the company decides to accept the proposal it is serially numbered and entered in the Proposal Register and Review Slip is made. For every proposal a different file is made containing review slip and other particulars related to the proposal.

SENDING ACCEPTANCE LETTER

The acceptance letter is sent by the insurance company to the proposer. The reminder of the payment of the premium due is also sent to the insured from time to time by the insurance company.

ISSUE OF FIRST PREMIUM RECEIPT

After the acceptance of proposal and payment of premium by the proposer, the insurance company will send First Premium Receipt to the proposer.

POLICY WRITING

The policy is usually written in a special department whose main task is to issue written contracts in accordance with the instructions from the underwriting department. They also keep a register of policies for future reference. These days, insurance companies are using computers to keep records of clients, the payment of premium and other particulars.

SERVICING OF POLICY-HOLDERS

Servicing of policy holders include:

(1) Proof of age

(2) Nomination

(3) Assignment

(4) Alteration / Changes

(5) Paid up value & surrender value

PROOF OF AGE

The age of the life assured must be proved either during the period of the policy or after the claim arises, because age is an important factor for calculating at the rate of premium to be charged for a particular policy. The age is generally admitted by the following proofs.

(i) Certified extract from Municipal or other records made at the time of birth.

(ii) Original horoscope prepared at the time of birth. If it is found that the horoscope has been prepared for the specific purpose of proving the assured's age, the same should not be accepted.

(iii) Certificate of school or college records if the age or date of birth is stated therein.

(iv) Certificated extracts from the Service Registers of the reputed employer.

(v) Indemnity Cards issued by the Defence Department for its employees.

(vi) Passport issued by Passport Authority of India

(vii) Marriage certificate in case of Roman Catholics issued by Roman Catholic Church.

Cases where admission of age proof is required necessarily at the time of issue of policy.

The age should be proved at the time of issue of policy where the age of the life assured is below 20 or 50 and above, Children's

Deferred Assurance Policies, Annuity Policies and policies issued under Salary Saving Scheme. Proof of age is an important issue for insurer as the older people have higher probability of death than the younger ones. So premium rates are calculated on the basis of age groups. Where the insured is unable to give any of the standard age proofs, the insured may accept the age on the basis of a 'Declaration of age' executed by an elderly relative or friend who has personal knowledge of the assured's date of birth. The declaration is required to be adequately stamped according to the stamp regulations. It must be signed by the declarant in the presence of a Magistrate or an officer empowered to administer oaths.

On submission of an age proof, age admission certificate is issued to the policyholder. In case of any difference in recorded age and actual age, the proposal review slip and policy register sheet are corrected accordingly. In case the actual age proves to be lower the excess of premiums charged from the policyholder will be refunded to him.

ASSIGNMENT AND NOMINATION

The Policyholder should be advised for nomination, if no nomination was effected. When nomination or assignment is effected by a policyholder, it should be scrutinized thoroughly to see whether it was in order or not. If there is any material omission or mistake, it may be returned to the policyholder or the assignee with a covering letter giving instructions as to the corrections to be made in the assignment or nomination. When a document is sent for correction, reminders should be sent every fortnight until the requirements are complied with. The policyholder should follow the instructions printed on the back of assignment or nomination.

NOMINATION

Nomination is the process of identifying a person to receive the policy money in the event of the death of the Policyholder. Nomination can be done at the beginning of the Policy by giving details of nominee in the proposal form. However, if the nomination is not given at the beginning, the policyholder can give it at a later date. For that purpose a prescribed form is to be filled up and nomination can be endorsed on Policy Bond.

Change in Nomination

Change of nomination can be done by the policy holder any time during the term of the policy and any number of times he wants to. Procedure of nomination is same every time.

Withdrawal of nomination

Nomination can be withdrawn by the policy holder without giving prior notice to the nominee.

Nomination can be done only by a policyholder who has attained majority and on a policy on his life. Under Nomination, the Nominee gets only the right to receive the policy money in the event of the death of the Policyholder.

Death of the Nominee If the nominee dies and the policyholder is still surviving then the nomination would be ineffective. If Nominee dies after the death of the Policyholder but before receiving policy money, then also Nomination becomes ineffective and only the legal heirs of the policyholder can claim money.

Nomination at a later date After the policy is prepared and issued and if no Nomination has been given the assured can give the nomination only by an endorsement on the policy itself. A nomination is not required to be stamped. Nomination in favour of a stranger cannot be given as there is no insurable interest involved in that case. For nomination in favour of wife and children, specific names of wife and children should be given.

Successive Nominee

Where it is mentioned in nomination that the policy money should be paid to "Nominee A failing him to Nominee B whom failing to Nominee C, etc.", such nomination is called successive nomination. Such nomination would be in favour of one individual in the order mentioned. All such Nomination would mean that if Nominee A were dead at the time in question the Nominee B would take the whole amount and that if both Nominees A and B were then dead then Nominee C would take the whole amount and so on.

A Minor Nominee

In view of the Insurance (Amendment Act) 1950, the Life Assured has the right, where a nominee is a minor, to appoint any person as the Appointee to receive the moneys secured by the policy in the event of the assured's death during minority of the nominee.

The person so appointed will not be a guardian of the minor Nominee's power will be limited to the right to receive the policy money in the event of the assured's death during the minority of the Nominee.

The appointment must be a major. The appointment of Appointee must be communicated to the insurance company. So his name can be registered with the company. The appointment can be cancelled or changed by the life assured any time before the maturity of the policy.

ASSIGNMENT

Assignment is a means whereby the right and title under a policy gets transferred from assignor to assignee. Assignor is the policyholder who transfers the title and assignee is the person who gets the title of the policy from the assignor. Assignment can be made either by endorsement on the policy or on a separate paper duly stamped. Assignor must be a major. Assignment must be in writing and assignor's signature along with a witness is required. Notice of assignment should be submitted to the insurer by the assignor. Assignment can be of two types:

1. Absolute Assignment: In which all the rights, title and interest of the assignor in the policy passes on to the assignee without the possibility of cancellation of the same.
2. Conditional Assignment: In which the assignor and the assignee may agree that in case specified event or events happen, the assignment would be cancelled or ineffective in part or as a whole.

Impact of Assignment

In assignment, assignor gives all the rights over the policy to the assignee that becomes the owner of the policy. The assignee has the right to reassign that policy.

In the event of Death of the Assignee

If the assignment is conditional assignment and the assignee dies, the assignment becomes ineffective and all the rights and title of the policy goes back to the life assured if he is alive. If the life assured is not surviving, the benefit goes back to the life assured's nominee. In case of absolute assignment, if the assignee dies, all the rights entitled of the policy are given to legal heirs of the assignee.

Cancellation of Assignment

An assignment once executed cannot be cancelled, however, if an assignee during the term of the policy reassigns the interest and title of the policy to the previous assignor such reassignment will result in cancellation of assignment and the benefits of the policy go back to the original assignor.

Procedures of Assignment

A standard form of Assignment is issued to the policyholder who wants to effect an assignment of his policy. Necessary instructions are there for executing the assignment which is then registered by the insurance company. Points to be checked by the insurance company for affecting assignment:

(1) Check whether the assignment is executed on the Policy or on a separate paper and if it is executed on a separate paper that the paper is adequately stamped. If it is unstamped or inadequately stamped inform the assignor and get it corrected.

(2) Check whether notice of assignment is received from the assignor; if the notice is not received or it is defective, inform the assignor.

(3) Check the signatures of assignor affixed to the assignment and notice with the specimen of his signature in the proposal papers to see that they tally. If the signature differs then for writing letter to the person concerned, inform the assignor.

(4) If the assignment is executed on a separate paper, ensure that the paper should be stamped, in accordance with the stamp regulations.

(5) Check that the data and place of execution on Assignment are mentioned. If they are not mentioned the assignment may be registered, if otherwise in order, but while returning the Assignment to the party concerned he should be asked to have the necessary particulars inserted in the Assignment under the Assignor's.

If the assignment is in order and that the notice there of has been duly received the particulars of assignment must be entered in the space provide for the purpose in the Policy Ledger Sheet under the heading "Nominations and Assignments".

Also the appropriate rubber stamp is affixed at the foot of assignment write the date on which the assignment and the notice are received.

ALTERATIONS

After issue of a Policy, the Policy holder desires an alteration in the terms thereof to suit his convenience, e.g., an alteration in the mode of payment of premiums, Plan of Assurance, reduction in the premium-paying period, etc. An alteration may be allowed provided the policy is in force and has not become fully paid up.

It is stated in the prospectus that no alteration from one class of Assurance to another subject to a lower scale of premium is permissible.

However, an alteration from the with profits Limited Payment plan to the with profits Endowment Assurance Plan with premiums payable for a term not exceeding the original premium-paying term will be allowed even if the premium payable on alteration is lower. Alterations from certain Classes of Assurance to certain other Classes are not allowed at all.

Frequently requested alterations by the policyholders are:

(1) Alteration in Name;

(2) Reduction in the Sum Assured;

(3) Adding Double Accident Benefit and Extended Disability Benefit.

(4) Alteration in Class or Term;

(5) Removal of an extra premium;

(6) Alteration in the Mode of Payment of Premiums;

(7) Alteration form Without Profits Plan to With Profits Plan;

(8) Correction in Policies;

No alteration will be permitted within one year of the commencement of the policy, except the few cases like:

(1) Compulsory alterations such as alteration in name, correction in policies, alteration in currency of payment of policy moneys and alterations age proving higher or lower than that stated at the time of proposal.

(2) Requests for addition of Double Accident Benefit, Extended Disability Benefit.

(3) Change in the mode of payment of premium to 'monthly' so as to bring the policy under Salary Saving Scheme or to finance the same from Provident Fund Account.

(4) Conversion of ordinary policies to those issued under Married Women's Property Act, as provided in the Manual on the subject of 'Married Women's Property Act'.

ALTERATION FEE

"Alteration fee" is required in the following cases;

(1) Alteration in the mode of payment whereby there is an increase in the frequency of payment of premium installments, e.g., alteration from yearly to half-yearly, quarterly or monthly, etc.;

(2) When policyholder wants to add Double Accident Benefit or Extended Disability Benefit after the issue of the Policy and such Benefit is not granted from the commencement;

(3) Reduction in the Sum Assured;

(4) When policyholder wants to add Premium Waiver Benefit under a Child Deferred Annuity policy after its issue and such Benefit is not granted form the commencement.

No fee is required for Alterations of the following types:

(1) Where the alteration should necessarily be made in age of the policyholder, as age stated in the policy is not correct. The age stated in the policy may be understated or overstated.

(2) Where policyholder wants to reduce the frequency of payment of installments of premiums in the year.

(3) Where change or correction is required in the name of the assured, nominee, assignee etc., in the policy.

Loan on Policy

Most of the insurance companies give facility to the policyholders to get loans on Life Insurance policies according to rules. The policyholder can apply for a loan in a prescribed form and has to give policy bond along with the completed form.

The loan amount that the policyholder can get is calculated according to surrender value of the policy at the time of taking the loan. Rate of interest charged on the loan by the insurance company may vary from time to time and may depend upon the rules of the insurance company. For loan the policy should be assigned absolutely in favour of the insurance company.

Repayment of Loan

The life assured can repay the loan either in full or in part anytime during the term of the policy. If the loan is not repaid during the term of the policy, the amount of loan and its interest will be subtracted from the claimed amount on the policy and the balance will be given to the policyholder.

When a loan is granted, it is entered with the particulars in the Policy Register Sheet of the insurance company. When the policyholder repays the loan in full or part, the particulars are entered in the Policy Ledger Sheet. Separate loan bond should be made and given to the policyholder for the purpose of granting more than one loans. However, only one cheque may be issued for all the loans.

Generally, the loans are not allowed for the following policies.

1. Immediate Annuity and Deferred Annuity Policies.
2. Children's Deferred Assurance policies during deferment period.
3. Janata Policies.
4. Where the assured or the assignee is incompetent to contract.

5. Where policies carry conditions or endorsements taking away the right of raising loans from the assured.
6. Policies issued under Married Women's Property Act.
7. Where the policies are lost or damaged.

SURRENDER VALUE

If the insured is unwilling or unable to pay the premium of the policy, he may surrender the policy and ask for its surrender value. Surrender value is the cash value payable by the insurance on voluntary termination of the policy contract by the life assured before the expiry of the term of the policy. Surrender value depends on the type of policy and number of premia paid. A policy can be surrendered only when the premia is paid for the three years.

PAID UP VALUE

When a policyholder wants to terminate the policy, he may convert the same into paid-up policy. In this case, the amount of paid-up value is payable to the insured only after the full term (maturity) of the policy. The option of converting the policy into paid up policy and stop paying the further premiums can be taken only if the policy has been in force for at least two years.

7

PRICING AND CHANNELS OF DISTRIBUTION

Pricing of Life Insurance

Pricing of insurance product is a complex task as premium rates to be charged depend upon variety of factors namely, expected losses, operating expenses, income from investments and profit margin of the insurance company. Actuaries employed by the insurer calculate and determine the premium rates to be charged for different policies and from people of different age.

If the premium charged is very low, the company would not be able to collect sufficient amount to pay claims, bear expenses and earn some profit. On the other hand, excessively high premium charged will result in loss of prospective clients of the insurance company because company may lose the prospective insurer to its competitors in the market. Pricing also depends on the market forces of demand and supply of insurance products. Pricing refers to the methods used to calculate rate of premium to be charged on insurance products. Premium is a price for which the insurer is willing to accept the risk. The payment of premium by the proposer is acceptance of the price charged by the insurer for providing the life insurance cover.

PRICING OBJECTIVES

The following are the objectives kept in mind while deciding upon the pricing of various insurance products:

Adequacy of Rates

The premium rates fixed by the insurance company should be adequate in order to pay the benefits promised to the policyholders and meet all the operating expenses. In other words the rates charged must be sufficient to collect the premium incomes the insurance company required to pay various operating expenses, to pay the claims and at some profit margin. Insurers do conduct periodic reviews to assess whether the initial premium levels established are equitable and not too high i.e. adequate.

Fairness and Rate Equity

The insurance rates must be fair and equitable. The rates charged to the policyholders with the same expected losses and other costs should be equal.

This is known as rate equity. It means that the insurance company should charge premiums in accordance with the expected payment of benefits and expenses.

The rates must be same for homogenous groups and must not be same for heterogeneous groups (say of different age groups).

If the two individuals of different ages, say one 25 years and other 50 years intend to purchase same policy for the same time period with same terms, the insurer will be charging the higher rate of premium from the person who is 50 years old as there is comparatively higher death probability of the older client. In the case of the young person of 25 years the company cannot associate very high death probability.

If there are two persons of the same age who want to take same policy with same terms and conditions but one person is chronically ill, the insurer must charge them different rates as the ill person has higher probability of dying at a certain age (so should be giving higher premium).

Reasonableness

The rates of the premium charged to the policyholders should not be too high because it will lead to loss of insurance business to the competitors in the industry. Charging excessive premium is therefore unfair to the customers.

Simplicity

The premium rates charged should be simple to understand and should not change very frequently.

LIFE INSURANCE PRICING ELEMENTS

1. Rate of death of large number of insured persons.
2. Administration cost and other expenses of the insurer.
3. Income from investment of premium.

Rate of Death of Large Number of Insured Persons

The mortality rates depend on the age, occupation, life style, and medical history of the insured. The premium rates charged are calculated on the basis of rate of deaths of very large number of persons insured, i.e., the past experience of large number of cases is taken into consideration before deciding on mortality rate.

Administration Cost and Other Expenses of the Insurer

Every insurer incurs certain expenses or administrative costs related to the service provided. The administration cost incurred may depend on frequency of payment of premium and the volume of records kept. If the premium is paid annually, cost is lesser as compared to quarterly and half yearly or monthly payments.

Income from Investment of Premium

Premium collected by the insurance company from various policyholders is again invested and the income earned on the same helps the insurance company to bear various expenses incurred and benefits given to policyholders.

CHANNELS OF DISTRIBUTION

Marketing includes all those activities carried on to transfer the goods and services from manufacturer to the consumer.

Marketing mix is a unique combination of basic ingredients of marketing viz.

1. Product
2. Price
3. Place (channels of distribution)
4. Promotion

It is designed for the best realization of the objectives of marketing management. In marketing management the term place is used to refer to channels of distribution i.e. intermediaries which fetch products/services from the place of the manufacture to the place of ultimate consumers.

The channel of distribution (place) is an important ingredient of marketing mix as however useful the product might be and how so ever suitable its price be, unless and until the products/ services are mad available to consumers at 'centres of convenient buying' the consumers will not be buying the same. Insurance being a service business requires marketing department to play a key role in delivery of service.

The marketing department conducts research for identification of target customers, help in maintaining and promoting the distribution system and also plays an active role in development of new products. It is the most vibrant department in an insurance organization since it has to necessarily deal with all the other department of the organization.

Insurance business is business of law of large numbers. The law requires the insurer to attract a sufficient number of exposures to allow credible ratio prediction.

The major task of sales managers in charge of the sales section of insurance company is the supervision of the sales functions of the branches. This section is also responsible for spreading awareness among the general public about the benefits of life Insurance. Sales training section is entrusted with responsibility for training in product, in selling and sales planning in the personnel such as development officers and agents.

Insurance policies are mainly sold by the agents of insurance company. We can take example of Life Insurance Corporation of India in particular to understand sales and distribution function of the corporation.

Job Description

What does an LIC Agent Do?

Most people have their first contact with an insurance company through an insurance agent. These workers help individuals, families, and businesses select insurance policies that provide the best protection for their lives, health, and property. Insurance sales who agents work exclusively for one insurance company are referred to as captive agents. Independent insurance agents or brokers represent several companies and place insurance policies of their clients with the company that offers the best rate and coverage. In either case, agent prepares reports, maintain records, seek out new clients, and in the event of a loss, help policyholders settle their insurance claims. Increasingly, some are also offering their client financial analysis or advice on ways the clients can minimize risk.

Insurance sales agents commonly referred to as "producers" in the insurance industry offer one or more types of insurance, such as property and casualty, life, health, disability, long-term care. Property and casualty insurance agents sell polices that protect individual and businesses from financial loss resulting from automobile accidents, fire, theft, storm and also cover injured workers' compensation.

Life Insurance agents specialize in selling policies that pay beneficiaries when a policyholder dies. Depending on the policyholder's circumstances, a cashvalue policy can be designed. Different policies provide retirement income, funds for the education of children, or other benefits. Insurance agents also sell annuities that promise a retirement income. Health insurance agents sell health insurance policies that cover the costs of medical care and loss of income due to illness or injury. They also may sell dental insurance and short and long term disability insurance policies.

The growth of the Internet in the insurance industry is gradually altering the relationship between agent and client. In the past, agents devoted much of their time to marketing of products to new clients, a practice that is now changing. Increasingly, clients are obtaining insurance quotes from a company's web site and then contacting the company directly to purchase policies. This interaction gives the client a more active role in selection of policy at the best price, while reducing the amount of time agents spend actively seeking to meet clients. Insurance sales agents also obtain many new accounts through referrals. It is important that they maintain regular contact with their clients to ensure that the clients' financial needs are being met. Developing a satisfied clientele that will recommend an agent's services to other potential customers, is a key to success in this field.

Training

Agents go through both generic and specific, professional training programs that help them remain well-informed and knowledgeable about the company's products in the market. There is further focus on soft skills such as communication, managing long-term relationship selling skills, which are very relevant in a service-driven industry like life insurance.

State-of-the-art infrastructure training facilities coupled with an excellent faculty, guarantee exceptional learning environment for agents who might be occupied with their business/professional routines.

A 17-18 day training schedule covers the mandatory IRDA training requirements and product training module. Revision session ensure that the candidate thoroughly understand the course contents and are well prepared for the licensing examination. Theoretical training benefits programmes and other State and Central Government regulations can affect insurance needs of clients and the way in which agents conduct business. Agents can enhance their selling skills and broaden their knowledge of insurance and other financial services taking courses at colleges and universities and by attending institutes, conferences, seminars sponsored by insurance organizations. IRDA also has mandatory education requirements focusing on insurance on insurance laws, consumer protection, and the technical details of various insurance policies.

Insurance sales agents should be flexible, enthusiastic, confident, disciplined, hard working and willing to solve problems. They should communicate effectively and inspire customer confidence. Because they usually work without supervision, sales agents must be able to use their time well and have the initiative to locate new clients.

An insurance sales agent who shows ability and leadership may become a Development officer in a Branch Office. However, many who have built up a good clientele prefer to remain in sales work.

8

WORKING CONDITIONS, TRAINING AND REWARD SYSTEM

WORKING CONDITIONS

Most insurance sales agents are based in offices, from which they contact clients and provide information on the policies they sell. However, much of their time may be spent outside their offices, traveling locally to meet with clients. Agents usually determine their own hours of work and often schedule evening and week end appointments for the convenience of clients. Although most agents work a 40-hour week some work 60 hours a week or longer. Commercial sales agents, in particular, may meet clients during business hours and then spend evenings doing paperwork and preparing presentations to prospective clients.

Employment

Insurance sales agents held about 11, 00,000 jobs in 2005. Although most insurance agents specialize in life or general insurance, a growing number of "multi-line" agents sell all types of insurance.

Training, Other Qualifications and Advancement

For insurance sales agent jobs, most companies and independent agencies prefer to take college graduates-especially those who have majored in business or economics.

Training may help agents grasp the technical aspects of insurance policies and fundamentals and procedures of selling insurance. Many colleges and universities offer courses in insurance and a few schools offer a bachelor's degree in the field. College courses in finance, mathematics, accounting, economics, business law, marketing and business administration enable insurance sales agents to understand how social and economics conditions relate to the insurance industry. Courses in psychology and public speaking can prove useful in improving sales techniques. In addition, because companies provide instantaneous information on a wide variety of financial products and greatly improve agent's efficiency, familiarity with computer and popular software packages has become important.

Insurance sales agents must obtain a license from IRDA. Separate licenses are required by agents to sell life and general insurance. Licenses are issued only to applicants who complete specified pre-licensing courses and who pass IRDA examinations covering insurance fundamentals and insurance laws. A number of organizations offer professional designation programs that certify one's expertise in specialties such as life, health and general insurance as well as financial consultancy. Although voluntary, such programs assure clients and employers that an agent has a thorough understanding of the relevant specialty. Agents are usually required to complete a special number of hours of continuing education to retain their designation.

Employers also are placing greater emphasis on continuing professional education so that diversity of financial products sold by insurance agents increases. It is important for insurance agents to keep up to date on issues concerning clients.

Career

Career development is emphasized upon from the very day the agent joins the system. Though individual meetings with his or her Development Officer, the agent can discuss various issues related to business development and career enhancement, expectations from organizations in terms of chalking a career in the insurance industry are also discussed.

Absorption into the management is another career enhancement option provided at LIC program helps agent build a full time career as a Development Officer in the organization offering great potential for managing a team of agents and personal development.

Rewards and Recognition

LIC agents are constantly recognized and rewarded for their performance. Depending on the level of business the agent achieves in a year, he or she will become a member of various clubs such as the Corporate Club, the Chairman's club, etc. Of these clubs have specific performance criteria for qualification and members of these are entitled to attend seminars held at exotic international and domestic locations.

BENEFITS OF BECOMING AN LIC AGENT

1. Rewarding Career: Agent will help people realize their dreams by fulfilling their financial goals. The difference made to their lives is very rewarding and satisfying.
2. A Successful Team: Agent will be a part of the country's finest team of life insurance Agents.
3. Attractive Remuneration: Agents get the best remuneration systems in the industry that not only takes care of current earnings, but also guarantees an earning for the future.
4. World-Class Training: LIC provides the best-in-class training systems, since that is what differentiates LIC Agents from the rest. Even if they don't have previous experience in selling, multidimensional training programme conducted by qualified in-house training personnel make them specialists in life insurance sales.
5. Infrastructure Support: LIC has invested in creating a state-of-the-art infrastructure at each of the Branch office. Agents have access to the necessary tools, technology and people support that enables to build a profitable longterm business.

GUIDELINES ON HOW TO BECOME AN AGENT

(a) Eligibility:

12th standard pass

Age 18 and above

(b) Process:

Person intending to be the agent should contact your nearest Branch Office and meet the Development Officer there. The Branch Manager will conduct an interview, and if found suitable, person will be selected for training at Divisional/Agency Training Centre. The training is for 100 hours and covers all aspects of Life Insurance Business. After successful completion of training, person will have to sit for Pre-Licensing examination conducted by the Insurance Regulatory and Development Authority (IRDA). After successful completion of the examination person will awarded a License by the IRDA to work as an insurance agent. Candidates will be appointed as an agent by the Branch Office and he will be a part of the team under the Development Officer.

The Development Officer will impart him field training and other valuable inputs, which will help him in the market place.

(c) Attractions:

- Unlimited earning potential
- A clear career path
- All round support through excellent advertising
- In house consultant
- World class training
- A comprehensive benefit package
- Rewards & Recognition

They are a key source of business for the organization, and are the continuing link with clients. That is why company takes a lot of care in recruiting and developing the agency force to set higher standards of quality in service and salesmanship. To cater the needs of the knowledge-oriented marketplace, company look for graduates who are good communicators and enjoy meeting new people. Prior sales experience is added benefit.

(d) Qualities of an agent:

- Self-motivation
- A master communicator
- A go-getter
- Ambitious
- Likes meeting people

ALTERNATIVE DISTRIBUTION CHANNELS OF LIC

Alternate Distribution channel has emerged as a strong alternative to the existing distribution channels. The high averages i.e. FP per policy SA per policy and FP per 000 SA recorded. Through alternate channels indicates that the new channel is able to target new market segments and high net worth individuals by leveraging the large customer base and the reach of Banks and Corporative Agents.

In a highly competitive market environment for the year 2004-2005 alternate channels posted and impressive performance under writing 140615 policies with a sum assured of 1401.46 crore and first premium income of 194.40 crore registering highest ever growth rates of 229.32% & 364.05% in policies sun assured & first premium income respectively.

Banks have emerged as strong business partners amongst alternate channels in terms of first premium mobilization. LIC has tied up with 3 banks having 10175 outlets, 646 corporate Agents operating through 1920 outlets & established relationship with 100 Brokers across the country. Some of the permanent Banks are Corporation Bank, UCO Bank, Central Bank of India, Allahabad Bank, Indian Overseas Bank, Oriental Bank of Commerce, Bank of Punjab and City Union Bank. During the current year our focus is on enlarging and consolidating the bancassurance channel resulting in more tie ups with banks in addition to supporting the Corporate Agencies and Brokers. By leveraging the large dedicated customer base of Bank partners and corporate agents LIC is confident of increasing market share through alternate channels and also greater presentation of high end, unit linked and pension markets.

INFORMATION RELATING TO PRIVATE INSURANCE (LIFE)

Bank of Punjab (BoP) announced its tie up with the state-owned life insurance major LICI for distributing the latter's insurance products. The Indian Cricket Board will launch a unique insurance policy offered by LICI for its players wherein their returns would rise by 43 percent annually compared to an existing benevolent fund.

Vijaya Bank, Punjab National Bank (PNB), the Principal Financial Group of the US and a leading tyre company have signed a memorandum of understanding (MoU) and have applied to IRDA for a license for a life insurance venture.

Private insurance players are targeting Non-resident Indians (NRIs) as the premiums coming from this segment of society are huge. Birla Sun Life Insurance Company and SBI Life Insurance are coming up the special insurance-cum-investment products targeted at NRIs. The Supreme Court has ruled that an insurance company which has issued a Third Party (TP) liability policy has to pay compensation to the victims of a road accident even if the driver of the vehicle which meets with an accident had a fake driving license. LIC is looking at extending insurance cover to HIV-infected women under the Jeevan Bharati plan. The life insurance company will need national level data on AIDS/HIV infection and relevant statistical information to take any decision on extending insurance cover to women affected by this disease. IRDA has granted in principle permission to the Sahara Group to enter the life insurance business, subject to the latter fulfilling some regulatory requirements.

In the context of declining interest rates, Senior citizens are awaiting for the launch of LIC's pension scheme, guaranteeing an annual return of 9% in the form of monthly pension scheme.

Summary

Life Insurance provides risk coverage to the life of assured. It is an instrument of protection as well as investment. On death of the assured the insurer offers protection against loss of income and compensates the titleholder of the policy. Life Insurance is a contingent contract and not a contract of indemnity. Diverse life insurance policies are offered to take care of insurance requirements of persons in different situations in life. Various documents are prepared by insurance company for life insurance contract. The settlement of claims arises due to the death of the policyholder or due to maturity of the policy. While underwriting new business department is to decide whether to accept or reject a risk and to determine the terms on which risk is to be accepted. Proper pricing of insurance lays a strong foundation for financial viability as well as the solvency of the insurance company.

Glossary

Premium: Price or consideration of insurance policy.

Sum Assured: Sum Payable by insurance company to the assured / his beneficiary

Maturity Date: Date at which insurance policy expires.

First Premium Receipt: Receipt given to the assured after the risk has been accepted by the insurer and first premium has been paid by insured.

Claimant: Nominee / Assignee or nearest legal heir of the deceased.

Insurable interest

Indemnity

Annuity

Assignment

Nomination

Underwriting

Mortality rate

Proposal Form: Standardized Form to be completed by the prospective insured in his own handwriting and signed in the presence of the agent to enter into insurance contract.

9

NON-LIFE INSURANCE

INTRODUCTION

As we have discussed that insurance is an important aid to minimize the effect of uncertainties of life as well as property. With the increasing complexities in our personal and professional life, the range of risks that the insurance companies accept has also expended substantially. The broadest classification of insurance is in terms of Life Insurance and non-Life Insurance (General insurance).

A non-life insurance contract is different from a life insurance contract. A life insurance contract is a long term contract, while general insurance contract is a one-year renewable contract. The risk namely 'death' is certain in life insurance. The only uncertainty is as to when it will take place, whereas in general insurance, the insured event may or may not take place. It is difficult to determine the economic value of life, whereas the financial value of any asset to be insured under a general insurance policy can be determined. Because of these peculiar features, a non life insurance contract is different from a life insurance contract. In this lesson we will learn in detail the treatment of each type of non-life insurance.

Section 2(6B) of the Insurance Act 1938, defines general insurance business. According to this general insurance business means fire, marine, or miscellaneous insurance whether carried separately or in combination. General Insurance Corporation of India (GIC) was set up with exclusive privilege for transacting General Insurance business. After the passage of IRDA Act 1999, GIC has been delinked from its subsidiaries and has been assigned the role of Indian reinsurer.

MEANING AND IMPORTANCE OF NON-LIFE INSURANCE

Non-life insurance refers to the property and liability insurance. Fire insurance covers stationary property. Marine insurance covers mobile property. Bonding is a special coverage that guarantees the performance of the contract by one party to another. Casualty coverage includes accident and health insurance besides the above mentioned categories. Miscellaneous Insurance business means all other general insurance contracts including therein motor insurance.

The role of insurance is two fold. Insurance achieves both risk transfer and risk reduction. The insurer collects the premium from a group of business firms who wants to protect their property against the damage caused by fire. Insurer will then indemnify the firm that suffers a loss to property due to fire out of the premium so collected.

So the collective contributions of this entire group of the insured have been utilized to pay for the losses of the unfortunate few who sustain losses.

Insurance also acts as a risk reduction mechanism in various senses. Firstly, the individual risks have been shifted to the insurance company by way of pooling. Secondly, firm's risk exposure is well spread out because insurer has an access to the reinsurance market making possible a further spread of risk. If an aircraft is destroyed, the airline company will have a big hole in its financials. If the aircraft is insured, the loss would be spread out among a large number of insurance companies throughout the world.

Every business enterprise is exposed to a large number of risks and uncertainties to its premises, plant and machinery, raw materials, finished stock and other things. Goods may be damaged or lost in the process of transportation and may be destroyed due to fire or flood while in storage. As a matter of fact, business means risk and uncertainties.

Some of the risks can be avoided by timely precautions but some are unavoidable and are beyond the control of a businessman. For those types of risks, Insurance is the best protection. By providing protection against at least some of these risks, the insurance industry helps him better manage his risks and contributes to capital formation in the economy. After transferring risks and uncertainties of the business to the insurance company, the entrepreneur can focus on his core activity-of running the business.

Also, the insurance companies bring their experience and expertise to the field of risk management. Thus, they are able to add value to the customer's business processes.

Objectives

After going through this lesson you should be able to:

- Define the contract of fire insurance.
- Explain the characteristics of fire insurance contract.
- Understand the meaning of the term 'fire'.
- Describe the special policies under fire insurance.
- Write about fire claims and the procedures followed to settle a fire claim.
- Define the contract of marine insurance.
- Explain different types of perils that can affect a marine adventure.
- How to assign a marine policy.
- What are various clauses of a marine policy.
- Explain the difference between express and implied warranties.
- Describe different types of marine policy.
- Know the claim procedure to be followed for marine insurance.
- Define the contract of health insurance.
- Describe the various health insurance policies.
- The future of health insurance in India.
- Define the contract of Motor insurance.
- Explain the basic principles of motor insurance.
- Describe the motor insurance policies.
- Mention the classification of motor vehicles.
- Understand the operation of motor accident claims tribunal.

- Explain various types of insurances under miscellaneous insurances like personal accident insurance, Fidelity Insurance, Travel Insurance, Workmen's Compensation Insurance, Wedding Insurance, Employee State Insurance Scheme, Unemployment Insurance, Personal Liability Insurance, Credit Insurance, Burglary Insurance etc.

Fire Insurance

Fire is hazardous to human life as well as property. Loss of life by fire is covered under Life insurance and loss of property by fire is covered under fire insurance. Fire causes enormous damage by physically reducing the materials to ashes.

A fire insurance policy provides protection strictly against fire. There could be enormous reasons for fire. In practice certain other related perils are also covered by the fire insurance policy. The General Insurance Act (Tariff) recommends the form of the contract in which a fire insurance is to be written. The policy form contains a preamble and operative clause, general exclusions and general conditions.

Fire Insurance comes under tariff class of business. All India Fire Tariff is the revised fire insurance tariff, which came into force on May1, 2001. Now a single policy was introduced to cover all property risks called standard fire and special peril policy in the place of three standard policies i.e. A, B&C.

Definition

A contract of fire insurance can be defined as a contract under which one party (the insurer) agrees for consideration (premium) to indemnify the other party (The insured) for the financial loss which the latter may suffer due to damage to the property insured by fire during a specified period of time and up to an agreed amount.

The document containing the terms and conditions of the contract is known as 'Fire Insurance Policy'. A fire policy contains the name of the parties, description of the insured property, the sum for which the property is insured, amount of premium payable and the period insured against. The premium may be paid either in single instalment or by way of instalments.

The insurer is liable to make good the loss only when loss is caused by actual fire. The phrase 'loss or damage by fire' also includes the loss or damage caused by efforts to extinguish fire.

Scope of Cover

Standard Fire and special perils policy usually cover loss due to the following perils:

1. Fire: Destruction or damage to the property insured by its own fermentation, natural heating or spontaneous combustion or drying process can not be treated as damage due to fire.
2. Lightning: It may result in fire damage or other type of damage, such as cracks in a building due to a lightning strike.
3. Explosion: An explosion is caused inside a vessel when the pressure within the vessel exceeds the atmospheric pressure acting externally on its surface. This policy, however, does not cover destruction or damage caused to the boilers or other vessels where heat is generated.
4. Storm, cyclone, typhoon, hurricane, tornado, landslide: These are all various types of violent natural disturbances accompanied by thunder or strong winds or heavy rain fall. Loss or damage directly caused by these disturbances are covered excluding those resulting from earthquake, volcanic eruption etc.
5. Bush fire: This covers damage caused by burning of bush and jungles but excluding destruction or damage caused by forest fire.
6. Riot, strike, malicious, and terrorism damages: Any loss or physical damage to the property insured directly caused by such activity or by the action of any lawful authorities in suppressing such disturbance is covered.
7. Aircraft damage: Loss, destruction or damage caused by Aircraft, other aerial or space devices and articles dropped there from excluding those caused by pressure waves.
8. Overflowing of water tanks and pipes etc.: Loss or damage to property by water or otherwise on account of bursting or accidental overflowing of water tanks, apparatus and pipes is covered.

General Exclusions

Policy does not Cover

1. The first 5% of each and every claim subject to a minimum of Rs. 10,000 in respect of loss arising out of "Act of god perils" such as Lightning, Landslide etc.
2. Loss, destruction or damage caused by war, invasion, act of foreign enemy, mutiny, war like operations, civil war, military rising etc.
3. Loss, destruction or damage caused to the insured property by pollution or contamination.
4. Loss, destruction or damage to the stocks in cold storage premises caused by change of tempreture.
5. Loss of earnings, loss by delay, loss of market or other indirect loss or damage of any kind whatsoever.
6. Any loss or damage caused by or through or in consequence directly or indirectly due to earthquake, volcanic eruption etc.
7. Loss by theft during or after the occurrence of any insured peril except as provided under Riot, Strike and Terrorism Damage cover.
8. Loss, destruction or damage to any electrical machine, apparatus, fixture, or fitting arising from or occasioned by over-running, excessive pressure, short circuiting etc.
9. Expenses necessarily incurred on (i) Architect's, surveyor's and consulting engineer's fees and (ii) Debris removed by the insured following the loss to the property insured by an peril insured in excess of 3% and 1% of the claim amount respectively.

Add-on Covers

The insurer can issue the standard fire policy with added benefits at the option of the policyholders by charging additional premium. These added benefits are as follows:

1. Architects, Surveyors and Consulting engineer's fees (in excess of 3% claim amount)
2. Debris removal (in excess of 1% of claim amount)
3. Deterioration of stocks in cold storage due to power failure

4. Forest fire
5. Spontaneous combustion
6. Earthquake as per minimum rates and excess applicable as specified in the tariff.
7. Omission to insure additions, alterations or extensions.

On the basis of judicial decisions, the following losses are also covered by fire insurance.

(a) Goods spoiled or property damaged by water used to extinguish the fire.

(b) Pulling down of adjacent buildings by the fire brigade in order to prevent the spread of fire.

(c) Breakage of goods in the process of removal from the building where fire is raging.

(d) Wages paid to persons employed for extinguishing fire.

The following types of losses, however, are not covered by a fire policy:

(i) Loss by theft during and after the occurrence of fire.

(ii) Loss caused by burning of property by order of any public authority.

(iii) Loss caused by underground fire.

(iv) Loss or damage to property occasioned by its own fermentation or spontaneous combustion.

(v) Loss happening by fire which is caused by earthquake, invasion, act of foreign enemy, warlike operations, civil wars, riot etc.

In all the above cases the insurer is not liable, unless specifically provided for in the fire insurance policy. The insurer can issue the standard fire policy as per the New Fire Tariff along with added benefits at the option of the policyholders by charging additional premium.

Meaning of Fire

Fire is not described in the policy. It should therefore, be taken in the general sense as an ignition of some kind. Damage by lightening or explosion is not covered unless these cause actual ignition which spread into fire. A claim for loss by fire must satisfy the following conditions;

A) The loss must be caused by actual fire or ignition and not just by high tempreture. There should be rapid combustion that produces ignition and may result in flames. Hence, chemical action producing heat but not actual fire and damage caused by an acid is not considered as fire damage.

B) The proximate cause of loss should be fire.

C) The loss or damage must relate to subject matter of the policy.

D) The fire must be accidental, not incidental. If the fire is caused through a deliberate act of the insured or his agents, the insurer will not be liable for the loss. Fire due to the negligence of the insured or his servant is however, covered by the policy. If a third party willfully sets fire to the insured's property, the loss is by fire and the insurer is liable.

E) The ignition must be either of the goods or of the premises where goods are kept.

The essential features of a contract of fire insurance are as under:

1) It is a contract under Indian Contract Act, 1872. Like other insurance contracts, fire insurance contracts are also governed by general provisions of Indian Contract Act, 1872. It implies that fire insurance also has to satisfy the essentials of a valid contract.
2) It is a contract of indemnity. The principal of indemnity implies that the insurer restores the insured to his position before incurring the loss caused by the fire. The insured can not claim anything more than the amount of actual loss. He can be indemnified only to the extent of damage incurred, not the entire value of the property insured.
3) It is a contract of utmost faith. It is a contract of 'uberrimae fidei', i.e. utmost good faith. Both the insured and the insurer must disclose everything which is in their knowledge and can affect the contract of insurance.
4) Existence of insurable interest. Insurable interest arises out of a pecuniary relationship between the insured and the subject matter of the insurance. The destruction or

damage to the latter involves the insured in financial loss. Insurable interest should exist at the time of taking a fire insurance policy and continue throughout the policy term. Claim can be made for the loss due to fire only when the insurable interest exists. The insurable interest in goods may arise out of ownership, possession or contract.

The following persons have insurable interest in the subject matter of insurance in case of fire policy:

1) A person has insurable interest in the property he owns.
2) Partner has insurable interest in the property of partnership.
3) A businessman has insurable interest in his stock, plant, machinery and building.
4) Agent has insurable interest in the property of his principle.
5) Mortgagee has insurable interest in the property which is mortgaged.

5) It is a yearly contract.

Generally, a contract of fire insurance is a contract from year to year only and the insurance automatically comes to an end after the expiry of the year. However, the contract can be renewed before the expiry of the contract.

Types of Fire Policies

The important fire insurance policies are discussed below:

1. Valued Policy. They are the exception in fire insurance. Under valued policy, the value declared in the policy is the amount the insurer will have to pay to the insured in the event of a total loss irrespective of the actual value of loss. The policy violates the principle of indemnity. The insurer has to pay a specified amount quite independent of the market or actual value of the property at the time of loss. So such a policy is very rarely issued. It may be issued only on artistic work, antiques and similar rare articles whose value cannot be determined easily.
2. Specific Policy. Under this policy, the insurer undertakes to make good the loss to the insured upto the amount specified in the policy. Supposing, a building worth Rs.2,00,000 is insured against fire for Rs. 1,00,000. If the

damage to the property is Rs.75,000 the insurer will get the full compensation. Even if the loss is Rs.1,00,000 the insurer will get the full amount. But if the loss is more than Rs. 1, 00,000 the insured will get Rs. 1,00,000 only. Hence, the value of property is not relevant in determining the amount of indemnity in case of a specific policy.

3. Average Policy. Under a fire insurance policy containing the 'average clause' the insured is liable for such proportion of the loss as the value of the uncovered property bears to the whole property. e.g. if a person gets his house insured for Rs. 4,00,000 though its actual value is Rs. 6,00,000, if a part of the house is damaged in fire and the insured suffers a loss of Rs. 3,00,000, the amount of compensation to be paid by the insurer comes out to Rs. 2,00,000 calculated as follows:

Amount of claim= Insured amount * Actual loss

Actual value of property

4,00,000 * 3,00,000 =2,00,000

6, 00,000

4. Floating policy. A floating policy is used for covering fluctuating stocks of goods held in different lots for one premium. With every transaction of sale or purchase, the quantities of goods kept at different places fluctuate. It is difficult for the owner to take a policy for a specific amount. The best way is to take out a floating policy for all the stocks of goods.
5. Reinstatement Policy. In such a policy, the insurer has the right to reinstate or replenish the property destroyed instead of paying compensation to the insured in cash. It may be granted on building, machinery, furniture, fixture and fittings only.
6. Consequential loss Policy. Sometimes the insured has to suffer a greater financial loss on account of dislocation of business caused by fire.e.g. close down business after fire for repair, to meet fixed expenses such as rent, salaries, taxes and other expenses as usual. Such considerable loss to the insured is not covered by the ordinary fire policy. In order to cover such loss by fire, the

'Consequential Loss Policy' has been introduced. The loss so suffered is separately calculated from the loss actually suffered.

7. Comprehensive policy. This policy covers the risks of the fire arising out of any cause that is civil commotion, lightening, riots, thefts, labor disturbances and strikes etc. It is also known as 'all insurance policy'.
8. A Blanket policy. This policy is issued to cover all the fixed and current assets of an enterprise by one insurance.
9. Declaration policy. In this policy, trader takes out a policy for the maximum value of stock which may be expected to hold during the year. At a fixed date each month, the insured has to make a declaration regarding the actual value of stock at risk on that date. On the basis of such declaration, the average amount of stock at risk in the year is calculated and this amount becomes the sum assured.
10. Sprinklers leakage policy. It covers the loss arising out of water leakage from sprinklers which are setup to extinguish fire.

Claim Procedure for Fire Insurance

In the event of fire the insured must immediately give the insurer a notice about the loss caused by fire. A written claim should be delivered with in 15 days from the date of loss. The insured is required to furnish all plans, invoices, documents, proofs and other relevant informations required by the insurer.

If the insured failed to submit these documents with in 6 months from the date of loss, the insurer has the right to consider it as no claim. On receipt of the claim the insurer verifies whether the essentials of a valid claim are satisfied or not. e.g. The cause of fire should be an insured peril. The insured completes the form, signs the declaration given in the form as to the truthfulness and accuracy of the information and returns the same. An official employed by the insurer investigates small and simple claims. For large claims, the insurance company employs independent loss surveyor. On the basis of the claim form and the investigation report, the company then settles the claim.

10

Marine Insurance

Insurance on the risks of transportation of goods is one of the oldest and most vital forms of insurance. The value of goods shipped by business firms each year cost millions of rupees. These goods are exposed to damage or loss from numerous transportation perils. The goods can be protected by marine insurance contracts. It is an important element of general insurance. It essentially provides cover from loss suffered due to marine perils. In India the marine insurance is regulated by the Indian Maritime Insurance Act 1963, which is based on the original English Act.

History of Marine Insurance

Marine insurance as we know it today can be described as mother of all insurances. It is believed to have originated in England owing to the frequent movement of ships over high seas for trade. In India, insurance has been in vogue for several centuries. History holds proof that these people had a system of pooling their contributions, if any one of their clan were to meet a tragedy in their voyages.

Today marine insurance has assumed a vast canvas due to the expanding trade across the globe, which involves large shipping companies that require protection for their fleet against the perils of the sea.

Definition

Marine insurance is a contract under which, the insurer undertakes to indemnify the insured in the manner and to the extent thereby agreed, against marine losses, incidental to marine adventures. It may be defined as a form of insurance covering loss or damage to vessels or to cargo during transportation to the high seas.

It follows from the above discussion the marine insurance is a contract between the insured and the insurer. The insured may be a cargo owner or a ship owner or a freight receiver. The insurer is known as the underwriter. The document in which the contract is incorporated is called "Marine policy". The insured pays a particular sum, which is called premium, in exchange for an undertaking from the insurer to indemnify the insured against loss or damage caused by certain specified perils.

The salient features of a contract of marine insurance are as follows:

1. It is based on utmost good faith. Both the insured and the insurer must disclose everything which is in their knowledge and can affect the contract of insurance.
2. It is a contract of indemnity. The insured is entitled to recover only the actual amount of loss from the insurer.
3. Insurable interest in the subject-matter insured must exist at the time of the loss. It need not exist when the insurance policy is taken. Under marine insurance, the following persons are deemed to have insurable interest:
   a) The owner of the ship.
   b) The owner of the cargo.
   c) A creditor who has advanced money on the security of the ship or cargo.
   d) The mortgagor and mortgagee.
   e) The master and crew of the ship have insurable interest in respect of their wages.
   f) In case of advance freight, the person advancing the freight has an insurable interest if such freight is not repayable in case of loss.
4. It is subject to the doctrine of causa proxima. Where a loss is brought by several causes in succession to one another, the proximate or nearest cause of loss must be taken into account. If the proximate cause is covered by the policy, only then the insurance company will be liable to compensate the insured.

5. It must contain all the essential requirements of a valid contract, e.g. lawful consideration, free consent, capacity of the parties, etc.

Meaning of Marine Perils

Maritime perils can be defined as the fortuitous (an element of chance or ill luck) accidents or casualties of the sea caused without the willful intervention of human agency. The perils are incidental to the sea journey that arises in consequence of the sea journey. There are different forms of perils, of which only a few are covered by insurance while others are not. Accordingly we have insured and uninsured perils.

Insured perils are storm, collision of one ship with another ship, against rocks, burning and sinking of the ship, spoilage of cargo from sea water, mutiny, piracy or willful destruction of the ship and cargo by the master (captain) of the ship or the crew, jettison etc. Uninsured perils are regular wear and tear of the vessel, leakage (unless it is caused by an accident), breakage of goods due to bad movement of the ship, damage by rats and loss by delay. All losses and damages caused due to reasons not considered as perils of the sea are not provided insurance cover..

Subject Matter of Marine Insurance

The insured may be the owner of the ship, owner of the cargo or the person interested in freight. In case the ship carrying the cargo sinks, the ship will be lost along with the cargo. The income that the cargo would have generated would also be lost. Based on this we can classify the marine insurance into three categories:

(a) Hull Insurance: Hull refers to the ocean going vessels (ships trawlers etc.) as well as its machinery. The hull insurance also covers the construction risk when the vessel is under construction. A vessel is exposed to many dangers or risks at sea during the voyage. An insurance effected to indemnify the insured for such losses is known as Hull insurance.

(b) Cargo Insurance: Cargo refers to the goods and commodities carried in the ship from one place to another. The cargo transported by sea is also subject to manifold risks at the port and during the voyage. Cargo insurance covers the shipper of the goods if the goods are damaged or lost. The cargo policy covers the risks associated with the transshipment of goods. The policy can be written to cover a single shipment. If regular shipments are made, an open cargo policy can be used that insures the goods automatically when a shipment is made.

(c) Freight Insurance: Freight refers to the fee received for the carriage of goods in the ship. Usually the ship owner and the freight receiver are the same person. Freight can be received in two ways-in advance or after the goods reach the destination. In the former case, freight is secure. In the latter the marine laws say that the freight is payable only when the goods reach the destination port safely. Hence if the ship is destroyed on the way the ship owner will loose the freight along with the ship. That is why, the ship owners purchase freight insurance policy along with the hull policy.

(d) Liability Insurance: It is usually written as a separate contract that provides comprehensive liability insurance for property damage or bodily injury to third parties. It is also known as protection and indemnity insurance which protects the ship owner for damage caused by the ship to docks, cargo, illness or injury to the passengers or crew, and fines and penalties.

Types of Marine Policy

There are different types of marine policies known by different names according to the manner of their execution or the risk they cover. They are:

1. Voyage Policy: Under the policy, the subject matter is insured against risk in respect of a particular voyage from a port of departure to the port of destination, e.g. Mumbai to New York. The risk starts from the departure of ship from the port and it ends on its arrival at the port of destination. This policy covers the subject matter irrespective of the time factor. This policy is not suitable for hull insurance as a ship usually does not operate over

a particular route only. The policy is used mostly in case of cargo insurance.

2. Time Policy: It is one under which the insurance is affected for a specified period of time, usually not exceeded twelve months. Time policies are generally used in connection with the insurance of ship. Thus if the voyage is not completed with in the specified period, the risk shall be covered until the voyage is completed or till the arrival of the ship at the port of call.
3. Mixed Policies: It is one under which insurance contract is entered into for a certain time period and for a certain voyage or voyages, e.g., Kolkata to New York, for a period of one year. Mixed Policies are generally issued to ships operating on particular routes. It is a mixture of voyage and time policies.
4. Valued Policies: It is one under which the value of subject matter insured is specified on the face of the policy itself. This kind of policy specifies the settled value of the subject matter that is being provided cover for. The value which is agreed upon is called the insured value. It forms the measure of indemnity in the event of loss. Insured value is not necessarily the actual value. It includes (a) invoice price of goods (b) freight, insurance and other charges (c) ten to fifteen percent margin to cover expected profits.
5. Unvalued policy: It is the policy under which the value of subject matter insured is not fixed at the time of effecting insurance but has to be ascertained wherever the subject matter is lost or damaged.
6. Open policy: An open policy is issued for a period of 12 months and all consignments cleared during the period are covered by the insurer. This form of insurance Policy is suitable for big companies that have regular shipments. It saves them the tedious and expensive process of acquiring an insurance policy for each shipment. The rates are fixed in advance, without taking the total value of the cargo being shipped into consideration. The assured has to declare the nature of each shipment, and the cover is provided to all the shipments. The assured also deposits

a premium for the estimated value of the consignment during the policy period..

6. Floating Policy: A merchant who is a regular shipper of goods can take out a 'floating policy' to avoid botheration and waste of time involved in taking a new policy for every shipment. This policy stands for the contract of insurance in general terms. It does not include the name of the ship and other details. The other details are required to be furnished through subsequent declarations. Thus, the insured takes a policy for a huge amount and he informs the underwriter as and when he makes shipment of goods. The underwriter goes on recording the entries in the policy. When the sum assured is exhausted, the policy is said to be "fully declared" or "run off".
7. Block Policy: This policy covers other risks also in addition to marine risks. When goods are to be transported by ship to the place of destination, a single policy known as block policy may be taken to cover all risks. E.g. when the goods are dispatched by rail or road transport for shipment, a single policy may cover all the risks from the point of origin to the point of destination.

Assignment of Marine Policy

A marine insurance policy may be transferred by assignment unless the terms of the policy expressly prohibit the same. The policy may be assigned either before or after loss. The assignment may be made either by endorsement on the policy itself or on a separate document. The insured need not give a notice or information to the insurer or underwriter about assignment. In case of death of the insured, a marine policy is automatically assigned to his heirs.

At the time of assignment, the assignor must possess an insurable interest in the subject matter insured. An insured who has parted with or lost interest in the subject matter insured can not make a valid assignment.

After the occurrence of the loss, the policy can be assigned freely to any person. The assignor merely transfers his own right to claim to the assignee.

Clauses in a Marine Policy

A policy of marine insurance may contain several clauses. Some of the clauses are common to all marine policies while others are included to meet special requirements of the insured. Hull, cargo and freight policies have different standard clauses. There are standard clauses which are invariably used in marine insurance. Firstly, policies are constructed in general, ordinary and popular sense, and, later on, specific clauses are added to them according to terms and conditions of the contract. Some of the important clauses in a marine policy are described below:

1. Valuation Clause. This clause states the value of the subject matter insured as agreed upon between both the parties.
2. Sue and Labour clause. This clause authorizes the insured to take all possible steps to avert or minimize the loss or to protect the subject matter insured in case of danger. The insurer is liable to pay the expenses, if any, incurred by the insured for this purpose.
3. Waiver Clause. This clause is an extension of the above clause. The clause states that any act of the insured or the insurer to protect, recover or preserve the subject matter of insurance shall not be taken to mean that the insured wants to forgo the compensation, nor will it mean that the insurer accepts the act as abandonment of the policy.
4. Touch and Stay Clause. This clause requires the ship to touch and stay at such ports and in such order as specified in the policy. Any departure from the route mentioned in the policy or the ordinary trade route followed will be considered as deviation unless such departure is essential to save the ship or the lives on board in an emergency.
5. Warehouse to warehouse clause. This clause is inserted to cover the risks to goods from the time they are dispatched from the consignor's warehouse until their delivery at the consignee's warehouse at the port of destination.
6. Inchmaree Clause. This clause covers the loss or damage caused to the ship or machinery by the negligence of the master of the ship as well as by explosives or latent defect in the machinery or the hull.

7. F.P.A. and F.A.A. Clause. The F.P.A. (Free of Particular Average) clause relieves the insurer from particular average liability. The F.A.A. (free of all average) clause relieves the insurer from liability arising from both particular average and general average.
8. Lost or Not Lost Clause. Under this clause, the insurer is liable even if the ship insured is found not to be lost prior to the contact of insurance, provided the insurer had no knowledge of such loss and does not commit any fraud. This clause covers the risks between the issue of the policy and the shipment of the goods.
9. Running down Clause. This clause covers the risk arising out of collision between two ships. The insurer is liable to pay compensation to the owner of the damaged ship. This clause is used in hull insurance.
10. Free of Capture and Seizure Clause. This clause relieves the insurer from the liability of making compensation for the capture and seizure of the vessel by enemy countries. The insured can insure such abnormal risks by taking an extra 'war risks' policy.
11. Continuation Clause. This clause authorizes the vessel to continue and complete her voyage even if the time of the policy has expired. This clause is used in a time policy. The insured has to give prior notice for this and deposit a monthly prorate premium.
12. Barratry Clause. This clause covers losses sustained by the ship owner or the cargo owner due to willful conduct of the master or crew of the ship.
13. Jettison Clause. Jettison means throwing overboard a part of the ship's cargo so as to reduce her weight or to save other goods. This clause covers the loss arising out of such throwing of goods. The owner of jettisoned goods is compensated by all interested parties.
14. At and From Clause. This clause covers the subject matter while it is lying at the port of departure and until it reaches the port of destination. It is used in voyage policies. If the policy consists of the word 'from' only instead of 'at and

from', the risk is covered only from the time of departure of the ship.

Warranties

Besides the three important principles i.e. good faith, indemnity, and insurable interest, it is necessary that all the marine insurance contracts must fulfil the warranties also. Warrantee means a condition which is basic to the contract of insurance. The breach of which entitles the insurer to avoid the policy altogether. If the warranty is not complied with by the insured, the contract comes to an end. There are two exceptions where the breach of warranty is excused and does not affect that insurer's liability:

(i) Where owning to change in the circumstance the warranty is inapplicable and

(ii) Where due to enactment of a subsequent law the warranty becomes unlawful.

Kinds of Warranties

Warranties are of two types:

(i) Express, and

(ii) Implied.

An express warranty is one which is expressed or clearly stated in the contract and it can be easily ascertained whether it has been fulfilled or not. For instance a marine policy usually contains the following express warranties:

(i) The ship will sail on a specified day.

(ii) The ship is safe on a particular day.

(iii) The ship will proceed to the port of destination without any deviation.

(iv) The ship is neutral and will remain so during the voyage.

The implied warranty, on the other hand, is not expressly mentioned in the contract but the law takes it for granted that such warranty exists. An express warranty does not exclude implied warranty unless it is inconsistent therewith. Implied warranties do not appear in the policy documents at all, but are understood without being put into words, and as such, are automatically applicable. These are included in the policy by law, general practice, long established custom or usage. The important implied warranties are discussed below:

(a) Sea-Worthiness of the ship.: A ship is sea worthy when it is in a fit condition as to repair, equipment, crew, etc. to encounter the ordinary perils of the voyage. This implies that the ship must be suitably constructed, properly equipped and manned, sufficiently fuelled and provisioned and capable of withstanding the ordinary strain and stress of the voyage. It must not be overloaded.

(b) Legality of Voyage.: The journey undertaken by the ship must be for legal purposes. Carrying prohibited or smuggled goods is illegal and therefore, the insurer shall not be liable for the loss.

(c) Non-deviation of the ship route.: It is assumed that the ship will maintain the same route as stated in the policy in ordinary course, but in case of peril it is permitted to deviate. If the ship does not follow the usual route, the insurer will not be liable even if the ship regains her route before any loss takes place. However, the insurer remains liable for any loss which might have occurred prior to the deviation.

Types of Marine Losses

A loss arising in a marine adventure due to perils of the sea is a marine loss. Marine loss may be classified into two categories:

(1) Total loss: A total loss implies that the subject matter insured is fully destroyed and is totally lost to its owner. It can be Actual total loss or Constructive total loss. In actual total loss subject matter is completely destroyed or so damaged that it ceases to be a thing of the kind insured. e.g. sinking of ship, complete destruction of cargo by fire, etc.

In case of constructive total loss the ship or cargo insured is not completely destroyed but is so badly damaged that the cost of repair or recovery would be greater than the value of the property saved. e.g. a ship dashed against the rock and is stranded in a badly damaged position. If the expenses of bringing it back and repairing it would be more than the actual value of the damaged ship, it is abandoned.

(2) Partial loss: A partial loss occurs when the subject matter is partially destroyed or damaged. Partial loss can be general average or particular average. General average refers to the sacrifice made during extreme circumstances for the safety of the ship and the cargo. This loss has to be borne by all the parties who have an interest in the marine adventure. e.g. A loss caused by throwing overboard of goods is a general average and must be shared by various parties.

Particular average may be defined as a loss arising from damage accidentally caused by the perils insured against. Such a loss is borne by the underwriter who insured the object damaged. e.g. If a ship is damaged due to bad weather the loss incurred is a particular average loss.

Marine Insurance in India

There is evidence that marine insurance was practiced in India since long time. In earlier days travellers by sea and land were exposed to risk of losing their vessels and merchandise because of piracy on the open seas. It was the British insurers who introduced general insurance in India, in its modern form. The first company known as the Sun Insurance Office Ltd. was set up in Calcutta in the year 1710. This followed by several insurance companies of different parts of the world, in the field of marine insurance. In India marine insurance is transacted by the subsidiaries of the General Insurance Corporation of India-New India Assurance, National Insurance, Oriental Insurance and United India Insurance. Marine and hull insurance contribute 20% to the total premium of the general insurance industry in India.

11

HEALTH INSURANCE

A systematic plan for financing medical expenses is an important and integral part of a risk management plan. With rising health care costs, it was no longer possible for an individual to meet the heavy cost of treatment involving hospitalization.

The reasons for rise in health care costs are:

(a) Increase in medical treatment costs.

(b) Technological advancements in medical equipment.

(c) High labour costs.

Definition

"Health insurance is an insurance, which covers the financial loss arising out of poor health condition or due to permanent disability, which results in loss of income."

A health insurance policy is a contract between an insurer and an individual or group, in which the insurer agrees to provide specified health insurance at an agreed upon price (premium). It usually provides either direct payment or reimbursement for expenses associated with illness and injuries. The cost and range of protection provided by health insurance depends on the insurance provider and the policy purchased..

Health Insurance Policies

The health insurance policies available in India are:

(a) Mediclaim policy (individuals and groups)

(b) Overseas mediclaim policy

(c) Raj Rajeshwari Mahila Kalyan Yojna

(d) Bhagyashree Child Welfare Policy

(e) Cancer Insurance Policy

(f) Jan Arogya Bima Policy

Mediclaim Policy (individuals and groups)

Mediclaim policy is offered to individuals and groups exceeding 50 members. It covers the hospitalization for diseases or sickness and for injuries. Under group mediclaim policy, group discount is allowed to groups exceeding 101 people.

The medical expenses will be reimbursed only if the insured is admitted in the hospital for a minimum duration of 24 hours. Cost of treatment includes consultation fee of doctors, cost of medicines and hospitalization charges.

Health insurance in India is available at very economical rates. It is very popular among professionals like Chartered accountants, Advocates, Engineers etc. It is very suitable for self-employed persons because it covers risks against several general and serious diseases.

Overseas Mediclaim Policy

In 1984, the Overseas Mediclaim Policy was developed. This policy will reimburse the medical expenses incurred by Indians upto 70 years of age while traveling abroad. The premium will be charged based on their age, purpose of travel, duration and plan selected by the insured under the policy. This policy is provided is provided to businessmen, people going on holiday tour, traveling for educational professional and official purposes.

Raj Rajeshwari Mahila Kalyan Yojna.

It is a personal accident policy offered by an insurance company for the welfare of women. It is offered to women residing in rural and urban areas. Women between 10-75 years of age are eligible for this policy irrespective of their occupation and income level.

Bhagyashree Child Welfare Policy

It is offered to girls between 0-18 years. The age of the parents of the girls shouldn't be more than 60 years. It provides coverage to one girl child in a family who loses her father or mother in an accident.

Cancer Insurance Policy

It is designed for cancer patients aid association members. The persons insured under this policy will pay premium to their association along with the membership fee. This policy will offer coverage to the insured in case he develops cancer. All the expenses incurred for treatment of cancer not exceeding the sum insured will be paid directly to the insured person.

Jan Arogya Bima Policy

This policy provides medical insurance to poorer section of the people. This policy covers illness like heart attack, jaundice, food poisoning, and accidents etc. that requires immediate hospitalization.

Future of Health Insurance

During the last 50 years, India has made considerable progress in improving its health status. Still it is in a developing stage. The increasing health care costs in the country are likely to contribute to the development of more health insurance products. Health insurance is not at the present recognized as a separate segment in Indian insurance industry. Privatization of insurance industry is likely to encourage the development of this segment. Health insurance in India has indeed a long way to go.

12

Motor Insurance

There has been a sudden rise in the motor accidents in the last few years. Much of these are attributable to increase in the number of vehicles. Every vehicle before being driven on roads has to be compulsorily insured. The motor insurance policy represents a combined coverage of the vehicles including accessories, loss or damage to his property or life and the third party coverage.

Persons driving vehicles may cause losses and injuries to other persons. Every individual who owns a motor vehicle is also exposed to certain other risks. These include damage to his vehicle due to accidents, theft, fire, collision and natural disasters and also injuries to himself.

In 1939, motor vehicle act came into force in India. Compulsory insurance was introduced by motor vehicle act to protect the pedestrians and other third parties. Claims for damages may arise due to possession of car, usage and maintenance of car. Motor insurance policy will pay the financial liability arising out of these risks to the insured person.

Definition

Motor insurance policy is a contract between the insured and the insurer in which the insurer promises to indemnify the financial liability in event of loss to the insured.

Motor Vehicles Act in 1939 was passed to mainly safeguard the interests of pedestrians. According to the Act, a vehicle cannot be used in a public place without insuring the third part liability. According to Section 24 of Motor Vehicles Act, "No person shall use or allow any other person to use a motor vehicle in a public place, unless the vehicle is covered by a policy of insurance."

Classification of Motor

Vehicles As per the Motor Vehicles Act for the purpose of insurance the vehicles are classified into three broad categories such as.

Private Cars

a) Private Cars-vehicles used only for social, domestic and pleasure purposes

b) Private vehicles-Two wheeled
   1. Motorcycle / Scooters
   2. Auto cycles
   3. Mechanically assisted pedal cycles Commercial vehicles
      1) Goods carrying vehicles
      2) Passengers carrying vehicles
      3) Miscellaneous & Special types of vehicles

The risks under motor insurance are of two types:

1) Legal liability due to bodily injury, death or damage caused to the property of others.
2) Loss or damage to one's own vehicle\ injury to or death of self and other occupants of the vehicle.

Basic Principles of Motor Insurance

Motor insurance being a contract like any other contract has to fulfill the requirements of a valid contract as laid down in the Indian Contract Act 1872. In addition it has certain special features common to other insurance contracts.

They are:

- Utmost good faith
- Insurable interest
- Indemnity
- Subrogation and contribution
- Proximate cause

Utmost good Faith

The principle of Utmost good faith casts an obligation on the insured to disclose all the material tracts. These material facts must be disclosed to the insurer at the time of entering into the contract. All the information given in the proposal form should be true and complete.e.g. the driving history, physical health of the driver, type of vehicle etc. If any of the mentioned material facts declared by the insured in the proposal form are found inappropriate by the insurer at the time of claim it may result in the claim being repudiated.

Insurable Interest

In a valid insurance contract it is necessary on the part of the insured to have an insurable interest in the subject matter of insurance. The presence of insurable interest in the subject matter of insurance gives the person the right to insure. The interest should be pecuniary and must be present at inception and throughout the term of the policy. Thus the insured must be either benefited by the safety of the property or must suffer a loss on account of damage to it.

Indemnity

Insurance contracts are contracts of indemnity. Indemnity means making good of the loss by reimbursing the exact monetary loss. It aims at keeping the insured in the same position he was before the loss occurred and thus prevent him from making profit from insurance policy.

Subrogation and Contribution

Subrogation refers to transfer of insured's right of action against a third party who caused the loss to the insurer. Thus, the insurer who pays the loss can take up the assured's place and sue the party that caused the loss in order to minimise his loss for which he has already indemnified the assured. Subrogation comes in the picture only in case of damage or loss due to a third party.

The insurer derives this right only after the payment of damages to the insured. Contribution ensures that the indemnity provided is proportionately borne by other insurers in case of double insurance.

Types of Motor Insurance Policies

The All India Motor Tariff governs motor insurance business in India. According to the Tariff all classes of vehicles can use two types of policy forms. They are form A and form B. Form A which is known as Act Policy is a compulsory requirement of the motor vehicle act. Use without such insurance is a penal offence. Form B which is also known as Comprehensive Policy is an optional cover.

1. Liability only policy – This covers third party liability and / or death and property damage. Compulsory personal accident covers for the owner in respect of owner driven vehicles is also included.
2. Package policy – This covers loss or damage to the vehicle insured in addition to 1 above.
3. Comprehensive policy-Apart from the above-mentioned coverage, it is permissible to cover private cars against the risk of fine and / or theft and third party/ theft risks.

Every owner of motor vehicle has to take out a policy covering third party risks but insurance against other two risks is optional. When insurance policy covers third party risks, third party who has suffered any damages, can sue the Insurance company even though he was not a party to the contract of insurance.

Insurance policies for the vehicles subject to the purchase agreements, lease agreements and hypothecation are to be issued in the joint names of the hirer and owner, lease and lessor, owner and pledge respectively. In case of policy renewal a notice of one month in advance before the date of expiry is issued by the insurers. The notice gives the details of premium payable for renewal.

Transfer of Ownership

In case of any sale of vehicle involving transfer of policy, the insured should apply to the insurer for consent to such transfer. The transfer is allowed, if within 15 days of receipt of application, the insurer does not reject the plea. The transferee shall apply within fourteen days from the date of transfer in writing to the insurer who has insured the vehicle, with the details of the registration of the vehicle, the date of transfer of the vehicle, the previous owner of the vehicle and the number and date of the insurance policy so that the insurer may make the necessary changes in his record and issue fresh

Certificate of Insurance

Insurer's Duty to Third Party

It is obligatory on the part of the insurer to pay the third party since, the insurer has no rights to avoid or reject the payment of liability to a third party. The duties of the insurer towards a third party are provided in section 96(1). The court determines the third party liability and accordingly compensation is paid. The liability is unlimited.

Cancellation of Insurance

The insurer may cancel a policy by sending to the insured seven days notice of cancellation by recorded delivery to the insured's last known address and the insurer will refund to the insured the pro-rata premium for the balance period of the policy. A policy may be cancelled at the option of the insured with seven days notice of cancellation and the insurer will be entitled to retain premium on short period scale of rates for the period for which the cover has been in existence prior to the cancellation of the policy. The balance premium, if any, will be refundable to the insured.

Double Insurance

When two policies are in existence on the same vehicle with identical cover, one of the policies many be cancelled. Where one of the policies commences at a date later than the other policy, the policy commencing later is to be cancelled by the insurer concerned. If a vehicle is insured at any time with two different offices of the same insurer, 100% refund of premium of one policy may be allowed by canceling the later of the two policies. However, if the two policies are issued by two different insurers, the policy commencing later is to be cancelled by the insurer concerned and pro-rata refund of premium thereon is to be allowed.

Calculation of Premiums

In the case of Comprehensive Insurance Cover, for the purpose of premium, vehicles are categorized as follows:

Private Car

This is used for personal purposes. Private cars are lesser exposed than taxis, as the latter is used extensively for maximum revenue. The premium is computed on the following basis

1. Geographical area of use: Large cities have higher average claim costs followed by suburban areas, smaller cities, and small towns or rural areas. In India, the geographical areas have been classified into Group A and Group B.
2. Cubic capacity: The more the cubic capacity, the higher the premium rate.
3. Value of the vehicle.: The premium rate is applied on the value of the vehicle. Owner has to declare the correct value of the vehicle to the insurer. This value is known as the Insured's Estimated Value (IEV) in motor insurance and represents the sum insured. Two-wheeler

It is used for personal purpose only. Premium is calculated on cubic capacity and value of vehicle. Theft of accessories is not covered, unless the vehicle is stolen at the same time.

Commercial Vehicle

This is the vehicle used for hire. For goods carrying commercial vehicle, premium is calculated on the basis of carrying capacity i.e. gross vehicle weight and value of the vehicle. For passenger carrying commercial vehicles, premium is calculated on the basis of again carrying capacity i.e. number of passengers and value of the vehicle.

Accessories extra, as specified. Heavier vehicles are more exposed to accidents since the resultant damages they incur are more. Similarly, vehicles with higher carrying capacity expose more passengers to risk. Therefore heavier vehicles attract higher premium rate.

Claim Settelement

Claim Arise When

1) The insured's vehicle is damaged or any loss incurred.
2) Any legal liability is incurred for death of or bodily injury
3) Or damage to the third party's property.

The claim settlement in India is done by opting for any of the following by the insurance company

- o Replacement or reinstatement of vehicle
- o Payment of repair charges

In case, the motor vehicle is damaged due to accident it can be repaired and brought back to working condition. If the repair is beyond repair then the insured can claim for total loss or for a new vehicle. It is based on the market value of the vehicle at the time of loss.

Motor insurance claims are settled in three stages. In the first stage the insured will inform the insurer about loss. The loss is registered in claim register. In the second stage, the automobile surveyor will assess the causes of loss and extent of loss. He will submit the claim report showing the cost of repairs and replacement charges etc. In the third stage, the claim is examined based on the report submitted by the surveyor and his recommendations. The insurance company may then authorize the repairs. After the vehicle is repaired, insurance company pays the charges directly to the repairer or to the insured if he had paid the repair charges.

Section 110 of Motor Vehicle Act, 1939 empowers the State Government in establishing motor claim tribunals. These tribunals will help in settling the third party claims for the minimum amount

13

FURURE PROSPECTS OF INSURANCES

In addition to life, fire and marine Insurance, several other general types of insurances are available today. The nationalized general insurance companies have also been offering special schemes meant for rural areas such as crop insurance, cattle insurance, insurance for huts, poultry etc. There is also a social security group accident scheme covering weaker sections of the society. Some of these are described below:

Personal Accident Insurance

All of us are exposed to the risk of accident, which is a threat to our financial security, and therefore it is prudent to have adequate personal accident cover to manage this contingency. For handling accident risks, personal accident policy, Janata personal accident policy and Gramin personal accident policies are available in India.

Scope of Cover

Personal accident policy pays compensation to the insured in the event of happening of one or more of the following listed below which may be selected by insured at the time of taking policy:

- On death
- On permanent total and partial disability and
- On temporary total disability

In case of accident death during the policy period, the policy in addition covers funeral expenses of the insured person. Permanent total disablement occurs when an individual is unable to perform his regular duties for the remaining part of his life.

Permanent partial disablement may result when a person loses any part of his body due to accident.

When an individual is injured in an accident and as a result he is unable to perform his normal duties for a certain period we can describe it as temporary total disablement. This policy can also be extended to reimburse the medical expenses due to accidents up to 10% of the insured amount or 25% of the claim amount or expenses incurred for treatment of the insured person whichever is less.

Personal accident policy does not cover the injuries resulting out of war, self-inflicted injury, diseases or insanity, death due to war operations, attempted suicides, accident in armed forces, aircraft accidents, accidents due to nuclear weapons etc.

Janata personal accident policy is meant for weaker section of the society. Thus premium charged under this policy is comparatively less. Gramin personal accident policy is designed for the rural people in the country. It is a contract of Insurance under which the insurer agrees to pay a specific sum of money to the insured in case of bodily injury by accident and to the heirs of the insured in case of death by accident. A contract of personal accident insurance is not a contract of indemnity and the insurer has to pay a fixed sum of money on the death or total disablement of the insured or provide medical benefits for recovery from the injury.

In case of accidental death during the policy period, the policy in addition covers funeral expenses of the insured person. Permanent total disablement occurs when an individual is unable to perform his regular duties for the remaining part of his life. Permanent partial disablement may result when a person loses any part of his body due to accident. It does not cover the injuries resulting out of war, diseases, attempted suicides etc.

Fidelity Insurance

Under this type of insurance contract the insurer undertakes to compensate the insured against the loss caused by misappropriation of funds or goods or damage to the property caused by his employees. Such a policy is useful to the employers who fear embezzlement, forgery, fraud and dishonesty on the part of their employees. Under it the insured is required to furnish all material facts about the employees and also to notify any change in the condition of their service. The policy can be taken for specific positions rather than names, e.g., accountant, cashier etc. Blanket cover is also available for entire staff or group of employees.

Burglary Insurance

Such a policy provides protection against loss or damage caused by housebreaking, robbery or theft. It is also known as 'robbery, theft or larceny insurance'. For this purpose a comprehensive policy may be taken or each risk may be separately insured. Full details of the article insured are given in the policy. Insured items include gold and gold ornaments and other assets including household items such as TV, fridge, air conditioner etc. A burglary policy for business premises would provide cover against loss to damage by house breaking and burglary of stock-in-trade, goodsin-transit, cash-in-safe, fixture and fittings etc.

Credit Insurance

Credit insurance policy is taken to cover the loss which may arise due to bad debts or non-payment of dues by the debtors. This insurance is very useful to businessmen who sell goods on credit. It protects them from loss arising out of insolvency of their debtors. In India, Export Credit and Guarantee Corporation (ECGC) provides credit insurance to exporters.

Workmen's Compensation Insurance

In India, Workmen's Compensation Act was passed in 1934 and 1946. According to this act, an employer is required to pay compensation to his workers who receive injuries or contract occupational diseases during the course of their work. An employer may obtain an insurance policy to cover such liability. The premiums are payable usually on the basis of wages. It is also known as 'Employers Liability Insurance'. This policy is essential to every employer who employs 'workmen' as defined under the Workmen's Compensation Act in order to protect himself against the legal liabilities arising out of death or bodily injury to this workman. It also extends coverage through reimbursement of medical, surgical and hospitalization expenses including transportation costs on the payment of additional premium. The National Insurance Company Ltd, United India Insurance Company Ltd, Oriental Insurance Company Ltd, and the New India Assurance Company Ltd offer workmen's compensation policies.

Travel Insurance

Travel insurance covers travel related accidents also. While traveling outside India, individuals face risks such as loss of baggage, accidents involving injuries, illnesses and medical emergencies requiring hospitalization treatment. All this can pose serious consequences to the overseas travellers. A rational person should therefore secure the required coverage before leaving his home country. In India travel insurance has become popular among International travellers. The coverage offered under travel insurance policies in India are as follows

Wedding Insurance

These days, weddings have become quite an expensive and elaborate affair. People do take care to make this once-in-a-lifetime event a memorable one. In case of any postponement or cancellation, there is a certain risk of monetary loss. The wedding insurance package can compensate for the monetary loss. This unique product covers the specific risks related to weddings. This Policy can protect you against certain types of financial losses you may incur in the event of unpredictable situations during the period leading up to and including your wedding day.

The period of insurance will be 24 hours prior to the start of the customary functions or rituals or programmes of events mentioned in the printed invitations till the end of the function or five days from the beginning whichever occurs earlier.

This policy provides cover for expenses actually and already incurred or advances paid in connection with marriage hall, catering, pandit, guests, music parties, photos and videography, loss on cancellation of travel tickets etc. Liability is restricted only when such cancellation arises out of cancellation or postponement of marriage.

The policy does not cover any loss arises when marriage is cancelled or postponed because of dispute between marriage parties, willful negligence and criminal misconduct of the bride, bridegroom or their parents.

Employee State Insurance Scheme

The Employee State Insurance Scheme (ESIS) is an insurance system which provides both the cash and medical benefits. It is managed by the Employee State Insurance Corporation (ESIC), a wholly government-owned enterprise. It was conceived as a compulsory social security benefit for workers in the formal sector. The original legislation creating the scheme allowed it to cover only factories which has been using power and employing 10 or more workers. However, since 1989 the scheme has been expanded, and it now includes all such factories which are not using power and employing 20 or more persons. Mines and plantations are explicitly excluded from coverage under the ESIS Act.

Unemployment Insurance

Unemployment insurance is designed to provide short term protection for regularly employed persons who lose their jobs and who are willing and able to work. Unemployment insurance has several basic objectives:

1) Provide cash income during involuntary unemployment.
2) Help unemployed workers find jobs.
3) Encourage employees to stabilize employment.
4) Help stabilize economy.

Unemployment insurance is a popular concept in developed countries like U.S. where they have well defined laws and regulations. However in India it will take a long time to come.

Personal Liability Insurance

Personal liability insurance provides protection against the legal liability, which arises due to insured's personal acts. The insurance company will pay for legal defense to third party damages or injuries up to policy limit. Except legal liability, which arises due to automobile accidents and professional liability, most other personal acts are covered under personal liability insurance.

The personal liability insurance covers damages caused to properties and injuries to other people due to the negligence of the insured. Under this policy, the insurance company is bound to defend the insured, should the matter go to court of law. It can also settle the matter out of court by negotiating with parties for a settlement within the policy limit. Personal liability policy offers very wide coverage. The following instances of loss, damages or injuries caused by an insured individual come under the purview of personal liability insurance in which coverage will be available up to the policy limit.

- Accidental fire to neighbors house as a result of insured's negligence
- Accidental injury to a third party while playing
- Damaging costly antique accidentally belonging to neighbor
- Injuring another person while riding a bicycle

Summary

We have seen that the entire non-life business has been divided into three segments, namely, Fire, Marine and Miscellaneous insurance. Motor and Health are part of Miscellaneous insurance.

Fire insurance is the protection against a loss suffered by the insured as a result of damage caused by fire to the property covered by the policy. Like any other insurance contract it has to satisfy the essentials of a valid contract. e.g. indemnity, insurable interest, utmost good faith etc. Then we have seen the meaning of fire, different types of fire policies and claim settlement procedure.

In marine insurance, the insurer undertakes to indemnify the insured against the losses incidental to marine adventure. Then we have seen characteristics of general insurance, common to marine insurance. The meaning of marine perils, different marine insurance policies, types of marine insurance and types of losses, Clauses and Warranties are also explained. We have tried to understand how the concept of marine insurance evolves specially in India.

Health insurance is a safeguard against rising medical costs. Different types of health insurance policies have been explained.

In India, motor insurance is classified as miscellaneous. It comes under tariff category and it offers policies and coverage at standard premium rate. We have also covered the basic principles of motor insurance, classification of vehicles, risks under motor insurance and claim settlement procedure.

Miscellaneous insurance is a large portfolio and has numerous types of policies floated by different insurance companies. For the purpose of this lesson, miscellaneous insurance has been explained through Personal accident insurance, Fidelity insurance, Burglary insurance, Credit insurance, Travel insurance, Workmen's Compensation insurance, Wedding insurance, Employee State Insurance Scheme, Unemployment Insurance and Personal liability Insurance.

14

LIFE INSURANCE CORPORATION OF INDIA

Life Insurance Corporation of India (LIC) was established on 1 September 1956 to spread the message of life insurance in the country and mobilise people's savings for nation-building activities. LIC with its central office in Mumbai and seven zonal offices at Mumbai, Calcutta, Delhi, Chennai, Hyderabad, Kanpur and Bhopal, operates through 100 divisional offices in important cities and 2,048 branch offices. LIC has 5.59 lakh active agents spread over the country. The Corporation also transacts business abroad and has offices in Fiji, Mauritius and United Kingdom. LIC is associated with joint ventures abroad in the field of insurance, namely, Ken-India Assurance Company Limited, Nairobi; United Oriental Assurance Company Limited, Kuala Lumpur; and Life Insurance Corporation (International), E.C. Bahrain. It has also entered into an agreement with the Sun Life (UK) for marketing unit linked life insurance and pension policies in U.K.

The total new business of the Corporation during 1998-99 was Rs 75,316 crore of sum assured under 148.43 lakh policies. LIC's group insurance business up to 31 March 1999 was Rs 66,085 crore (provisional) providing cover to 219 lakh people.

SOCIAL SECURITY GROUP SCHEME

A Social Security Fund (SSF) administered by the LIC was set up in 1989-90 to meet the insurance requirements of the weaker and vulnerable sections of the society. As on 31 March 1999, about 49 lakh people belonging to 24 occupational groups/areas have been covered under various social security group schemes financed from the SSF. Under these schemes people in the age group of 18-60 years are covered for a sum of Rs 5,000 on death due to natural causes, and Rs 25,000 on death caused by accident. While the SSF subsidises 50 per cent of the premium, the beneficiary has to pay the remaining 50 per cent.

Under Landless Agricultural Labourers Group Insurace Scheme (LALGI) in operation since 1987, the heads of the families in the age group of 18 to 60 years and not appearing as a land holder in the revenue records and not having inheritable right in agricultural land are eligible to be covered for an insurance cover of Rs 2,000 payable only on death before 60 years. Upto 1 April 1990, it was operated by LIC on behalf of the Central government which used to reimburse to LIC the premium payable by the beneficiaries. However, with effect from 1 April 1990 the entire premium payable by the beneficiaries is being met out of the SSF. At present, about 1.2 crore landless agricultural labourers are covered under the Scheme. During 1998-99, 47,122 claims were settled.

All over the country, the Integrated Rural Development Programme (IRDP) beneficiaries between the age group of 18 to 60 years are covered under a Group Life Insurance Scheme being operated by the LIC for which the entire premium is paid by the Central government. An amount of Rs 5,000 is payable to the beneficiary in case of normal death and Rs 10,000 in case of accidental death. During 1998-99, 5,896 claims were settled. The Rural Group Life Insurance Scheme (RGLIS), announced on 15 August 1995, is a group insurance scheme which provides a life cover of Rs 5,000 for persons in rural areas. The premium payable is Rs 60 per year for those who enroll up to the age of 40 years and Rs 70 per year for those who enroll beyond40 years and up to 50 years. The entry age is restricted to 20 years (mininum) and 50years (maximum). Deaths occurring after 60 years are not covered. Nor is there any saving element in the Scheme. There are two types of scheme: (i) General Scheme-for persons between the age 20 and 50 years where premiums are to be paid by the members in full and (ii) Subsidised Scheme-for persons between the age of 20 and 50 years who belong to a household below-poverty line. Only one member of such a household is eligible under the scheme where 50 per cent of the premium is shared by the Central government and State government in equal proportions. Intermediate Level Panchayats are designated as the nodal agencies for its implementation. LIC provides incentives to village level workers of Rs six for enrolment of a new member and Rs three on renewal of insurance cover for an existing member in the subsequent year. From 15 August 1997 to 14 August 1998, 3,09,252 persons were enrolled and 73,925 persons renewed their membership. Among them 2,98,917 and 70,183 persons were under subsidised category respectively 5,047 claims were settled up to 31 March 1999.

INSURANCE REGULATORY AUTHORITY

On the recommendations of the Malhotra Committee, Government has set up an interim Insurance Regulatory Authority (IRA), with a view to activate an insurance regulatory apparatus essential for proper monitoring and control of the insurance industry. The IRA is headed by a Chairman who is also Controller of Insurance and Chairman of TBC. The other Members of the IRA, not exceeding seven in number of whom not more than three shall serve full time, shall be nominated by the Central government.

GENERAL INSURANCE CORPORATION OF INDIA

The general insurance industry in India was nationalised and a government company known as General Insurance Corporation of India (GIC) was formed by the Central Government in November 1972. With effect from 1 January 1973 the erstwhile 107 Indian and foreign insurers which were operating in the country prior to nationalisation, were grouped into four operating companies, namely, (i) National Insurance Company Limited; (ii) New India Assurance Company Limited; (iii) Oriental Insurance Company Limited; and (iv) United India Insurance Company Limited. All the above four subsidiaries of GIC operate all over the country competing with one another and underwriting various classes of general insurance business except for aviation insurance of national airlines and crop insurance which is handled by the GIC. From 799 offices in 1973, the network grew to 4,208 offices as on 31 March 1998.

Besides the domestic market, the industry is presently operating in 17 countries directly through branches or agencies and in 14 countries through subsidiary and associate companies. The wholly-owned subsidiary of GIC known as India International Insurance Private Limited set up in 1988 in Singapore has grown into a leading company in the Singapore market. The gross premium income of the general insurance industry in India during 1997-98 was Rs 7,736 crore as against Rs 7,021 crore during 1996-97 representing a growth of 10.2 per cent over the premium income of 1996-97. The net premium income of the general insurance industry in India during 1997-98 was Rs 6,725 crore as against Rs 6,041 crore during 1996-97 representing a growth of 11.3 per cent over the net premium income of 1996-97. The gross profit of the industry during 1997-98 were Rs 1,623 crore as against Rs 1,084 crore in 1996-97 recording a growth of 49.7 per cent over the previous year. The net profits of the industry during 1997-98 were Rs 1,255 crore as against Rs 719 crore in 1996-97 representing a growth of 74.5 per cent over the previous year.

Hut Insurance Scheme for Poor Families in Rural Areas provides fire insurance cover for huts and belongings of landless labourers, small farmers, artisans and other poor families in rural areas. Under the Scheme, compensation is provided for an amount not exceeding Rs 1,000 for a hut and Rs 500 for belongings in the hut destroyed by fire. The Central Government is bearing the entire premium in respect of the scheme. During the year 1997-98, 40,554 claims involving an amount of Rs 4.85 crore were settled.

Mediclaim Insurance Policy has recently been revised. The revised policy does away with the sub-limits under the various sub-heads and offers just one sum-insured ranging from Rs 15,000 to Rs 3,00,000. The cover provides for reimbursement of medical expenses incurred by an individual towards hospitalisation/domicillary hospitalisation for any illness, injury or disease contracted or sustained during the period of insurance. Premium is calculated on the basis of age of the proposer and the sum insured opted forJan Arogya Bima Policy which is primarily meant for the larger segmentof the population who cannot afford the high cost of medical treatment,was introduced with effect from 12 August 1996. The limit of cover per person is Rs 5,000 per annum. The premium payable is very low depending on the age of the person covered ranging from Rs 70 to Rs 140 per person per year and Rs 50 per dependent child below 25years. The cover provides for reimbursement of medical expenses incurred by an individual towards hospitalisation/domicillary hospitalisation for any illness, injury or disease contracted or sustained during the period of insurance.

The existing Overseas Mediclaim Policy offering emergency medical expenses cover to overseas travellers has been extended to include In-flight Personal Accident cover up to US $ 10,000 and Loss of Passport cover upto US $ 150 from 1 April 1997.The extended cover will be available without payment of additional premium under Business and Holiday cover and under the Corporate Frequent Travellers cover. A more comprehensive policy with additional benefits has also been devised.

A new policy called Videsh Yatra Mitra covering supplementary benefits besides providing indemnity for medical expenses during the period of overseas travel, has been introduced by the general insurance industry with effect from 1 January 1998.Two types of policies—one offering limit of benefits upto US $ 2,50,000 for worldwide travel but excluding USA and Canada and the other offering limit of benefits up to US$ 5,00,000 for worldwide travel including USA and Canada are available under the Scheme.

In addition to medical coverage, the policy also provides coverage for: (i) Personal Accident up to US $ 25,000; (ii) Loss of Personal Baggage up to US $ 1,000; (iii) Delayed Baggage up to US $ 100 and (iv) Personal Liability up to US $ 2,00,000. The premium under the policy is only 14 per cent more than that under the existing Overseas Mediclaim Policy (OMD), while the medical benefits will be increased five times in addition to supplementary benefits.

Bhagyashree Child Welfare Policy covering girl child in the age group of 0 to 18 years whose parents' age does not exceed 60 years, was introduced with effect from 19 October 1998. In case of each of the girl child or both parents, an amount of Rs 25,000 would be deposited in the name of the girl child with a financial institution. Fixed annual disbursements to the girl child up to the age of 18 years would be made from the amount to her credit, and the balance amount to her credit would be disbursed on attaining the age of 18 years.

Raj Rajeshwari Mahila Kalyan Yojana offering security to women in the age group of 10 to 75 years irrespective of their occupation was introduced with effect from 19 October 1998. For a premium of Rs 15 per annum, the policy provides a cover of Rs 25,000 for permanent total disablement of the insured woman. The policy also provides a cover of Rs 25,000 for the death of her husband. For the death of an unmarried woman, the policy provides a cover of Rs 25,000 which will be payable to her nominee/ legal heir.

Crop Insurance Scheme was introduced from 1985 Kharif season. The scheme is implemented in 15 States and two UTs. The scheme is administered by GIC on behalf of Central government. The premium and claims are shared by the Central and State governments in the ratio of 2:1 respectively. There are 11 Crop Insurance Cells at State capitals and UTs under GIC. These cells maintain close liaison with the State governments and monitor the implementation of the scheme.

The susbsidiaries of GIC have introduced Jald Rahat Yojana with an objective to expedite payment of compensation to road accident victims. Under the scheme a claimant is not required to go to Motor Accident Claims Tribunal for claiming compensation and can directly approach concerned insurance company. Non-fatal injury claims involving accident victims of 18 years and above are taken up. The scheme is in operation in Ahmadabad, Mumbai, Bangalore, Calcutta, Delhi, Kochi, Chennai and Pune.

DISINVESTMENT IN PUBLIC SECTOR ENTERPRISES

For the year 1998-99 a target of Rs 5,000 crore was set for realisation through disinvestment of government's equity in public sector enterprises. the disinvestment programme of 1998-99 included offerings from Container Corporation of India (CONCOR), Gas Authority of India Limited (GAIL), Videsh Sanchar Nigam Limited (VSNL) and Indian Oil Corporation (IOC). The CONCOR offering was completed during November 1998 in the domestic market in which FIIs also participated. By divesting 90 lakh shares, the Government has realised about Rs 222 crore.

The Government holding in company stands at about 63 per cent. In case of VSNL, the GDR/domestic offering of GAIL was completed in the first week of February 1999 and an amount of Rs 785 crore approx. was realised.

The domestic offering of GAIL was completed in the first week of February 1999 and an amount of Rs 182 crore was realised. The disinvestment in IOC was deferred due to adverse market conditions. To have better synergies among the Oil Sector PSUs, ONGC, IOC and GAIL cross purchased each others shares among themselves realising about Rs 4,200 crore for the Government. The total amount realised from the disinvestment during the year 1998-99 was Rs 6,000 crore (approx.) against the target of Rs 5,000 crore..

Life Insurance is a contract for payment of a sum of money to the person assured (or failing him/her, to the person entitled to receive the same) on the happening of the event insured against. Life Insurance in its existing form came to India from the United Kingdom with the establishment of a British firm Oriental Life Insurance Company in Calcutta in 1818 followed by Bombay Life Assurance Company in 1823.

The Indian Life Assurance Companies Act,.1912 was the first statutory measure to regulate life insurance business. Later in 1928 the Indian Insurance Companies Act was enacted to enable the Government to collect statistical information about both life and non-life insurance business transacted in India by Indian and foreign insurers including provident insurance societies. In 1938 with a view to protecting the interest of insuring public earlier legislation was consolidated and amended by the Insurance Act 1938 with comprehensive provisions detailed and effective control over the activities of insurers. The Act was amended in 1950 resulting in far reaching changes in the insurance sector.

By 1956, 154 Indian insurers, 16 foreign insurers and 75 provident societies were carrying on life insurance business in India. On January 19, 1956, the management of life insurance business of 245 Indian and foreign insurers and provident societies then operating in India was taken over by the Central Government. Life Insurance Corporation was formed in September 1956 by LIC Act 1956 of Parliament, with a capital contribution of Rs.50 mn.

The then Finance Minister Mr. C.D.Deshmukh while piloting the bill for nationalization outlined the objectives of LIC thus:

"To conduct the business with utmost economy with the spirit of trusteeship; to charge premium no higher than warranted by strict actuarial considerations; to invest the funds for obtaining maximum yield for the policy holders consistent with safety of capital; to render prompt and efficient service to policy holders thereby making Insurance widely popular."

Today, although that objective remains same, the vision of LIC is to become 'A trans-nationally competitive financial conglomerate of significance to societies and Pride of India.'

Objectives of LIC

- Spread Life Insurance much more widely and in particular to the rural areas and to the socially and economically backward classes with a view to reaching all insurable persons in the country and providing them adequate financial cover against death at a reasonable cost.
- Maximise mobilisation of people's savings by making insurance-linked savings adequately attractive.
- Bear in mind, in the investment of funds, the primary obligation to its policyholders, whose money it holds in trust, without losing sight of the interest of the community as a whole; the funds to be deployed to the best advantage of the investors as well as the community as a whole, keeping in view national priorities and obligations of attractive return.
- Conduct business with utmost economy and with the full realisation that the moneys belong to the policyholders.
- Act as trustees of the insured public in their individual and collective capacities.
- Meet the various life insurance needs of the community that would arise in the changing social and economic environment.
- Involve all people working in the Corporation to the best of their capability in furthering the interests of the insured public by providing efficient service with courtesy.

- Promote amongst all agents and employees of the Corporation a sense of participation, pride and job satisfaction through discharge of their duties with dedication towards achievement of Corporate Objective.

INSURANCE IN INDIA

What is Insurance?

Insurance is also referred to as Assurance and in the early part of the 17th century the term Ensurance (French) was quite prevalent. The term Assurance is basically the earlier term and was used alike for both life and general insurance. The term insurance was initially used in 1635 in connection with Fire insurance and was quickly adopted as extensively as Assurance. In 1826, it was proposed that the term insurance be used for general insurance and the term assurance restricted for life insurance.

The origin of practice of insurance is probably lost forever in the mists of antiquity. References to practices similar to insurance are found in the ancient Indian texts of Rigveda. Rigveda refers to the concept of "Yogakshema"-loosely meaning 'the well being, prosperity and security of people'.

Archaeological excavation at the site of Aryan civilisation has yielded evidence of a practice similar to insurance, insuring loss of profits in industry. The codes of Hammurabi and of Manu had recognised the importance and advisability of some practice akin to provision for sharing of future losses or Yogakshema.

The Insurance sector in India governed by Insurance Act, 1938, the Life Insurance Corporation Act, 1956 and General Insurance Business (Nationalisation) Act, 1972, Insurance Regulatory and Development Authority (IRDA) Act, 1999 and other related Acts.

The insurance sector in India has come a full circle from being an open competitive market to nationalisation and back to a liberalised market again. Tracing the developments in the Indian insurance sector reveals the 360 degree turn witnessed over a period of almost two centuries.

A Brief history of the Insurance Sector

The business of life insurance in India in its existing form started in India in the year 1818 with the establishment of the Oriental Life Insurance Company in Calcutta.

Some of the important milestones in the life insurance business in India are:

- 1912: The Indian Life Assurance Companies Act enacted as the first statute to regulate the life insurance business.
- 1928: The Indian Insurance Companies Act enacted to enable the government to collect statistical information about both life and non-life insurance businesses.
- 1938: Earlier legislation consolidated and amended to by the Insurance Act with the objective of protecting the interests of the insuring public.
- 1956: 245 Indian and foreign insurers and provident societies taken over by the central government and nationalised. LIC formed by an Act of Parliament, viz. LIC Act,
- 1956, with a capital contribution of Rs. 5 crore from the Government of India.

The General insurance business in India, on the other hand, can trace its roots to the Triton Insurance Company Ltd., the first general insurance company established in the year 1850 in Calcutta by the British.

Some of the important milestones in the general insurance business in India are: 1907: The Indian Mercantile Insurance Ltd. set up, the first company to transact all classes of general insurance business.

- 1957: General Insurance Council, a wing of the Insurance Association of India, frames a code of conduct for ensuring fair conduct and sound business practices.
- 1968: The Insurance Act amended to regulate investments and set minimum solvency margins and the Tariff Advisory Committee set up.
- 1972: The General Insurance Business (Nationalisation) Act, 1972 nationalised the general insurance business in India with effect from 1st January 1973.

107 insurers amalgamated and grouped into four companies viz. the National Insurance Company Ltd., the New India Assurance Company Ltd., the Oriental Insurance Company Ltd. and the United India Insurance Company Ltd. GIC incorporated as a company.

The Insurance Regulatory and Development Authority, India.

Reforms in the Insurance sector were initiated with the passage of the IRDA Bill in Parliament in December 1999. The IRDA since its incorporation as a statutory body in April 2000 has fastidiously stuck to its schedule of framing regulations and registering the private sector insurance companies.

The other decisions taken simultaneously to provide the supporting systems to the insurance sector and in particular the life insurance companies was the launch of the IRDA's online service for issue and renewal of licenses to agents.

The approval of institutions for imparting training to agents has also ensured that the insurance companies would have a trained workforce of insurance agents in place to sell their products, which are expected to be introduced by early next year.

Since being set up as an independent statutory body the IRDA has put in a framework of globally compatible regulations. In the private sector 12 life insurance and 6 general insurance companies have been registered.

INSURANCE OUTSOURCING: INDIA GAINS MOMENTUM AS OFFSHORING INTENSIFIES

The insurance industry is facing myriad challenges arising from intense competition, rising regulatory compliance and growing payouts due to fraud and natural disasters. It's expected that competitive pressures will make offshoring of information technology (IT) and business processes a growing imperative in the insurance industry.

Compared to mainstream banking and financial services, where the early adoption of automation and IT helped facilitate outsourcing, first in IT services and later in BPO, the insurance industry has lagged behind. This is one reason why insurance companies have been more conservative in their attitude to "business process outsourcing", and especially to offshoring.

With expected cost savings of 30% to 40%, and other advantages such as focusing on core competencies and access to skilled labor, we believe that the insurance offshoring industry is poised for significant growth in the next three to four years.

THE OPPORTUNITY FOR INDIA

Indian revenues from offshore insurance BPO services are slated to rise from $690 million in 2006 to about $2 billion by 2010. During the period, employment in Indian insurance offshoring is likely to increase from 41,600 in 2006 to 100,500 by 2010.

INSURANCE OFFSHORING: THE GROWTH OPPORTUNITY

- Insurance carriers currently dominate the buyer landscape. However, in the future, we may also see offshoring from intermediaries and re-insurance companies.
- Buyers in the UK and Europe will increase their share in the insurance offshoring market, while the share of business from US buyers is expected to fall by 2010.
- As the industry achieves greater offshoring maturity, the share of higher value services such as underwriting support and analytics will increase. Because billing rates are higher in these "knowledge"-based services compared to traditionally offshored tasks, the rise in employment in the industry will be lower than revenue growth.

OUTSOURCE-ABILITY AND OFFSHORABILITY

Support functions such as accounting and human resource were among the first processes offshored by insurance carriers. Vendors typically require less insurance domain expertise for these functions than for some of the other transaction processing functions. The table below shows processes that have been finding their way offshore.

In the last two to three years, a large number of activities in claims processing functions have found their way offshore. Relatively, processes in underwriting, adjudication, fund management and actuarial processes are not yet being offshored in significant volumes, though this is likely to change.

Table: Typically offshored processes.

New business acquisition	*Policy management*	*Claims processing*	*Financial accounting*	*Support functions*
• Proposal acquisition • Digitalization • Policy issuance • Risk assessment	• Policy holder correspondence • Mailroom services • Record changes	• Claim set up • Account settlement • Validation and eligibility • Excess re-insurance	• Closed book accounting • Fund performance analysis • Compliance verification	• Help desk • Broker support • Payroll processing • Facilities management

Source: ValueNotes Research

THE INDIAN SERVICE PROVIDER LANDSCAPE

Historically, the industry owes its roots to the captives of large companies such as GE and Conseco, which first set up offshore centers in India to provide insurance processes. Subsequently, the captives of these companies became third party players — Genpact and EXL Service. Today they dominate the insurance service provider landscape by virtue of their size, domain expertise and offshoring capabilities.

The insurance BPO provider landscape comprises large, mid-size and small service providers. The larger BPO companies are diversified across many verticals; but as a result of their size, they have acquired deep domain expertise in multiple verticals, including insurance.

They have significant global reach, with marketing and delivery centers spread across the world. We expect this group to continue to dominate the insurance provider landscape in the next two to three years.

Many of the mid-size players have grown considerably in the last two years. They have diversified into additional insurance segments (life, healthcare and property and casualty) and broadened their service offerings. Some of these players, especially the BPO offshoots of IT companies, have good potential to grow both in size, and specialization in the next two to three years.

Table: Expected winners among third-party offshore vendors.

Large Players	*Rationale for high growth prediction*
Genpact	The largest BPO in terms of revenues. Is aggressively bidding for insurance contracts after attaining third-party status. Scale, BPO knowledge and process maturity make Genpact a formidable competitor.
EXL Service	Player with a strong banking, financial services and insurance focus (BFSI); has been scaling up in research and analytics. Has recently bought Inductis. NASDAQ listing in 2006 expected to provide funds for growth.
Cambridge	Large presence outside India; is trying to build up India presence. Not limited in terms of funds. We expect this company to increase competitiveness aggressively by building its India presence.
TCS BPO	Backing of the largest Indian IT company and large business house. Is acquiring companies focused in BFSI and leveraging its capabilities such as offshoring knowledge and process maturity very aggressively.
Wipro BPO	Has been scaling up its insurance practice. Diversifying into non-voice business, and insurance transaction processing will be an area of focus. Scale and outsourcing knowledge will give it an edge.
WNS Global Services	One of the largest Indian insurance BPO players. Has very strong insurance focus. We expect WNS to continue to scale up aggressively in the insurance vertical, backed up the recent cash through the NYSE listing.
Mid-size players	*Rationale for high growth prediction*
Infosys BPO (formerly Progeon)	Strong margins have been its forte. It will look to scale up rapidly and build capabilities in insurance, especially analytics and research. The Infosys parentage implies strong financial backing and offshoring know-how.
TransWorks	Has recently acquired Minacs, one of the largest call centers in Canada; has focused plans for BFSI capability building. Backing from the industrial house Birla means that funds won't be a constraint.
Xansa	Strong presence and client base in the European market where growth is expected, especially among UK-based insurance companies. Will ramp up in the insurance vertical in the next few years.

IBM Daksh	Not very focused on insurance as yet, but scaling up rapidly. Has the backing of global IT giant IBM in terms of funding and client base. Daksh is likely to build up strong insurance capabilities in the near future.

Source: ValueNotes Research.

Apart from the large, differentiated players, there are a number of tier 2 and 3 vendors of smaller sizes and capabilities. Some of these small BPO vendors — those that have been able to differentiate their offerings — are growing rapidly, at rates much higher than the industry average. However, this is on a typically tiny base, and their ability to manage scale isn't yet evident.

Key Trends in the Insurance BPO Industry

The insurance offshoring industry is definitely poised for higher growth than it has witnessed so far. According to ValueNotes' estimates, the industry will grow at a CAGR of 30% a year up to 2010, compared to a CAGR of 23% in the last two years, driven by the need to reduce costs, differentiate products in an increasingly competitive environment and ensure regulatory compliance.

Buyer Market to Shift Towards UK and Europe

As per our estimates, about 64% of the current offshore business is generated from insurance carriers based in the United States. Of the remainder, 28% of the business comes from the UK and Europe. We expect that by 2010, the US share will shrink to 54%, while that of the UK and Europe will increase to 36%.

Innovative Operating Models to Lead the Way in Contracts

We expect the number of contracts with "hybrid operating models" to show a large increase in the future. This will come at the expense of straightforward captive and third-party contracts from insurance companies.

Hybrid models will also have a large share of the additional employment generated in the insurance BPO industry in India. Among these, innovative arrangements such as the buy-out of the UK-based Pearl Group's insurance processing division by TCS will become more common.

Growth in Emerging Markets to Translate into More Business

The rising volume of insurance business due to globalization, in turn, promises greater opportunity for outsourcing vendors. In India itself, domestic insurance companies that have sprung up in the last decade have already begun to outsource. This trend is expected to accelerate with an increase in business volumes and intensifying competition.

Favorable Eco-system to Support Talent and Skill Availability in India

Following the privatization of the insurance sector in 2000, there's also evidence of greater skill development in insurance in India. This is likely to create a sustainable eco-system, which will provide the necessary talent and experience to fuel further growth in insurance BPO in India.

Research and Analytics Services to Provide Value Growth to BPOs

So far, knowledge services, especially the core insurance services, such as underwriting and actuarial support is restricted to the captives of large insurance carriers. But now, high-end knowledge based services such as analytics, data mining and research have also started to get offshored to third-party vendors in India.

While, services such as claims processing, policy management, etc. will continue to provide volume growth to offshore BPO services providers, services such as analytics and decision support will be the higher-end, higher billing rate-based services that will drive value growth for the BPO organizations.

Non-Voice Transaction Based Processes to go up Significantly

So far, knowledge services and the core insurance services such as analytics and decision support have been retained in-house or restricted to captives. However, this work is starting to get offshored to the larger Indian BPO vendors or niche service providers, which are rapidly acquiring capabilities in these areas.

While services such as claims processing, policy administration, etc. will continue to provide volume growth to offshore BPO services providers, it will be the higher-end, higher billing rate-based services that will drive value growth for BPO organizations in future. Pressure on billing rates coupled with the need to offer broadbase service offerings is expected to drive most Indian BPOs down this route in the future.

Convergence in vendor landscape expected

Mergers and acquisitions have become integral to growth strategies of insurance BPOs. Acquiring domain expertise, inheriting trained and skilled manpower and accessing newer markets and clients are the drivers for acquisitions. The broader trend, however, is towards acquiring expertise in banking, financial services and insurance as an integrated offering.

Third-party Administrator — BPO Service Provider Convergence?

Industry dynamics are pointing to the possibility of a "third-party administrator-BPO service provider" convergence. This convergence can be in either direction. TPAs, threatened by competitive pressures, may acquire offshore vendors to build a low-cost base in countries like India. On the other hand, some of the large third-party service providers may buy out TPAs, both for more business and to gain onshore presence and domain knowledge.

In Short

In the future, you can expect to see a rising trend towards outsourcing of higher-end processes such as underwriting, actuaries and analytics to the larger third-party BPO vendors, which are fast gaining capabilities in these areas. ValueNotes forsees greater offshoring of high-end, higher-value services like analytics, actuaries and underwriting to push industry average billing rates upwards by more than 25% in the next two to three years. Finally, by 2010 a large number of Indian vendors will have evolved into mature, end-to-end service providers, competing with multinational outsourcing companies. Players such as Genpact, WNS and EXL Services, as well as BPO offshoots of IT companies such as IBM, TCS, Infosys (Progeon) and Wipro will emerge as formidable global players.

Insurance in the 21st Century

D K Mehrotra, MD, LIC talks to Kumar Dawada about how insurance companies can retain business despite global competition. The strategy is to invest in customer-centric IT initiatives and to focus on customers by providing better products, services and returns.

We live in the information age. People are becoming more aware of the importance of insurance in their life. However, there is a paradox in the form of a growing need to educate people to buy insurance.

Today, natural disasters on a large scale occur regularly and even terrorism is increasing day by day. Specialised software is used in actuarial science to accurately predict life expectancy and mortality. But natural disasters are difficult to predict.

This has highlighted to the world that insurance is a basic and fundamental need for the safety and security of the family. Only a larger insurance cover can guarantee a better future.

However insurance claims for natural disasters are very low. This is because insurance coverage was too low, and those who really needed insurance had not taken it. There is the need to push insurance as a social responsibility for those who really need it.

Business and Social Objectives

When LIC was formed in 1956 through the amalgamation of 225 private companies, its business objectives complemented its social objectives. The main objective is to spread life insurance to every nook and corner of the country especially rural areas, to socially and economically backward classes and provide them reasonably-priced financial cover against death.

Other objectives include encouraging people to save for the future by making insurance-linked savings more attractive and secure. The funds created are then utilised and invested for nation building. The insurance business is conducted with the full realisation that LIC is only a trustee of the insured public and priority is given to meet the needs that arise due to change in the social and economic environments. Even today after 50 years, the core value of social commitment has not changed. What have changed in recent times are customers' expectations and the environment in which the life insurance sector operates. This is due to globalisation which has opened up the insurance sector to private players.

IT for Insurance

IT policy flows from the business and social objectives. IT usage covers all business activities of the organisation. This includes finance, investment, product development, actuarial, underwriting, customer relationship management, marketing, policy servicing, human resource development, office servicing, and estate management.

IT's role is not to automate processes. Rather, it is a strategic tool to simplify procedures and revamp processes. This helps create a very efficient customer service management system. It not only provides anywhere, any time service, it also provides greater accountability, transparency and responsiveness in all business processes.

In today's world, IT is a must for any industry to keep pace with the customer's changing expectations. This is especially relevant in the service industry. The insurance sector has to ensure that the technology it chooses does not lag behind where customer expectations are concerned.

In our case, LIC has more than 16 crore policy holders. So it has to induct the best IT products available and use them to cater to the needs of the customers and deliver anywhere any time service on demand and to add value to its new products. The trust and the goodwill of the customer gained in the last 50 years have to be consolidated by making all activities more customer-focused.

For instance, LIC has a corporate Web site to provide information on products, services, policy status, grievances and premium calculator. Other facilities include touch-screen information kiosks at central locations to provide 24 x 7 inquiry services to customers.

Info centres are set up at major cities to provide call centre type services. Alternate premium payment channels like ECS, Internet payment gateways as well as ATMs of major banks are also available. Push services like premium alerts and product information have been also been started through SMS.

A Customer-Centric Focus

As all the activities of insurance sector are customer-centric, any new technology implemented or process developed needs to be customer-focused. It is necessary to look at any IT implementation from the customer's perspective.

This approach ensures that the technology's benefits and convenience are passed on to the customers. The implementations should help customers minimise their effort in dealing with LIC and allow interactions and transactions from the comfort of their home or office any where and any time.

Future IT

Facilities exist to pay premiums and get information on policies online; however, there is a need to enhance the online service to include settlement of claims, policy surrender, distribution channel management and policy dockets.

There is a need to acquire CRM tools for better understanding of customers and their buying patterns. There is also a need to redesign business processes and centralise non-core functions, provide real-time processing, to have sound security policies and conform to international standards.

Initiatives to be implemented in the near future include Web portals dedicated to customers, sales intermediaries and employees. The process is afoot to set up a premium payment gateway for collecting insurance premia over the Internet as well as an online data store at a central level to make data available to requesting applications for online real-time transactions.This will provide MIS reports and help us deploy analytical and operational CRM.

Putting a document management system in place will eliminate the need to reference physical records and create the capability of extending anywhere, any time service to settle claims and other similar activities by using a repository of document images. Another aim is to conduct network audit, information security audits and achieve BS 7799 standards.

The feasibility of a BI solution from business objective and customer perspective is also being considered. Already the proper providers, technology and models are being considered as a precursor to a BI initiative. Work is also going on for a payment gateway which works both ways—payments and receipts, so that the customers can get their payments wherever they require.

For the CIOs

The insurance sector has to work with huge amounts of data on a daily basis through nationwide networks. There is a growing need to provide real-time services and transactions to customers. Hence the dependence of the business on IT will keep growing.

IT implementations will also have to be upgraded to align them with growing customer expectations and market needs which will, in turn, drive business objectives. Only those IT implementations that suit business needs and add value for customers will be adapted.

The customer should be the principal beneficiary of any technological or business process initiative. It is necessary to see things from a customer's perspective and only those technologies will be adapted which bring the organisation closer to the customer, which make the customer trust the organisation, which are user-friendly and convenient for the customer.

15

Insurance, the Future Boom Sector of India

The reforms in the insurance sector leading finally to the opening of the insurance sector for private participation have brought in its wake major changes not only in the design of the products available in the market but also the manner in which they are marketed. We have today a host of products coupled with a large number of intermediaries who market them.

The post-liberalized insurance industry panorama in India is witnessing dramatic changes in terms of a slew of latest products and services, new channels of distribution, greater use of I.T. as a service facilitator etc. There is also the phenomenon of noticeable shifts in consumer preferences impacting the product mix being offered by insurers. The market structure dominated by a few stabilized public sector players and the 'new' players in the market (some of whom claim their lineage from established international insurance behemoths) is in a state of flux-in terms of figure out market shares but is full of potential.

Added to these are the rising trends of convergence of financial services, especially in the areas like wealth management and evolution of newer risk management tools, particularly in the context of reinsurance management. Greater attention is also being bestowed on the areas like Agricultural Insurance and risk coverage of export-import trade. Then there is impact of visible socio-economic changes like greater urbanization, greater job mobility, growth of the services industry, weakening of traditional family structure, impact of globalization etc. All in all, interesting things are happening in the Indian insurance scene.

*Insurance undergone rapid and massive changes in all aspects of their business: product and services, sectoral structure, market segmentation, competitive environment.*It is believed that the information sharing has not taken its expected shape in the insurance industry for the purposes of practices, research and education. However, data is one of the most needed ingredients in the insurance business development as well as for research and consultancy. There have been regular efforts by IRDA for collection and sharing of the data and other information of public interest. The industry is facing problems in terms of data review as parliament need to register this beforehand. We believe that progress of the industry should not be constrained by any extraneous conditions in the interest of research and development in the area.

Manpower India today released the Manpower Employment Outlook Survey for the first quarter of 2006 revealing sustained positive hiring intentions of employers in India. India continues to lead all 23 countries surveyed this quarter, with a positive overall Net Employment Outlook of +27%. Even though this figure represents a decrease of 13 percentage points from the fourth quarter of 2005, the employment outlook remains extremely healthy. *For the first time since the Survey was launched in India, the Finance, Insurance and Retail industry sector emerged as the most optimistic sector for a quarter with a Net Employment Outlook of +32%, surpassing the Services sector.*

Privatization of insurance sector has allowed insurance companies to work in the market by depositing 100 crore rupees in the reserve of government. This has encouraged many overseas insurance companies, having a required amount in their reserve, to open their branch in our country. Introduction of the sector has changed the employment pattern, but people must know how to make profit from it. To be in the global market and have advantage of it, capital and skill as per the demand and knowledge of market is the requirement. It is necessary that institutions, which form a part of this financial system, have internal management, governance and accountability structures, which measure up to the highest standards.

Bibliography

Arrow, Kenneth J.: *Social Choice and Individual Values*, New York, Wiley, 1951.

Campbell, J.Y., Lo, A.W.: *The Econometrics of Financial Markets*, Princeton University Press, 1996.

Chaudhuri, Pramit: *The Indian Economy: Poverty and Development*, New York, St. Martin's Press, 1979.

Dhingra, C.: *The Indian Economy: Resources, Planning, Development, and Problems*, Delhi, Sultan Chand, 1983.

Greer, Douglas F.: *Industrial Organization and Public Policy*, MacMillan Publishing Company, 1992.

Ishwar, C.: *The Indian Economy: Resources, Planning, Development, and Problems*, Delhi, Sultan Chand, 1983.

Little, I.M.D.: *India: Macroeconomics and Political Economy, 1964-1991*, Washington, World Bank, 1994.

Mongia, J.N.: *India's Economic Development Strategies, 1951-2000 A.D.*. New Delhi, Allied, 1986.

Pranab, K.: *The Political Economy of Development in India*, Delhi, Oxford University Press, 1984.

Sargent, Thomas J.: *Dynamic Macroeconomic Theory*, Harvard University Press, 1987.

Tirole, Jean: *The Theory of Industrial Organization*, MIT Press, 1988.

Williamson, Jeffrey G.: *American Inequality: A Macroeconomic History*, New York, Academic Press, 1980.

Xavier Sala-i-Martin: *Economic Growth*. McGraw-Hill, 1995.

INDEX

□□□